THE DEVELOPMENT OF FREUD'S THOUGHT:

From the Beginnings (1886-1900)
through Id Psychology (1900-1914)
to Ego Psychology (1914-1939)

by Reuben Fine, Ph.D.

JASON ARONSON, INC.   New York

Dedicated to
Benjamin I. Weininger, M.D.
In gratitude for his lifelong courage,
originality and inspiration

PREFACE

Almost fifty years have passed since the publication of Freud's last major book, *The Problem of Anxiety* (1926). In that period psychoanalysis has, as Freud predicted, bypassed its native Vienna and encircled the globe. It has virtually absorbed clinical psychiatry, to such an extent that most laymen today do not know the difference between a psychiatrist and a psychoanalyst. In psychology, psychoanalysis has become the dominant influence in the clinical field, which in turn is responsible for the enormous growth of psychology since World War II. Social work schools habitually teach the doctrines of psychoanalysis, although on paper at least they may often be opposed to it. Much of the generally educated public has come to realize, with Philip Reiff, that Freud's work is the "most important body of thought committed to paper in the twentieth century." Organizationally the fully trained psychoanalysts have become the most prestigious body of practitioners of the mental healing arts in the world, a far cry from the psychiatrist of Freud's day who, with the exception of the ship's doctor, was at the bottom rung of the medical hierarchy. Even if much of the profession is not fully trained, and many adopt techniques which would make Freud wince or shudder, the concepts of psychoanalysis have penetrated the thought of the social sciences to such an extent that, as the poet W. H. Auden has said, a whole new climate of opinion has been created.

Yet a curious gap persists: few people know what Freud really said. It is to fill this gap that this book has been written. In it I set out to examine the whole body of Freud's thought, to clarify what he said, and to review his ideas critically in the light of the best available existing knowledge. In this process of criticism I have tried to specify which aspects of Freud have stood the test of time, and which have not.

It is surprising that no comparable attempt has ever been made, with the exception of Ernest Jones' monumental three-volume work, which is in a different category. Freud has become a totem figure, to be deified or reviled, not a human being with a profound message that has to be understood.

Freud's writings cover a period of more than half a century, and the *Standard Edition*, which contains all his works on psychoanalysis, runs to twenty-four volumes; all but the Index have by now been published. That he would propound many theories that were later to be amended or discarded, and that he would handle some problems so thoroughly that little else remained to be done while others would be treated only superficially, was scarcely to be avoided. Furthermore, much new knowledge has been gained in psychoanalysis, psychology, and psychiatry since his death.

Freud looked upon himself as the founder of a new science: psychoanalysis, a branch of psychology. Today psychoanalysis could be equated with dynamic psychiatry, basic psychodynamics, psychoanalytic psychology, or even the major portion of clinical psychology. In all these fields, whatever has happened to science, the foundations were still laid by Freud. As Rado once put it, Freud skimmed the surface of *everything*.

Psychoanalysis is far from the unchanging monolithic structure its opponents would have us believe it to be. It is a living science, none of whose tenets would remain if they were not warranted by the evidence. Nor is it true that, as is often alleged, Freud would permit no differences of opinion. In a letter to Lou Andreas-Salome in 1914 he wrote:[1]

> I have never objected to differences of opinion among members of the psychoanalytic circle, especially as I myself usually have several views on a matter, until, that is to say, I have expressed one of them in print. But one must stick to the fundamental core; otherwise it becomes something else.

In a later letter to her, in 1926, he wrote:[2]

> It does no harm for people to realize that we have not yet earned the right to dogmatic rigidity and that we must be ready to till the vineyard again and again.

Freud was basically an empirical scientist who generalized from the observations, primarily clinical, that he made. A large number of his generalizations were profound and sound; many were not. I agree with Kubie that as scientists we should neither be *for* Freud nor *against* him, but should make every effort to build on his discoveries.

Nevertheless, as time has shown, it is extraordinarily difficult to remain dispassionate about Freud. Even if, as almost always happens, it requires a serious distortion of his views, people in and out of the field *are* either for him or against him. In this process of vehement argumentation four major errors are commonly found on the contemporary scene.

1. The *culturalist school* conducts a constant diatribe against his "biological" orientation. This loses sight of the fact that when Freud was writing Darwin was the great intellectual hero of the day, so that everyone in the field had a biological bias, and that furthermore the distinction between "cultural" and "biological" was not a significant one at that time. When the question did come up, as with Adler, Freud in the early 1900's accused him of being too biological, and ignoring the psychological factors in such doctrines as organ inferiority. Even Freud's sexual theories were subordinated to his emphasis on psychology. Thus when Reich in 1928 began his attempts to resurrect the early Freud, the latter wrote to Lou Andreas-Salome:[3]

> We have here a Dr. Reich, a worthy but impetuous young man, passionately devoted to his hobby-horse, who now salutes in the genital orgasm the antidote to every neurosis. Perhaps he might learn from your analysis of K. to feel some respect for the complicated nature of the psyche.

2. The *Freudians*, motivated primarily by their wish to defeat the culturalists, have in turn under-stressed the role of cultural and sociological factors in personality structure and neurosis. Furthermore, they show a strong tendency to put all of Freud's writings on an equal basis, ignoring both the period in which they were written and the evidence adduced by Freud for his theories. Thus the concept of psychic energy is adhered to today by most Freudians, with numerous references to the *Project for a Scientific Psychology of 1895*, even though this book was never published by Freud, and even though, as Strachey has shown in his preface in the *Standard Edition*,[4] Freud was consistently ambiguous about the concept in this book, not even using the same terminology throughout, thus never making it clear whether he was thinking of psychic energy as somatic or as psychic or some combination of the two. In his cultural writings frequent reference is made to a superficial piece of work such as *Civilization and Its Discontents* (1930), which Freud himself scarcely took seriously. Again in a letter to his confidante, Lou Andreas-Salome, he wrote about this book:[6, 7]

> It . . . strikes me, no doubt rightly, as very superfluous—in contrast to earlier works, which always sprang from some inner necessity. But what else can I do?

Certainly *Civilization and Its Discontents* cannot even remotely be compared with *Totem and Taboo* (1913) which is basically a cornerstone of modern anthropology, in spite of disclaimers to the contrary by anthropologists.[8]

3. The *general public* has consistently pulled many of his ideas out of context, or simply indulged in bald misrepresentation. A good example is the current attack on Freud's views of women by many members of the Women's Liberation Movement. Typical is a statement by Dr. Naomi Weisstein:[9]

> Psychology has nothing to say about what women are really like, what they need and what they want, essentially, because psychology does not know.

Gone with one stroke of the pen is the great Freudian revolution of the twentieth century, which has demonstrably played a significant role in liberating women sexually, socially, and morally, and helped to place them in a position that they never knew before in history.

4. The *innovators* as a rule take one aspect of Freudian theory and make a whole system of it, disregarding the historical experience. Thus Reich goes back to the early Freud of the 1890's, with his emphasis on the Aktual-neurosis, or somatic consequences of sexual malpractices, including abstinence, a position which on the basis of further clinical experience has been abandoned by all other analysts.

The historical record shows that what Freud created was essentially a wholly new science. He has precursors who dimly glimpsed some of his ideas; among them he placed Shakespeare first and foremost. But he can scarcely be said to have any real predecessors, in spite of numerous efforts to read 19th century psychiatry,[10] Jewish mysticism,[11] Janet's unconscious,[12] and many other ideas into him.

Inevitably the concept of "psychoanalysis" has been used in one or more of four different meanings, all stemming from Freud: 1. a system of psychology, emphasizing particularly the unconscious and dynamic forces; 2. a technique of therapy, relying mainly on the analysis of transference and resistances; 3. a philosophical approach to life and happiness; 4. various schools within each of these. For clarity of thought it is essential to keep these four meanings sharply separate from one another.

It is one of my theses in this book that the division of psychoanalysis into different schools is an historical error. All too often a viewpoint is announced as new because of wholly erroneous interpretations of Freud.

When his work is looked at more carefully, it turns out that the author has reworded the traditional position and then added a new idea or a different emphasis. The result has been enormous waste and confusion. Within the main body of psychoanalytic doctrine there always have been and there are today large areas of difference which are hotly debated, as new analysts come along who "till the vineyard again and again." To designate these as "schools" may serve a propagandistic purpose in convincing the ignorant that something novel has been proposed, but for scientific work it merely beclouds the issues.

It is my conviction, which I have tried to document in this book, that today we are all Freudians, regardless of the name used. To call oneself Freudian, however, by no means implies that all the problems of psychology are solved; quite the opposite. By building on Freud's fundamental insights psychologists and psychiatrists can move on most readily to empirical research, thereby constructing a more satisfactory science of psychology.

I wish to express my thanks to Dr. Jason Aronson for his kind encouragement of this work, to Mr. Kennett Rawson, for his patience and assistance at a difficult time in the life of this book, to my wife Charlotte for her long-suffering forbearance with the literary side of my life, and to my children, Benjamin and Ellyn, for their amazing familiarity with Freud's theories of psychosexual development.

Reuben Fine

Notes

1. Sigmund Freud and Lou Andreas-Salome: *Letters,* p. 19, Basic Books, 1964.

2. Ibid., p. 163.

3. Ibid., p. 174.

4. *Standard Edition of Freud's Works,* Vol. 1, pp. 283-293, The Hogarth Press, 1966.

5. For a recent summary of the major arguments pro and con the theory of psychic energy, see A. Applegarth: "Comments on Aspects of the Theory of Psychic Energy," *J. Amer. Psychoanalytic Assn.,* 19, pp. 379-416, 1971.

6. Sigmund Freud and Lou Andreas-Salome: *Letters,* p. 181, Basic Books, 1964.

7. E. Jones: *The Life and Work of Sigmund Freud,* Vol. 3, p. 148, Basic Books, 1957.

8. M. Harris: *The Rise of Anthropological Theory* is typical of those who have misunderstood the basic meanings of Freud's contribution. For further discussion, see the text, chapter 9, T. Y. Crowell, 1968.

9. R. Morgan, Ed.: *Sisterhood Is Powerful,* p. 208, Random House, 1970.

10. H. Ellenberger: *The Discovery of the Unconscious,* Basic Books, 1970.

11. D. Bakan: *Sigmund Freud and the Jewish Mystical Tradition.* Van Nostrand Reinhold, 1958.

12. L. L. Whyte: *The Unconscious Before Freud,* Barnes and Noble, 1967.

CONTENTS

CONTENTS

Part I.

THE BEGINNINGS OF PSYCHOANALYSIS
1886–1900

Chapter I. HISTORICAL ANTECEDENTS

Sigmund Freud was born in Freiberg, in what is now Czecho-slovakia, on May 6, 1856. The street on which he was born was later renamed Freudova Ulice in his honor. At the age of four he and his family moved to Vienna, where he remained until 1938 when the Nazi persecution forced him to flee to England, a year before his death.

Freud was the son of a poor Jewish merchant. To his Jewish background he himself attributed his ability to cling to an unpopular position in the face of enormous calumny.

Outwardly there is relatively little to relate about Freud's life. He was always a very bright student and from an early age seemed destined for an academic or intellectual career. He studied at the University of Vienna in the Faculty of Sciences and eventually did research under the famous physiologist, Brücke. Because the financial rewards for pure research were so limited that he was unable to support himself, he turned to medicine and took his M.D. degree in 1881.

For several years thereafter he served as a physician in various hospital departments. In 1885 he received a traveling grant to go to Paris for several months' study with the Frenchman, Jean Charcot, the most famous neurologist of his time.

In 1886 he set himself up in private practice as a neurologist in Vienna. That same year he married Martha Bernays, by whom he had six children. The youngest, Anna Freud, is today one of the world's leading figures in psychoanalysis.

In 1885 he was appointed *Privatdocent* (roughly Lecturer) in Neuropathology at the University of Vienna. Some twenty years later he was made a *Professor extraordinarius* (Associate Professor), and in 1920 he became a full Professor. All these honors came to him as a result of his work in neurology. His psychoanalytic labors received no official recognition from the university until long after his death.

In 1923 he contracted a cancer of the jaw, which after many operations and much suffering ultimately proved fatal in 1939.

Such, in brief outline, are the details of his life. The reader who looks for more excitement in Freud's biography finds none because there was none. His epic lay in his intellectual adventure, the founding of psychoanalysis.

The dominant influence in Freud's thought, as in that of most scholars of his day, was the implicit faith in the scientific method and the scientific spirit. Let science attack the problems that beset mankind, and they will disappear, was the virtually universal belief. Even toward the end of his life, in 1932, when he considered the relationship of psychoanalysis to philosophy, Freud maintained that psychoanalysis had no need of any special Weltanschauung, since it was a part of science. And science alone is sufficient, without any metaphysical speculation.

In physiology, where Freud began, the two major forces that shaped thought in that day were, first, the reduction of physiology to physics and chemistry and, second, the extraordinary explanatory value of evolution. Brücke, Freud's first master, was an outstanding member of the far-reaching movement known as Helmholtz's School of Medicine. Du Bois, another member of that school, wrote in 1842:

Brücke and I pledged a solemn oath to put into effect this truth: "No other forces than the common physical-chemical ones are active within the organism. In those cases which cannot at the time be explained by these forces one had either to find the specific way or form of their action by means of the physical-mathematical method or to assume new forces equal in dignity to the chemical-physical forces inherent in matter, reducible to the force of attraction and repulsion." [1]

The science of physics, in the 1870's and 1880's, was much simpler than it is today. It was still dominated by the brash certainty of the Newtonian world system, which led some scientists of the day to proclaim that in principle all problems had been solved, only the details had still to be worked out. In this view material particles affected one another in a determinable way, which could be summed up in various laws, in a closed system. The Einsteinian revolution, which revealed the much greater complexity of nature and led to statistical predictions and open systems, was still more than a quarter of a century away. In the type of thinking that Freud adopted he remained closer to Newton than to Einstein, though he by no means ignored the later developments in science.

By now the impact of Darwin and the theory of evolution on science has been so thoroughly assimilated that we can scarcely conceive how world-shaking it seemed to the young intellectuals of Freud's day. Finally man could be included within the scope of the cosmic process and be studied just like any other natural phenomenon. The social sciences, which up to then had relied on physical models, turned to evolution for the explanatory principles that could clarify all the problems related to man.

These two ideas—the scientific method, especially as exemplified in Newtonian physics, and the explanatory power of evolution— were the major formative influences in Freud's thought. They remained fundamental to him to the end.

Nevertheless, it must be remembered that psychoanalysis, like evolution and relativity, is an essentially novel idea in human history, although it has many antecedents. In Freud's writings, as will be seen, there is often manifest a conflict between his realization that he had created something entirely new and his wish to reconcile it in some way with what the revered teachers of his youth had taught him.

Freud's work can be divided into four major periods:

1. The period of the exploration of neurosis, from the inception of his practice (1886) until the publication of the Studies on Hysteria (1895);

2. The period of self-analysis, 1895-1899;

3. The period of the elaboration of the psychoanalytic system of psychology, based primarily on *The Interpretation of Dreams* (1900) and the *Three Essays on Sexuality* (1905), which lasted roughly until 1914;

4. The final period involving a considerable extension and elab-

oration of the earlier ideas, lasting from 1914 until his death in 1939. While there is naturally a great deal of overlap among these stages in the development of Freud's thought, it is helpful to get a bird's-eye view of his life's work and to fit individual ideas into this broad scheme.

NOTES ON CHAPTER I

The only adequate biography of Freud in any language is the monumental three-volume work by Ernest Jones: *The Life and Work of Sigmund Freud* (New York: Basic Books, 1953-1957). A one-volume abridgment by Trilling and Marcus was issued in 1961. Other biographies, such as H. W. Puner: *Freud: His Life and Mind* (New York: Grosset and Dunlap, 1947), are poorly informed and badly documented. Much of the literature on Freud's life rests upon unsubstantiated speculations and statements which have led to the grossest misunderstandings.

For the general intellectual background a number of excellent texts are available. The most scholarly is J. H. Randall: *The Making of the Modern Mind* (Boston: Houghton Mifflin, 1940). A stimulating intellectual history of ideas from Leonardo to Hegel is J. Bronowski and B. Mazlish: *The Western Intellectual Tradition* (New York: Harper and Bros., 1960). A personal interpretation by one of the leading philosophers of our time is Bertrand Russell: *A History of Western Philosophy* (New York: Simon and Schuster, 1945). Unfortunately no standard historical work displays any real understanding of the full significance in the history of thought of Freud and psychoanalysis. For a reflective psychoanalytical appraisal of the historical process, see especially two books by Franz Alexander: *Our Age of Unreason* (Philadelphia: Lippincott, 1942), and *The Western Mind in Transition: An Eyewitness Story* (New York: Random House, 1960).

For the psychological material the standard text is G. Murphy: *Historical Introduction to Modern Psychology* (New York: Harcourt, Brace, 1949). For the psychiatric history, see G. Zilboorg: *A History of Medical Psychology* (New York: Norton, 1941).

Chapter II. THE EXPLORATION
OF NEUROSIS—1886–1895

Legend has it that Archimedes discovered the principle of specific gravity when he was taking a hot bath, and that the idea of universal gravitation occurred to Newton when he saw an apple fall from a tree. No such good fortune attended the birth of psychoanalysis. It was rather a groping, fumbling, testing process, extending over many years.

The field of the neuroses, which Freud entered as soon as he began his private practice in 1886, was at that time a virtual terra incognita. Various symptoms had been described by different authors, but there was no systematic knowledge and no treatment that was other than a hit-or-miss affair.

Only two of Freud's predecessors provided anything from which he could learn. One of them was the Frenchman, Jean Martin Charcot, then the leading neurologist of Europe; the other was the Viennese physician, Josef Breuer.

During Freud's stay in Paris in the winter of 1885-1886 he was particularly impressed by two of Charcot's ideas: that hysteria was a demonstrable disease, and that hypnotism had valid uses. Both of these ideas were bitterly fought by the majority of the medical profession at the time, and both encountered severe opposition when Freud attempted to bring them back with him to Vienna. Charcot, who was primarily a brain anatomist and neurologist, and not a psychologist, did not go any further; he did not try to determine any of the psychological factors operative in hysteria, nor was he especially interested in doing so, and his use of hypnotism was quite limited.

The second influence on Freud, Josef Breuer, has come to assume a somewhat exaggerated role in the history of psychoanalysis because Freud, out of excessive modesty, attributed too much to him in the early days. As time goes on, Breuer's role seems less and less important. Nevertheless, he did make several fundamental observations. In the period from 1880 to 1882 he treated Anna O., a young girl suffering from hysteria, and obtained a considerable improvement in her symptoms. He communicated his experiences and theories to Freud, who urged him to go on with them; but Breuer was a general practitioner and did not care to delve more deeply into the problems of the neuroses. It was not until 1893 that, under the persistent urging of his younger colleague, Breuer finally published his findings, although even then only in conjunction with Freud.

Breuer treated his young patient, Anna, by placing her under hypnosis and then inquiring into the circumstances under which her symptoms had arisen. In the course of this so-called cathartic method, he discovered that the girl's symptoms disappeared when she had related the nature of their origin. He was, however, not a scientist in the sense that Freud was; as he himself said later:

> My merit lay essentially in my having recognized what an uncommonly instructive and scientifically important case chance had brought me for investigation, in my having persevered in observing it attentively and accurately, and my not having allowed any preconceived opinions to interfere with the simple observation of the important data.[2]

Freud learned certain essential facts about hysteria from Breuer. He learned that both the release of repressed emotion, which was called abreaction, and the making conscious of what was unconscious had therapeutic effects. Apparently Breuer never again treated a case at such depth; in fact, he vowed that he would not again go through such an ordeal as he had had with Anna O. Thus it was not at all clear whether the findings of Breuer and Freud were peculiar to this one patient or were, in general, characteristic of hysteria. It remained for Freud alone to investigate the matter on a much wider scale.

When he began, Freud's therapeutic arsenal consisted of only two weapons—electrotherapy and hypnotism. Electrotherapy (which is different from the severe electric shocks of electroshock therapy as practiced today) he soon discovered to be a total waste. He says in his *Autobiography:*

My knowledge of electrotherapy was derived from W. Erb's textbook, which provided detailed instructions for the treatment of all the symptoms of nervous diseases. Unluckily I was soon driven to see that following these instructions was of no help whatever and that what I had taken for an epitome of exact observations was merely the construction of fantasy. The realization that the work of the greatest name in German neuropathology had no more relation to reality than some Egyptian dream book, such as is sold in cheap bookshops, was painful, but it helped to rid me of another shred of the innocent faith in authority from which I was not yet freed. So I put my electrical apparatus aside . . .[3]

Accordingly the only method of treatment that remained at Freud's disposal was hypnotism. In 1889 he made a special trip to Nancy, in France, to visit Bernheim, then probably the leading expert on the subject. Freud practiced hypnotism for a number of years, until he finally discarded it in 1896 and replaced it entirely by the psychoanalytic method. He had to invent an entirely new technique for studying and treating the neuroses.

Freud's first major discovery was that *the key to neurosis lies in psychology.* This can be stated in many different ways. Through an understanding of psychopathology we reach normal psychology; through psychology we can explain the manifestations of neurosis as well as of normal behavior. While he realized that there must be a physiological basis for all psychological functioning, after some initial hesitation Freud always insisted that the phenomena he described must be understood in purely psychological terms.

In the posthumously discovered letters to his friend, the Berlin physician Wilhelm Fliess, Freud's preoccupation with setting up a new system of psychology comes out over and over again. In one he wrote (May 25, 1895):

My tyrant is psychology; it has always been my distant, beckoning goal and now, since I have hit on the neuroses, it has come so much nearer. I am plagued with two ambitions: to see how the theory of mental functioning takes shape if quantitative considerations, a sort of economics of nerve-force, are introduced into it; and secondly, to extract from psychopathology what may be of benefit to normal psychology. Actually a satisfactory theory of neuropsychotic disturbances is impossible if it cannot be brought into association with clear assumptions about normal mental processes.[4]

Or again, in the letter of April 2, 1896:

When I was young, the only thing I longed for was philosophical knowledge, and now that I am going over from medicine to psychology I am in the process of attaining it. I have become a therapist against my will; I am convinced that granted certain conditions in the person and the case, I can definitely cure hysteria and obsesssional neurosis.[5]

Then in a more despairing moment he confessed (October 10, 1898): "... how can I ever hope to gain an insight into the whole of mental activity, which was once something I proudly looked forward to?"[6]

As he well knew, the transition to psychology signified a sharp break with the past. Where were the physico-chemical forces that Brücke had taught him to look for? What was the bodily basis of all these conflicts, traumas, and defenses that he kept seeing?

True to his traditions, he attempted a grand physiological theory according to which psychology would be put on a firm neurological basis. He called it a "Psychology for Neurologists" and sent a draft of it to Fliess. For a while he was wildly enthusiastic. On October 20, 1895, he wrote:

Now listen to this. One strenuous night last week when I was in the stage of painful discomfort in which my brain works best, the barriers suddenly lifted, the veils dropped, and it was possible to see from the details of neurosis all the way to the very conditioning of consciousness. Everything fell into place, the cogs meshed, the thing really seemed to be a machine which in a moment would run of itself. The three systems of neurones, the "free" and "bound" states of quantity, the primary and secondary processes, the main trend and the compromise trend of the nervous system, the two biological rules of attention and defense, the indications of quality, reality, and thought, the state of the psycho-sexual group, the sexual determination of repression, and, finally, the factors determining consciousness as a perceptual function—the whole thing held together, and still does. I can naturally hardly contain myself with delight.[7]

Ten days later he was less enthusiastic and referred to his paper as a preliminary draft. After another month he gave it up altogether. On November 11, 1895, he wrote to Fliess:

I no longer understand the state of mind in which I concocted the psychology; I cannot conceive how I came to inflict it on you. I think you are too polite; it seems to me to have been a kind of aberration. The clinical explanation of the two neuroses will probably stand, after some modifications.[8]

The project was then completely abandoned. Freud did not ask Fliess to return the manuscript, and never tried to repeat it or to publish it. It came to light only after his death when his letters to Fliess were discovered.

Freud kept on hoping that someday a physiological explanation for his findings would emerge. In fact, one motive for his friendship with Fliess was his respect for the latter's scientific knowledge which Freud expected to be able to apply to his own work. In the letter of June 30, 1896, he makes a direct plea for help:

Anxiety, chemical factors, etc.—perhaps you may supply me with solid ground on which I shall be able to give up explaining things psychologically and start finding a firm base in physiology.[9]

Evidently Fliess encouraged him to keep up the search for the physiological underpinnings. But eventually Freud gave this up and looked to psychology. On September 22, 1898, he wrote:

I am not in the least in disagreement with you, and have no desire at all to leave the psychology hanging in the air with no organic basis. But, beyond the feeling of conviction (that there must be such a basis), I have nothing, either theoretical or therapeutic, to work on, and so I must behave as if I were confronted by psychological factors only. I have no idea yet why I cannot yet fit it together (the psychological and the organic).[10]

To have seen the close interconnection between psychology and psychiatry was in itself a bold and original conception. Today this concept is so familiar to us that we find it hard to imagine how foreign it was to the thinking of Freud's colleagues. For a century and more psychiatrists had been convinced that all mental illness was the result of brain pathology. Most of them thought that the major cause of neurotic and psychotic disturbances was some hereditary weakness or degeneration, and the only hope, if there was any, was that someday biochemical research would solve the problem. To bring in psychology seemed to many to be a return to that outmoded demonology which had created such a tragic chapter in human history.

Psychologists, on the other hand, had little interest in psychiatry. To them it was a recital of facts about "abnormal" people, who were markedly different from the "normal" person who was the major subject of psychological inquiry.

Both these attitudes have since undergone vast changes as a result of Freud's work, although many traces of them remain.

But if he was to pursue psychology, what kind was it to be? The psychology of the schools, which he generally referred to as philosophy, had virtually nothing to offer him. He rightly saw that he had to invent a whole new science. After reviewing the literature on dreams, he wrote to Fliess on February 9, 1898:

The only sensible thing on the subject was said by old Fechner in his sublime simplicity: that the psychical territory on which the dream process is played out is a different one. It has been left to me to draw the first crude map of it . . .[11]

It was indeed entirely new territory on which Freud ventured. Justifiably, he felt like a conquistador exploring a new world.

Freud's thought in the 1890's centers around one major clinical observation: *Neurosis involves a defense against unbearable ideas.* This concept of an inner conflict is an Ariadne's thread which runs through the whole history of psychoanalysis. After the initial formulation, Freud in 1900 noted the contrast between the primary process, which strives for immediate discharge, and the secondary process, which attempts to bind and control. In 1911 the concept was recast as the struggle between the pleasure principle and the reality principle. And in 1923 he introduced the terminology, which has since been the dominant one, of the ego and the id.

The two sides of the conflict between the defense and the unbearable idea can both be explored. Historically, Freud investigated the unbearable idea first and came to the defensive processes only much later.

Experience indicated that the unbearable idea lay in the past *unfinished*

rather than in the present. The neurotic had suffered a trauma or shock, which had not been properly dealt with. Whereas the normal individual, when he meets with something disturbing, releases some emotion and eventually forgets about it, the neurotic, by contrast, remembers the traumatic experience and builds up a pathological reaction. He does not *discharge* his feelings. As Freud and Breuer said in their *Studies on Hysteria,* "The hysteric suffers from reminiscences."

Hysteria is characterized by organic or bodily symptoms for which there is no demonstrable organic basis. If the underlying conflict is psychological there must be some way in which the psychic disturbance has been converted into the bodily disturbance. For this process Freud coined the term *conversion,* although the manner in which the conversion took place as yet remained unexplained.

At first, the unbearable idea was seen as any emotion. Very soon it was narrowed down to ideas of a sexual nature. Freud's first theory of neurosis, elaborated early in the 1890's, was a directly sexual one. According to this theory, neurosis is due to sexual frustration, and the various forms of neurosis are due to different forms of sexual frustrations. Although the concept of sexuality was later broadened to include all forms of bodily pleasure, and tenderness and affection as well, in the beginning sexuality was used in the ordinary sense of genitality, or activities relating to sexual intercourse.

To explain psychical processes Freud postulated a *psychic energy* Originally this term had a physiological meaning (the "quantity" of the project) but the physiology was soon dropped and it remained a psychic concept, although one frequently linked in some way with the body. Following Breuer, Freud specified two kinds of psychic energy, *bound* and *unbound.* Bound energy is that which is fixed in one area, while unbound can shift from one area to another.

The theory that sexuality or sexual frustration is the direct cause of neurosis was called on to explain the clinical facts. The fundamental characteristic of the neuroses is that they present a variety of pictures; hence it was necessary to correlate the various types of sexual frustration with the various types of neuroses. Freud attempted this correlation in his early theories. He drew up a classification which is typical of his dualistic approach; it is one of a number of instances where he overschematized his material and then later had to drop his schema.

The neuroses Freud divided into what he called the actual neuroses and the psychoneuroses. The *actual neuroses* are those which are due to the accumulation of physical tension owing to sexual frustration; these he looked upon as purely physiological manifestations, although, of course, they could have psychological consequences. The actual neuroses included neurasthenia and anxiety neurosis; he even went so far as to trace neurasthenia to excessive masturbation and anxiety neurosis to an excessive abstinence from sexual activity or heightened tension because of such abstinence.

Freud's early theory of the actual neurosis is not accepted by the majority of contemporary psychoanalysts, and is scarcely alluded to any longer.

The *psychoneuroses* consist of hysteria and obsessional neurosis. Hysteria is caused by a passive seduction in childhood, while obsessional neurosis results from an active seduction. Both are amenable to psychotherapy.

While in the 1890's sexuality was seen as the heart of the unbearable idea, Freud's views on this point went through a number of changes. Much will be said about sexuality in the further course of this book, but it will be helpful here to summarize the major changes that occurred in Freud's development with regard to this point:

1. In the beginning (1886-1900), Freud had a simple theory of the *sexual causation of neurosis*. Sexual difficulties cause neurosis; neurosis, in turn, is always caused by sexual difficulties.

2. Around 1900, for a variety of reasons, Freud began to abandon this simple, direct sexual theory and turned to the investigation of *infantile sexuality*.

3. At the same time the concept of sexuality was broadened, and the term *psychosexual* came to be used. The broadening involved, first, an extension of sexuality to all physical pleasure, and, second, its extension to affection, love, and all the tender emotions. This was crystallized in the *Three Essays on Sexuality*, published in 1905.

4. The newer concepts of sexuality led to a newer concept of neurosis, which Freud referred to as the *libido theory*, although this

term has several meanings. The direct sexual theory of neurosis was abandoned, except for the one instance of actual neurosis, that is, current sexual difficulties causing neurotic problems. Instead, a view of personality was put forth in which the individual's character structure is related in fairly definable ways to his instinctual drives and their life history. This theory dates mainly from 1905-1915.

5. In 1914, in the paper on narcissism, Freud revised the libido theory further with the assumption that the ego was libidinally charged or cathected. Up to that time he had assumed that the ego was the rational part of the person, which contained the self-preservative drives, while the libido was reserved for the sexual drives. This required further changes in theory.

6. In 1920, Freud postulated the existence of *two fundamental instincts*, sexuality and aggression, or, to use his own terms more precisely, Eros and the death instinct.

7. In 1923, Freud proposed a new theory of the mind, which has since been called *ego psychology*. Here character structure can be spoken of more precisely as the structure of the ego. This ego, in turn, can be broken down into a variety of component parts, and when it is carefully understood, it is seen to be far more complex than had been thought. If there is now a complex ego, and if there are now two instincts instead of one, the older theory of the causation of neurosis, the libido theory of 1905, must necessarily be revised. This revision is still in the process of being worked out by psychoanalysts, and there are still many differences of opinion on matters both of theory and of practice. Freud himself laid the foundation for the later thinking but did not himself pursue it to any great extent.

The other side of the conflict—defense—in this period received much less attention, as has been noted above. The term itself was soon replaced by *repression*.[*]

Repression was part of the concept of *unconscious processes*, which, with *The Interpretation of Dreams* in 1900, became a cornerstone of Freud's thinking. It is necessary, however, to make a rather

---

[*] In 1926 Freud reintroduced the term *defense* in *The Problem of Anxiety*. From then on repression has been seen as one of many possible defense mechanisms.

sharp distinction between the unconscious of the 1890's and that of the 1900's. In the earlier period it was a relatively simple idea, not too far removed from other psychologies of the time. In fact, it has been shown that there is a marked resemblance between Freud's early ideas and those set forth by Herbart seventy years earlier.[12] The only decisive new factor for the time being was Freud's concept of a dynamic unconscious, the tracing of which, under hypnosis and in psychoanalysis, had therapeutic effects. This unconscious, however, lacked the breadth and range of the unconscious as Freud, after his self-analysis, dream work, and discovery of infantile sexuality came to see it.

In *psychotherapy* Freud utilized and expanded two tools which he got from Breuer: *abreaction* and *making the unconscious conscious*, or insight. Initially these were both part of the hypnotic procedure. It was only gradually that he came to abandon hypnosis and to substitute psychoanalysis. The exact time of change is unclear; we are told only that after 1896 he no longer used hypnosis.[13] *Abreaction* means the release of emotion which has been repressed at the time of the traumatic experience. In the evolution of psychoanalysis after 1900 abreaction as such was relegated to a secondary role, and seen as subordinate to insight.[14] In the elaboration of his theories, however, it did lead Freud to lay primary stress on the discharge phenomenon and the *striving for discharge*.

Insight, or making the unconscious conscious, was still looked upon in rather rudimentary terms in the *Studies on Hysteria* (1895). It meant primarily hypnotizing the patient and leading him or her back to some repressed experience, often of relatively recent origin, and making that experience conscious. When the theory of the unconscious became much more elaborate, from 1900 on, insight came to have a much deeper meaning.

One of Freud's major contributions throughout his work was the clarification of the nature of *anxiety* and assigning to it the central role in all neurotic problems. His first theory of anxiety, propounded in this period, was that it is the transformation of physical sexual tension. He saw the mechanism of anxiety-neurosis in the deflection of somatic sexual excitation from the psychical field and in an abnormal use of it, due to this deflection. This toxicological theory, which was not fully abandoned until 1932, thus held on to some more intimate connection between body and mind than did other aspects of his theories.

Although Freud always liked to discount his therapeutic leanings, the transition from hypnosis to psychoanalysis signaled a considerable change in his attitude toward therapy.

Even as a hypnotist Freud had made significant contributions. The French school, which had experimented with hypnosis most widely, had only one therapeutic use for the technique, that of posthypnotic suggestion. To this Freud added Breuer's catharsis.

To Freud hypnosis, in addition to being a therapeutic device, was a psychological phenomenon of uncommon interest. Some patients could be hypnotized, others could not; this fact was well known. But exactly what was the difference between these two types of patients? There must be some psychological force, Freud reasoned, which led the patient to block the hypnotic process; further, this force must be connected with the relationship between the patient and the physician. Here are already apparent [15] the earliest observations of transference and resistance which later were seen to be key concepts in all psychotherapy.   "bound"

The concern with resistance was a new element in psychotherapy. The prevailing view of the etiology of neurosis and psychosis was organic. According to this position, if the neurotic got better, that was a lucky accident; if not, well, then, his brain had been damaged since birth. While Freud did not entirely discard the view that heredity is the cause of neurosis (echoes of it are to be found all through his writings) his contribution was, after all, the psychological one. If neurosis has a psychological basis, and if it can be understood dynamically or even cured by psychotherapy, then the constitutional factor becomes, to that extent, less significant.   devalued

Further, to concern oneself with therapeutic failure implied a denial, for practical purposes, of the hereditary factor and an affirmation of the psychological one. In this way a hitherto unknown therapeutic optimism, cautious at first, yet gradually growing stronger, was introduced into psychiatry. This attitude, that the patient who has not been helped is one who has not been sufficiently understood, rather than one who is beyond hope, persists to this day.

It has always been a fructifying attitude that has steadily broadened the horizon of the psychotherapist.   *Kabbala*

The replacement of hypnosis by psychoanalysis was made possible by one of Freud's most momentous discoveries, *free association.* He developed it somewhere between 1892 and 1896, and it soon displaced the cathartic method entirely.

In free association the patient is asked to say whatever comes to mind, no matter how trivial or embarrassing or irrelevant it may appear. That these associations should be significant is a direct out-growth of the assumption of science that everything has a cause. It follows pretty directly from the associationist school of psychology, the leading school in psychology for many centuries, and it is surprising that the discovery of the value of free association had to wait for Freud.

Theoretically, some free association should always be possible, as Freud had observed. It thus provides a marked contrast to hypnosis, which in a great many cases is not applicable. Then, if free association is always possible,* the therapist has not only a broader therapeutic approach but also an opening to that totality of mental functioning which was Freud's greater interest.

By no means the least, though a frequently underestimated, aspect of Freud's discoveries in this period, was the concept that neurosis is primarily a social, rather than a physiological, phenomenon. He himself was surprised by his findings, and in the *Studies on Hysteria* at one point he became somewhat apologetic about it. He wrote:

I have not always been a psychotherapist. Like other neuro-pathologists, I was trained to apply local diagnoses and electro-prognosis, and it still strikes me myself as strange that the case histories I write should read like short stories and that, as one might say, they lack the serious stamp of science. I must console myself with the reflection that the nature of the subject is evidently responsible for this, rather than any preference of my own. The fact is that local diagnosis and electrical reactions lead nowhere in the study of hysteria, whereas a detailed description of mental processes such as we are accustomed to find in the works of imaginative writers enables me, with the use of a few psychological formulas, to obtain at least some kind of insight into the course of that affection. Case

---

* Free association is often not feasible as a therapeutic tool, as, e.g., with children or schizophrenics. That, however, does not alter the fact that it is always possible.

play

histories of this kind are intended to be judged like psychiatric ones; they have, however, one advantage over the latter, namely, an intimate connection between the story of the patient's sufferings and the symptoms of his illness—a connection for which we still search in vain in the biographies of other psychoses.[16]

This concern with the intimate human side of the patient's life has ever since been characteristic of psychoanalysis as contrasted with other approaches to psychology.

Freud's numerous changes of view, his continuing fruitless search for a "firm basis in physiology" and his personal preoccupations led to a relative paucity of publications in this early period before 1900. There was one book, *Studies on Hysteria,* published in conjunction with Breuer in 1895, and a few papers, particularly "The Defense Neuro-Psychoses" (1894), "On the Grounds for Detaching from Neurasthenia a Particular Syndrome: The Anxiety Neurosis" (1894) and "Further Remarks on the Defense Neuro-Psychoses" (1896), which contain his principal views. In one form or another the *Studies on Hysteria* particularly contain the germs of all his later theories. Nevertheless, since he still lacked a clear theory of the unconscious, of infantile sexuality, and of transference this work must still be looked upon as part of the prehistory of psychoanalysis.

By 1895 Freud had established himself as a brilliant young neurologist. He had classified the major forms of neurosis, used hypnosis and particularly catharsis to attain much-improved therapeutic results, and formulated a number of concepts, such as trauma, conflict, defense, abreaction, and the toxic theory of anxiety which remained basic to his thinking. Nevertheless, he was still only a neurologist, concerned primarily with a special form of illness, like other specialists. While he was well ahead of the other neurologists of his day, there were many others who had somewhat similar ideas.

Available English Translations of Freud's Works Cited in Chapter II.

Studies on Hysteria. 1895.
    Standard Edition, Vol. II.
    Above issued as a separate volume: New York: Basic Books, 1957. Under title: "Studies in Hysteria." Nervous and Mental Diseases Monograph Series No. 61. New York and Washington: Nervous and Mental Diseases Publishing Co., 1936. Boston: Beacon Press (paperback).

The Origins of Psychoanalysis. 1887-1902.
Sigmund Freud's Letters, Drafts and Notes to Wilhelm Fliess, 1887-1902. Edited by Marie Bonaparte, Anna Freud and Ernst Kris. New York: Basic Books, 1954. New York: Doubleday Anchor (paperback).

The Defense Neuro-Psychoses. 1894.
Collected Papers, Vol. I, pp. 59-75.

On the Grounds for Detaching from Neurasthenia a Particular Syndrome: The Anxiety Neurosis. 1894.
Collected Papers, Vol. I, pp. 76-106.

Further Remarks on the Defense Neuro-Psychoses. 1896.
Collected Papers, Vol. I, pp. 155-182.

NOTES ON CHAPTER II

For a good brief description of knowledge of the neuroses before Freud see Chapter IX, "The Discovery of Neuroses," in G. Zilboorg: *A History of Medical Psychology* (New York: Norton, 1941). An authoritative historical account of the concept of neurasthenia is in H. A. Bunker: "From Beard to Freud," *Medical Review of Reviews,* 412th issue, March, 1930.

On Charcot, see Freud's own article: "Charcot," *Collected Papers,* Volume I, pp. 9-23. Also the recent biography by G. Guillain: *Charcot* (New York: Hoeber, 1959).

On Breuer, see P. F. Cranefield: "Joseph Breuer's Evaluation of His Contribution to Psychoanalysis," *International Journal of Psychoanalysis,* XXXIX, 1958, pp. 319-22.

For a recent critical discussion of the actual neurosis, see A. Blau: "In Support of Freud's Syndrome of Anxiety (Actual) Neurosis," *International Journal of Psychoanalysis,* XXXIII, 1952, pp. 363-72. C. Brenner: "An Addendum to Freud's Theory of Anxiety," *International Journal of Psychoanalysis,* XXXIV, 1953, pp. 18-24.

For a historical discussion of the roots of free association see L. Bellak: "Free Association: Conceptual and Clinical Aspects," *International Journal of Psychoanalysis,* XLI, 1961, pp. 9-20. In 1939 Carney Landis suggested that free association readily lends itself to experimental investigation (*Psychoanalysis as Seen by Psychoanalyzed Psychologists,* p. 28). For a recent experimental approach see K. Colby: "Experiment on the Effects of an Observer's Presence on the Imago System During Psychoanalytic Free Association," *Behavioral Science,* V, No. 3, July, 1960.

Chapter III. SELF-ANALYSIS—1895–1899

The few publications from Freud's pen in the period from the *Studies on Hysteria* (1895) to the *Interpretation of Dreams* (1900) were primarily reformulations of positions already established. What he was preoccupied with instead was, as we now know from biographical and autobiographical data, his own self-analysis. It was his analysis of himself that brought about the decisive change in his interest from neurology to psychology, and created a whole new science, psychoanalysis.

The role that Freud's own analysis played in the history of the science can scarcely be overestimated. It established the precedent for the contemporary training analysis, still the most essential part of the preparation of any psychoanalyst. It showed that the difference between the neurotic and the normal is a quantitative one of degree, not a qualitative one of kind. Freud had always had an inkling that this must be so. In 1882 he had written to his fiancée: "I always find it uncanny when I can't understand someone in terms of myself." [17] Now he was to prove his hunch.

Appreciation of the role that self-analysis played in Freud's development has come only gradually and late. He himself made but few allusions to it in his published writings, and in these he attached no real importance to what he had done. After his death in 1939 some scattered references to autobiographical data were brought to light and commented upon. Then his letters to Fliess, to which reference has already been made, were discovered and published in 1950.

Wilhelm Fliess was a Berlin physician who was a close friend of Freud's from 1887 to 1902. The two often met to discuss scientific matters and engaged in a lively correspondence. Fliess kept Freud's letters. After Fliess's death his widow sold them to a Berlin bookdealer named Stahl. During the Nazi regime Stahl fled to France, where he offered the letters to Marie Bonaparte. She immediately bought them, and though Freud advised her to throw them away, she kept them and eventually had them published. They appear in English as *The Origins of Psychoanalysis: Sigmund Freud's Letters to Wilhelm Fliess (1887-1902)*.

In Chapter XIV of Volume I of his biography of Freud, Ernest Jones gathered together the relevant details from these *Letters to Fliess*, added some other material, and gave a vivid description of the most intensive period of the self-analysis, from June to November, 1897.

However, remarkable as was Freud's self-analysis, it was described by him in an equally remarkable way—in *The Interpretation of Dreams*. Here he relies most heavily on his dreams, and reveals himself as no man has ever done before or since.

To co-ordinate the many aspects of Freud's life and work requires a great amount of careful research. This task has recently been performed by the French scholar, Didier Anzieu.[18] The following account is taken primarily from Anzieu.

In 1895, when his intensive self-analysis began, Freud was 39 years old. He was a successful neurologist, happily married, the father of five children, with a sixth on the way; his daughter, Anna, was born on December 3, 1895. To all outward appearances he was a happy man. His time was devoted to his practice, his family, and his friends. He read widely in many fields, and was a man of considerable cultural attainments, in addition to his medical specialty.

Inwardly however he was full of moods and fears. He was frequently depressed; he formed violent hatreds; he was afraid to travel, at times even afraid to cross the street. He had somatic symptoms, and alternated between diagnoses of stomach trouble and heart trouble. His dependence on Fliess was obviously not based on purely objective considerations.

Nevertheless, all Freud's inner fears and conflicts were scarcely different from those of other men in his community. He was what in modern parlance is called a "normal-neurotic" and one can give no compelling reason for his analysis. Like so many others before him, he might have shrugged off his problems by saying "That's life" or given himself some esoteric or medical diagnosis, or "taken up a hobby." Instead he entered on an intellectual adventure which opened up a whole new world, namely, the inner life of man. Once opened up, this new world now seems familiar enough to us, and so many others have followed in Freud's footsteps that we have lost sight of the revolutionary character of his undertaking. Freud's self-analysis, however, must rank as one of the greatest discoveries of all time. It is on a par with Darwin's theory of evolution and Einstein's principle of relativity.

Much as an analysis today begins with what later turns out to be a trivial symptom, Freud began with the wish to explore two ideas: free association, and the hypothesis that a dream is the fulfillment of a wish of the previous day. The dream of Irma's injection, on July 24, 1895,* revealed to him for the first time that dreams have meaning, and showed how this meaning could be extracted from them. It is from this dream and its interpretation that the beginning of his self-analysis is to be dated. Freud was well aware of the magnitude of his discovery at the time and jokingly suggested in a letter to Fliess that a tablet be placed on the house in which the meaning occurred to him, with the inscription:

ON JULY 24, 1895

THE SECRET OF THE DREAM

WAS REVEALED TO DR. SIGMUND FREUD

The interpretation of this dream showed Freud that he could apply the method of free association to himself. But in so doing he also made a supplementary observation (serendipity): There are unconscious wishes in the dream. The structure of the dream is similar to that of the neurotic symptom in that both are symbolic. This discovery came about in the course of the dream itself, thus offering a new illustration of the creative power of the dream. Finally, the particular dream, which is one of guilt and expiation,

* This has since been called the "dream specimen of psychoanalysis." See *The Interpretation of Dreams,* Chapter II and reference 61.

contains a new personal insight: Freud is haunted by feelings of guilt toward his patients, his colleagues, his family, and his friends.

Apart from all this, the dream set loose a process in Freud which was to continue throughout his entire life and work. Sooner or later psychoanalysis touches upon every human concern. It was no longer a matter of scientific research; it became an intense human experience.

The year 1895-6 was the one in which this transformation occurred. Freud finished his previous work. He resigned himself to the loss of Breuer, who was frightened by Freud's sexual theories, and moved closer to Fliess, whom he looked upon as an expert in biology and the chemistry of the sexual processes, and from whom he hoped to receive the enlightenment he needed on these subjects.

The death of his father in September 1896 created an upheaval from which it took him three years to recover. His dreams became more importunate and more precise. It was as though they embodied a dialogue which gave voice to his inner conflicts. A son necessarily experiences violent hostility toward his father, even the most beloved of fathers. This hostility Freud had denied and forgotten, and it was this hostility which his father's death reawakened in him. He was experiencing the "return of the repressed" which was to occupy such a central role in all his later thinking. The hostility explains the feelings of guilt which had been apparent since the dream of Irma's injection. Freud recognized his hostility and analyzed each of its forms: jealousy, rivalry, ambition, resentment; gradually he freed himself from their inevitable corollaries: shame, remorse, impotence, inhibition, and the wish to fail.

Much of this became clear to him in a time of trouble, during the summer of 1897. He could no longer work intellectually. His theories had collapsed; his practice was shrinking; he felt incapable of finishing an analysis he was engaged in; the difficulties of his patients aroused enormous personal repercussions. He again began to feel threatened by doubts about the future. He was even paralyzed in his correspondence with Fliess, toward whom he was beginning to experience the same ambivalence that analysis had revealed existed toward his father. The crisis was accompanied by an exacerbation of all his weak points: fear of cardiac illness and of approaching death, fear of railroad trips, depression to the point where he feared he was suffering from a neurosis.

Under this tension, his self-analysis turned toward his memories of childhood. In the course of his interpretations of dreams childhood memories cropped up with increasing frequency and helped to convince him that the unconscious wish in the dream stems from childhood as well as from the previous day. His personal experience made him certain that the unconscious of the adult is in large measure made up of the child that slumbers within the adult. The child is driven by his own desires and impulses which lead him to create imaginary satisfactions in a rich fantasy life; later the adult is no longer able to distinguish between fantasy and reality.

These two key areas of fantasy and of childhood were clarified in a period of intensive self-analysis at the end of September and the beginning of October, 1897, which followed the summer crisis. He reconstructed the libidinal emotions of his childhood: the incestuous wishes for his mother, sadism toward his niece Pauline, shame and fear of punishment by his nurse, and the corresponding aggressive feelings: jealousy of his father, wish to murder his younger brother Alexander, fierce competition with his nephew John, who happened to be a year older than he. The two sides of his nature he combined in his theory of the Oedipus complex.

The following period, from the fall of 1897 to the summer of 1898, saw the application ("working-through") of these insights to his neurosis, his friendships, his profession. His cardiac anxieties and fear of traveling disappeared. His dependence on Fliess changed into competition. He discarded hypnosis altogether and henceforth in his practice relied on dreams, free associations, and childhood memories. The wish to write a book on dreams became stronger. Brücke and Charcot ceased to be his models; instead he identified with Goethe. Like Goethe, he was beginning to extend his findings to the entire range of human activity.

Freud's inner life in the spring and summer of 1898 was marked by anal material: excremental dreams, reading of Rabelais and Zola, digestive difficulties, coarseness of images and memories. He was reliving the time of his toilet-training.

For a while Freud's interest in his own dreams diminished. He had already made his most significant discoveries, and was anxious to publish a book on the topic. A necessary review of the previous literature bored him but gave him the satisfaction of confirming once again that nothing of any consequence had ever been said on the subject. He began to turn to everyday slips of the tongue or pen or memory, and to think of his next book, *The Psychopathology of Everyday Life*.

Nevertheless, there were relapses. The fall of 1898 saw a new crisis: return of his inner suffering, intellectual paralysis. From this depression a dream * rescued him. He thought of all his vanished friends, and all the rivals on whom he had wished death.

But there was another side to his depression: his relation to his mother and the oral stage. A further dream † makes clear the ambiguity of the mother-image which he had re-experienced in his wife: giver of life and nourishment, but instrument of implacable death, inviting love and pleasure, but forbidding or punishing them at the same time.

After these dreams he could reconstruct the stages of his love-life: his attachment to Pauline, his first adolescent love-dream, his first erotic fantasies, his love-marriage and resentment toward his wife because of the difficulties in the relationship.

His difficulties were resolved by refinding the father-image, the serene authority who had ruled so happily in his childhood and the mother-image who gave him that sublime self-confidence which he always ascribed to the love which a mother gives to her first born and son.

Finally, surmounting his inner conflicts, he turned back to work. In the first nine months of 1899 he finished the manuscript of *The Interpretation of Dreams*. From then to the end of his life, with minor interruptions, he found his place in life as a calm and serene father. For the most part his symptoms disappeared, although he occasionally showed signs of depression and somatic difficulties throughout his entire life. In his personal life he found much happiness with his family. The break with Fliess finally came in 1900, although Freud tried to maintain the relationship for another two

---

* *Non vixit*: see *The Interpretation of Dreams*, pp. 421-5.
† The three fates: see *The Interpretation of Dreams*, pp. 204-8.

omnipotent → death-vulnerable

fiction

years. Henceforth Freud had disciples, but no longer any need for close friends. His fear of traveling was overcome. In 1901 he was able to visit Rome which he had previously felt compelled to stay away from. And in his work he was able to lay the foundation for the new science of psychoanalysis.

Although his immediate conflicts subsided ("his analysis was terminated"), in one sense self-analysis continued to the end of Freud's life. He told Jones at one time that he devoted the last half-hour of every day to this purpose.[19]

The effect of Freud's self-analysis on the further development of his views and the science in general was enormous. Two immediate consequences can be highlighted here.

First of all, Freud had reached his most important discoveries only through self-exploration. What had begun as a kind of intellectual game became a bitter internal struggle lasting five years, and in one sense continuing all his life. Since it was only after this struggle on his part that the meaning of his findings became clear to him, he made the same demand on others. In 1910 he stated:

Now that a considerable number of people are practising psychoanalysis and exchanging their observations with one another, we have noticed that no psychoanalyst goes further than his own complexes and internal resistances permit; and we consequently require that he shall begin his activity with a self-analysis and continually carry it deeper while he is making his observations on his patients. Anyone who fails to produce results in a self-analysis of this kind may at once give up any idea of being able to treat patients by analysis.[20]

The demand however goes further than the practitioner. Experience has shown that an intellectual grasp of the doctrines of psychoanalysis is extraordinarily difficult, because these doctrines involve such a drastic change in man's ways of thinking. The emotional heat generated by Freud is so great that many of the writers who have examined his views have not even been able to quote them accurately. It is this fact which has led to the suggestion that all workers in the social sciences should have some analysis. It is however quite possible that with the spread of public knowledge of psychoanalysis this difficulty will diminish.

A second consequence of Freud's self-analysis was the realization that the difference between the neurotic and the normal is one of degree rather than of kind. The neurotic is a person with troubles, not someone suffering from some obscure medical illness. This point of view has recently been most clearly formulated by T. S. Szasz in his book *The Myth of Mental Illness*.

Without detracting in any way from the magnificence of Freud's achievement, it is still necessary to examine Freud's self-analysis critically. The effect of Freud's personality on the historical development of psychoanalysis can of course hardly be exaggerated, and it was the self-analysis which produced the mature man.

In spite of his success, Freud doubted that he could analyze himself. In November, 1897 he had written to Fliess:

My self-analysis is still interrupted and I have realized the reason. I can only analyze myself with the help of knowledge obtained objectively (like an outsider). Genuine self-analysis is impossible; otherwise there would be no illness.[21]

And in 1936 he wrote:

In self-analysis the danger of incompleteness is particularly great. One is too easily satisfied with a part explanation, behind which resistance can easily keep back something that may perhaps be more important.[22]

Nevertheless, for a long time Freud was modest enough to believe that anybody could do what he had done. As late as 1914 he was still willing to accept self-analysis as adequate for analytic training.[23]

Experience, however, soon dashed the hope that everybody's self-analysis could flow even as smoothly as Freud's, which had not been too smooth. It quickly became all too apparent how seriously countertransferences came to interfere in analytic practice. After World War I the conviction grew that the only way to overcome these countertransferences was by a personal analysis by a more experienced analyst. Since that time, personal analysis has become an absolute requirement of every analytic training institute. Where at first it was held that anybody could do what Freud had done, it was finally concluded that nobody could.

In retrospect, certain gaps and biases can be pointed out in Freud's self-analysis also. By and large, Freud tended to stress his own personal kind of experience too much. The death of his father had precipitated his own great inner turmoil, and accordingly he wrote that the death of a man's father is "the most important event, the most poignant loss of a man's life." [24] But what if, unlike Freud, a man lost his mother first or a child or a beloved grandparent, or retained his parents but had his home uprooted?

More serious is Freud's predominant emphasis on male psychology and his astounding confessions of ignorance about women. His writings are replete with protestations about how little is known about women. As late as 1933 in an essay on "The Psychology of Women" he wrote:

Throughout the ages the problem of woman has puzzled people of every kind. . . . You too will have pondered over this question insofar as you are men; from the women among you that is not to be expected, for you are the riddle yourselves.[25]

Here are some other representative statements from earlier writings. In the 1923 paper on the phallic phase he wrote:

Unfortunately we can describe this state of things only as it affects the male child; the corresponding processes in the little girl are not known to us.[26]

In the *Three Essays* in 1905 he wrote:

The significance of the factor of sexual overvaluation can be best studied in men, for their erotic life alone has become accessible to research. That of women . . . is still veiled in an impenetrable obscurity.[27]

Thus, just as *The Interpretation of Dreams* was based largely on his own dreams, the theoretical description of infantile sexuality leaned most heavily on his understanding of his own development. It was not without reason that he once commented that much that is of general occurrence and clearly true can yet be overlooked by psychoanalysts in spite of decades of unremitting observation.[28]

In his self-analysis Freud made a host of fundamental discoveries: the unconscious, the Oedipus complex, the anal stage, infantile sexuality, how to interpret dreams, free associations, transferences, and resistances. This is assuredly a tremendous contribution for any one man to make.

Yet he omitted a number of others. He knew little about the oral stage, particularly the infant's hostility toward the mother, and maternal rejection of the infant. These are features of human development that have become subjects of interest and exploration only since about 1940.

Freud's masculine bias and professed ignorance of the psychology of women have already been noted. Equally surprising is his failure to examine more critically his relationships to his own children. In his self-analysis he was interested in his functioning as a child; how he behaved as a parent was apparently of no concern to him. His own conflicts with his parents he ascribed to a biological factor, namely, his instinctual impulses. In a sense his biological orientation had one root in his desire to exonerate his parents, particularly his mother. His main concern was to uncover his own instinctual development; how his parents handled these instincts was a secondary matter. Though it is readily implicit in psychoanalytic theory, it took a long time for him to get in more detail to the role which parents play in the formation of the Oedipus complex and of the child's personality in general.[29]

No doubt it was this neglect of the parental aspect which stopped Freud from undertaking the analysis of children. A natural opening for such an extension came with his analysis of the 5-year-old Hans. Hans was a little boy who developed a fear of horses which prevented him from going out on the street. Freud could have analyzed the child, but chose instead to work through the father. It remained for his daughter Anna and her colleague, Melanie Klein, to go on to the direct treatment of the child.

The particular problems which Freud was grappling with in his self-analysis had little relationship to the society in which he found himself. Accordingly, for a long time he tended to ignore the milieu and concentrate on the personal-individual features of the neurosis. This too was a gap that was filled in later.

Freud's self-analysis was conducted by means of dreams, free associations, and childhood memories. In all three of these he was astoundingly gifted. Modestly he assumed that others would be equally gifted; if they did not produce the material quickly he ascribed it to resistance. But subsequent history has shown that many people find it difficult to recall dreams, or to free-associate or to remember their childhood, in spite of the most intensive analysis of resistances. There has been a tendency to call those who could do to any degree what Freud did analyzable and those who could not unanalyzable. This is one of the factors which has led to the many controversies about analyzability.

Thus in more than one sense Freud's self-analysis is the matrix from which the whole science grew. It was here that he had the great insights which form the basis of psychoanalysis. And it was here too that he left broad gaps which he and other workers in the field were later to fill in.

Available English Translations of Freud's Works Cited in Chapter III

An Autobiographical Study. 1925. With Postscript, 1935.
Standard Edition, Vol. XX, pp. 7-70.
London: Hogarth Press and the Institute of Psychoanalysis, 1946. In *The Problem of Lay Analyses* (without 1935 Postscript). New York: Brentano, 1927, pp. 189-316.
Under title *Autobiography*. New York: Norton, 1935, 1952.

NOTES ON CHAPTER III

As mentioned in the text, the only fully adequate source for the self-analysis is D. Anzieu: *L'Auto-Analyse* (Paris: Presses Universitaires de France, 1959), which has not yet been translated from the original French. Vol. I of Jones's biography is of course invaluable. Freud himself never described his self-analysis in any systematic manner. His *An Autobiographical Study* (Standard Edition, Vol. XX, pp. 7-74) covers the development of the science, but not his inner struggles.

On self-analysis since Freud, see the subsequent parts of the work by Anzieu cited above. The feasibility and limits of self-analysis are still matters of considerable dispute among analysts. For different points of view, see K. Horney: *Self-Analysis* (New York: Norton, 1942). E. Pickworth Farrow: *A Practical Method of Self-Analysis* (London: Allen and Unwin, 1942), also has a foreword by Freud. E. Weigert: "Counter-Transference and Self-Analysis of the Psycho-Analyst," *International Journal of Psychoanalysis*, XXXV, 1954, pp. 242-6. M. Kramer: "On the Continuation of the Analytic Process after Psychoanalysis (A Self-Observation)," *International Journal of Psychoanalysis*, XL, 1959, pp. 17-25.

Part II.

ID PSYCHOLOGY: THE FIRST
PSYCHOANALYTIC SYSTEM—1900–1914

Chapter IV. THE UNCONSCIOUS

When the International Psychoanalytical Association was founded in 1910, the goals of the Association were declared to be to:

... foster and further the science of psychoanalysis founded by Freud, both as a pure discipline of psychology and in its application to medicine and the mental sciences. . . .[30]

The "pure discipline of psychology" which Freud had in mind, and which may be called the first psychoanalytic system, rested on three bases. These were: the unconscious, the libido theory, and transference and resistance as the basis of psychotherapy. The major works of Freud in which these concepts were developed were published between 1900 and 1914, although in a number of cases various additions were made afterward.

The unconscious was always for Freud one of the major pillars of psychoanalytic psychology. In every one of his popular presentations of psychoanalysis, which were quite numerous, he devoted most space to a delineation of the unconscious. If he had to refer to psychoanalysis briefly, he would call it the psychology of the unconscious or the psychology of the depths. Much of the opposition to psychoanalysis he attributed to its discovery of the unconscious and the consequent blow to man's fond narcissistic belief that he is in complete control of himself.

It is vital to understand that the unconscious is a concept which provides a theoretical framework that ties together a number of clinical observations. It is not an anatomical concept; as Freud noted over and over again, it has no anatomical locale. It is not reified, that is, it is not transformed into some entity with an independent existence. The unconscious is merely shorthand for "unconscious mental processes."

Furthermore, as a theory designed to explain the observed facts, it left Freud somewhat dissatisfied, and he was always preoccupied with the wish to make it much more consistent. In other words, it is a first approximation, although actually Freud's work on the unconscious was so thoroughly done that nothing of any fundamental importance has since been added. His own view was summed up in the paper on "The Unconscious" in 1915, in which he wrote:

Study of the derivatives of the unconscious will completely disappoint our expectations of a schematically clear-cut distinction between the two psychical systems. This will no doubt give rise to dissatisfaction with our results and will probably be used to cast doubts on the value of the way in which we have divided up the psychical processes. Our answer is, however, that we have no other aim but that of translating into theory the results of observation, and we deny that there is any obligation on us to achieve at our first attempt a well-rounded theory which will commend itself by its simplicity. We shall defend the complications of our theory so long as we find that they meet the results of observation, and we shall not abandon our expectations of being led in the end by those very complications to the discovery of a state of affairs which, while simple in itself, can account for all the complications of reality.[31]

To some extent the unconscious always played a role in the history of psychology. L. L. Whyte has recently summarized the pre-Freudian literature. Herbart, one of the dominant figures in German psychology, in the nineteenth century, actually used terms such as "unconscious" and "repressed" which were identical with Freud's terms, and it has been shown that Freud was exposed to textbooks of psychology written along Herbartian lines. Freud himself made a number of references to one of the leading German psychologists of his day, Theodor Lipps, who insisted that the unconscious was the real problem of psychology. The famous English psychologist, Francis Galton, had written a passage in 1880 that sounds almost like Freud:

Associated ideas lay bare the foundations of men's thoughts ... with more vividness and truth than he would probably care to publish to the world ... and the valid reason, therefore, to our believing in the existence of still deeper strata of mental operations, sunk wholly below the level of consciousness, which may account for such mental phenomena as cannot otherwise be explained.[32]

Nevertheless, it must not be supposed that the historical antecedents explain Freud's revolutionary use of the concepts. The same holds true of the unconscious as of other pathbreaking steps in the history of ideas, such as evolution or relativity: While there are many predecessors, it remains for some profound mind to come along and show how the concept can really be applied to the data at hand. This is Freud's real contribution. He made the unconscious a working tool for the psychologist, instead of a speculative device, as it had been in the past. Thereby he opened up a whole new world for psychological investigation.

Freud's early observations of the 1890's were deepened by his own self-analysis, which led to *The Interpretation of Dreams* (1900). Some further additions were made in *The Psychopathology of Everyday Life* (1904) and in the paper (1915) "The Unconscious." These three works summarize Freud's thinking on the unconscious.

Actually Freud's theory of the unconscious is relatively simple. It examines both the conscious and the unconscious, and considers the shifting balance between the two types of mental processes.

In order to understand a mental process in all its aspects one takes the *metapsychological* point of view. This metapyschological point of view embodies topographic, dynamic, and economic aspects.

The *topographic* aspect distinguishes three components of a mental process: the unconscious, the preconscious, and the conscious, commonly abbreviated as Ucs, Pcs, and Cs. The *dynamic* aspect presupposes that mental phenomena are looked upon as being the result of the interaction and counteraction of forces.

The *economic* aspect leads to the attempt to ascertain the fate of given volumes of excitation. It considers the quantitative element. It is an outgrowth of the concept of bound and unbound energy which stemmed from Freud's Breuer period.

When excitation is concentrated either positively or negatively in any given direction or area there results a *"cathexis"*; in other words, a cathected object is one that is either desired or feared. The term "cathexis" is a somewhat clumsy one; it was especially coined by Brill for his English translation of Freud. "Emotional charge" would have been a simpler form. However, "cathexis" is by now widely used and well understood.[33]

The kernel of the unconscious consists of instinct presentations, the aim of which is to discharge their cathexis. They are wishes or impulses. In the processes belonging to the unconscious are to be found exemption from mutual contradiction, timelessness, the substitution of psychic for external reality, and domination by the primary process.

In other words, the unconscious consists of a variety of wishes which press for discharge. These wishes originally stem from instinctual needs but may develop far beyond them. It is only when such wishes are discharged, in one form or another, either in phantasies, in dreams, in neurotic symptoms, or in overt active behavior of one kind or another, that the unconscious becomes known. Otherwise it acts silently and completely beyond the awareness of the observer.

The *primary process* is that which reigns in the unconscious. Study of the primary process reveals a type of mental functioning that is radically different from ordinary rational thinking. Its chief characteristic is the striving for immediate discharge. The whole stress is laid upon making the cathecting energy mobile and capable of discharge; the content and the proper meaning of the psychical elements to which the cathexes are attached are treated as of little consequence. The primary process seeks release above all, and thus helps to account for those phenomena that come out involuntarily or unconsciously.

The two major devices of the primary process are *condensation* and *displacement*. In condensation one idea comes to stand for a great many, much as symbols do in works of art. In displacement, ideas or feelings are shifted to some entirely different area which may have no intrinsic relation to it. Condensation and displacement help to explain why the unconscious is so unintelligible; conversely, by understanding these processes one can make the unconscious intelligible.

Contrasted to the primary process is the *secondary process* which is ordinary rational thinking. However, it adds the idea that rational thinking serves the purpose of handling the impulses that emanate from the primary process. While the primary process seeks for discharge, the secondary process attempts to inhibit the discharge and to transform the cathexis into a quiescent one or to stabilize it.

From this point of view consciousness functions as a sense organ which selects the material from the unconscious which does not arouse too much anxiety in the individual, and which rejects those impulses which do arouse too much anxiety. Nevertheless our consciousness acts as a very imperfect sense organ, and frequently the unconscious breaks through into consciousness even though such a break-through is not desired. This is the phenomenon which Freud called "the return of the repressed." Just why repressed material should be repressed most of the time and return at others becomes a ticklish theoretical question, yet this phenomenon is something that a great many clinical observations help to explain.

The theory of the unconscious includes a number of important findings:

The Motives for Repression

Repression is a protective process that wards off unpleasant experiences for the individual. It is part of the earliest observation that Freud made, namely, that neurosis involves a defense against unbearable ideas. The enlargement of the concept involves the recognition that repression is not confined to neurosis but is found in all human beings. Repression is tied up with the pleasure principle, which, in general, all psychologists have seen to be the basis of biological strivings; man, like other animals, is an organism that searches for pleasure. The pleasurable desires are called wishes; the unpleasurable ones are called fears. Repression maintains the balance in the individual; by its means he helps himself to seek pleasure and to avoid pain.

Manifestations of the Unconscious

With the realization that dreams are an expression of unconscious wishes, Freud arrived at a new and deeper understanding of the unconscious. Henceforth he liked to refer to psychoanalysis as the psychology of the depths, by which is meant that the unconscious penetrates to the deepest layers of the personality and is far more extensive than anybody had hitherto realized.

The first manifestations of the unconscious were observed in hypnosis. In the hypnotic situation, the subject can be given a suggestion to carry out after he comes out of the hypnotic trance. If he is also told that he will forget what happened during hypnosis, he will do so and will carry out the suggestion, even though he has no idea of why he is acting in this way, and even though the action may be totally inappropriate to the circumstances. This is known as "posthypnotic suggestion" and "posthypnotic amnesia." Here the unconscious is, so to speak, demonstrated experimentally.

The next area in which unconscious manifestations were recognized by Freud was neurosis. In psychotherapy free associations were seen as an avenue to the unconscious.

These phenomena are confined primarily to therapeutic or clinical situations. When Freud turned to dreams, however, he came squarely to grips with normal psychology, since everybody dreams, and people have always dreamed everywhere and in all ages. Thus his work on dreams represented for Freud a transition from psychopathology to normal psychology.

After dreams, Freud turned to two subjects which were totally foreign to the neurological and psychiatric thinking of his day, just as dreams had been. In 1904 he wrote *The Psychopathology of Everyday Life;* the next year he wrote a book about jokes and the unconscious. By the psychopathology of everyday life he meant the various slips of the tongue, errors of omission and commission, symptomatic actions, failures to carry out actions, and all other minor slips and mistakes which may perhaps be best summed up by the term *Freudian slips.* Freud's thesis is really that any slip is to be taken seriously. If, for example, a man should forget to come to his own wedding, everybody would assume that he is in the grip of some fear of getting married. Freud extended this thinking to all kinds of slips; even apparently minor lapses, such as losing a letter or misplacing a book, may be unconsciously determined. The need for gratification and wish-fulfillment, which is the basis of all mental life, breaks through.

That jokes can have intense meaning to the individual is a proposition that many can readily agree with, once it is pointed out. Freud's contribution here, apart from the technical means of discovering the mechanisms of jokes, is once again that the individual is in the grip of psychic conflicts which need discharge, and that the joke serves as a discharge phenomenon.

At about the same time that he wrote about jokes Freud also began to investigate the matter of artistic production. As early as 1904 he wrote a paper, "Psychopathic Characters on the Stage," which embodies many of the essential ideas in the psychoanalytic interpretation of art. In the theatrical performance both the performer and the audience find some gratification for their neurotic needs. The needs which are gratified are unconscious in nature; were they to become conscious, the attraction of the artistic performance both for the performer and for the audience would be lost.

And so the horizons continued to be broadened. In 1907 Freud wrote a paper about obsessional acts and religious practices, in which he called attention to the close similarity between the two. He showed that religion, too, is motivated by unconscious forces.

By this time he had begun to have some followers, and several of them, particularly Otto Rank and Hanns Sachs, did some essential work in the application of psychoanalysis to mythology and the social sciences. In 1912 Freud published his classic application to other societies of psychoanalytic thinking, Totem and Taboo, in which he demonstrated that the unconscious processes which are found in one form of society are not really dissimilar from those found in others. There are certain basic conflicts that are common to all human beings in all societies.

Still later some of his followers were able to apply the theory of the unconscious not merely to slips in everyday behavior but also to ordinary everyday behavior, such as the way a person walks, talks, dresses, and so on. They were able to show that everything has or can have an unconscious aspect to it.

Among the aspects of human living in which manifestations of the unconscious can be found are: hypnosis, neurotic symptoms, free associations, daydreams, dreams, slips of everyday life, jokes, art, religion, mythology, other societies, and behavior in general.

In other words, the unconscious is applicable to every area of human existence. This fact explains the claim that psychoanalysis can become the basis of a general psychology.

The Unconscious and Infantile Sexuality

The contents of the unconscious are related to the stages of psychosexual development. It is to be borne in mind that all elements of the Freudian theory are interconnected with one another; each reinforces the other, so that it is not possible to take one in isolation and consider it as a disconnected entity. If one part of the theory is dropped then the explanation that Freud gave for some other part must be replaced. If, for example, the existence of a primary process is questioned, then it will be necessary to find some other way to explain dreams, since the primary process fits in most neatly with the nature of dreaming. Again, if the theory of the unconscious is dropped or questioned, then some alternative to Freud's explanation will have to be offered. At a later stage Freud demonstrated the central similarity of dreams, neurotic symptoms, schizophrenic delusions, and productions of primitive peoples.

The Contents of the Unconscious. With its dependence on the theory of instinct, the subject of the contents of the unconscious remained for Freud the most uncertain part of his system, and has offered the greatest room for controversy among other psychoanalysts. Freud himself changed his theories about the contents of the unconscious in two vital respects. In 1917 he formalized the concept of the introject in his paper, "Mourning and Melancholia." From this time on not only feelings and ideas could be unconscious but people as well; that is, there can be an unconscious image of another person, essentially the unconscious image of the mother and the father. In 1920 Freud revised his theory of the instincts and introduced the dual theory, with its concept of a life wish and a death instinct with its attendant instinctual aggression; this dual theory again altered his view of the development of sexuality. Both of these changes belong to the period of ego psychology and will be discussed more fully (see Chapter XI).

Freud not only produced a theory of the unconscious; he also had a method for working with the unconscious, which is as important as the theory, since without such a method the unconscious would remain on a theoretical level that would make it inaccessible. Freud's method derives from the various manifestations of the unconscious. Since the primary process is ordinarily concealed by man's rational everyday thoughts, it is only when this rational mask is either removed or reduced to a minimum that the unconscious becomes manifest. One point at which everybody is deprived of the protection of his rationalizations is during sleep; hence Freud referred to dreams as the royal road to the unconscious. In general, fantasies are closer to unconscious needs than are everyday activities. In psychology proper these fantasies can be elicited and studied by means of what are called the projective techniques.

Even though the interpretation of the unconscious may in a general way be the same among different observers, in specific instances one is certain to find a good deal of disagreement. It is a cardinal principle of Freud's doctrine that unconscious material can be understood only when the *associations* of the individual are provided, so that a chain can be formed from the particular production to its unconscious origin. Such associations are most freely obtainable in the psychoanalytic treatment situation. Otherwise they can be reached only with difficulty, and the interpretation of the unconscious meaning of any particular fantasy or act is frequently open to much question.

The idea of an unconscious mind was fought with the most incredible arguments by Freud's colleagues. As he later came to realize, he had dealt the world a severe blow; in effect what he said to men was that they were not really masters in their own house. All of a sudden, the façade behind which they assure themselves that they are aware of all their motives collapsed, and it is understandable that such a shock should be ardently fought. In the course of time the essentially common-sense character of Freud's doctrine has come to be increasingly recognized, and today there is scarcely any school of psychology dealing with personality that does not accept the unconscious in one form or another. Differences naturally arise in the interpretation of unconscious material, but these are differences in detail rather than in the over-all conception.

Schools of thought which do not recognize the unconscious have proved to be almost totally sterile in their approach to human personality, and sooner or later have fallen back heavily upon psychoanalytic concepts.

THE INTERPRETATION OF DREAMS

The work in which his theory of the unconscious was first clearly formulated by Freud was *The Interpretation of Dreams*. This is universally regarded as Freud's greatest work. It is indeed a monumental achievement, since at one stroke it resolves the problem of the dream and formulates the theory of the unconscious. Both of Freud's achievements in this book have stood the test of time. They still form the basis of today's psychoanalytic psychology. The book can rightly be regarded as one of the classics of all scientific literature.

The book was published on November 4, 1899, but the publisher chose to put the date 1900 on the title page.[34]

Initially the book was almost completely ignored by the profession and by the lay public. Six hundred copies were printed; it took eight years to sell them. In the first six weeks after publication 123 copies were sold; in the next two years, 228. Then, as interest in psychoanalysis grew, new editions and revisions were called for. This was one of the two books (the other was *Three Essays on Sexuality*) that Freud continued to revise and keep up to date throughout his life. During his lifetime there were eight editions in all, the last in 1929. In the later editions no fundamental changes were needed. The most important addition contained a theory of symbolism in which Freud gave full credit to Stekel's stimulating ideas.

Usually modest and self-effacing in relation to his achievements, Freud made an exception of this book and was unusually proud of it. In a special preface to the English edition of 1932 he wrote:

This book, with the new contribution to psychology which surprised the world when it was published [1900], remains essentially unaltered. It contains, even according to my present-day judgment, the most valuable of all the discoveries it has been my good fortune to make. Insight such as this falls to one's lot but once in a lifetime.[35]

On the very first page of the book Freud sets forth a statement which can only be regarded as a sharp challenge to the contemporary neurologists and psychologists of his day:

Anyone who has failed to explain the origin of dream images can scarcely hope to understand phobias, obsessions, or delusions, or to bring a therapeutic influence to bear on them.[36]

Inasmuch as no one else at that time understood dreams at all or paid the slightest attention to them, Freud was obviously saying that his colleagues were all misinformed and incapable of treating neurotic problems adequately. Such a provocative position was rarely taken by Freud and it shows again how certain he was of the fundamental and revolutionary character of this work.

The first chapter reviews the previous literature as it had come down through the ages. As Freud later said, nothing except a single isolated remark of Fechner's was of any value. And, indeed, in any scientific discussion of the dream today it is customary to begin with Freud and to discard everything that had gone before.

In Chapter II, entitled "The Analysis of a Specimen Dream," Freud's novel technique for interpreting dreams is first elucidated by means of an illustration, using a dream of his own. In order to understand a dream the dreamer's associations are needed, and if these are not forthcoming it is in general not possible to understand what the dreamer is trying to say. Exceptions to this rule occur only for those dreams which employ primarily symbolism, or which are so-called "typical dreams," that is, dreams that occur in the same form to a great many people.

Novel ideas have a way of looking astoundingly simple once they have been pointed out, and yet of being totally obscure before they are pointed out. Freud rightly stated that his technique of getting associations to the dream elements was the really revolutionary contribution in his conception of the dream and its interpretaton. This idea, of course, is also part of the larger theory of interpreting unconscious material which in general cannot be understood without the associations of the individual.

The associations lead back to the hidden material, which at bottom expresses a wish. Thus in this chapter there are already presented the essentials of Freud's theory of the dream, namely that the dream is a disguised way of gratifying a wish, and that its meaning can be unraveled by paying close attention to the associations of the dreamer.

In Chapter III, "A Dream is the Fulfillment of a Wish," Freud elaborates this latter point more fully. It has often been supposed that, in his opinion, the only wishes that occurred in dreams were of a sexual nature. Freud does hold that most dreams embody sexual wishes, but he goes to great lengths to deny the idea that all of them do. Thus he writes:

> The more one is concerned with the solution of dreams, the more one is driven to recognize that the majority of the dreams of adults deal with sexual material and give expression to erotic wishes.[37]

At the same time, on the very next page he is constrained to declare:

> The assertion that all dreams require a sexual interpretation, against which critics rage so incessantly, occurs nowhere in my *Interpretation of Dreams*. It is not to be found in any of the numerous editions of this book and is an obvious contradiction to other views expressed in it.[38]

If a dream involves a disguised expression of wishes, this requires further investigation. Such further investigation is the subject of Chapter IV, "Distortion in Dreams." Here Freud makes his fundamental distinction between the *manifest* and the *latent* content of a dream. The manifest content is the dream as it appears to the dreamer, the latent content is the dream as it is ultimately unraveled through the series of associations. In this contrast between the manifest and the latent content is seen the interplay of two forces, the *wish* which is striving to break through into consciousness and the *censorship* which seeks to restrain this wish from doing so. It is to be noted that this contrast is an elaboration of Freud's first fundamental hypothesis about neurosis involving a defense against unbearable ideas. The *censor* is a term for the psychic agency which determines whether certain material breaks through to consciousness. In the later period of ego psychology the concept was abandoned; the term is no longer used today.

If a dream is the expression of a wish, a natural objection arises: How is a dream with a distressing content possible? To this the basic answer is that a *dream distortion* has occurred, and that the distressing content serves merely to disguise something that is wished for. This may arise in one of two ways. First, the person may be a masochistic individual and may be seeking to gratify masochistic or self-punishing wishes. Second, in anxiety dreams the anxiety is a transformation of repressed *libido*. (See above, pages 16-17.) In other words, every fear covers up some disguised wish. Through the anxiety-dream the individual is able at least to express the libidinal desire and to derive some gratification in that way.

In Chapter V, "The Material and Sources of Dreams," Freud analyzes the material and the sources of dreams. He considers recent and indifferent material in dreams, infantile material as a source of dreams, the somatic sources of dreams, and typical dreams. The essential points in this chapter are the following:

First of all, there are no indifferent dreams. "We do not allow our sleep to be disturbed by trifles." [39] If the material in the dream seems to be of a trivial or indifferent nature, that is part of the disguise process. Furthermore, there is always a point of contact with the previous day; that is, the dream is triggered off by something that happened within the past twenty-four hours. This stimulus is known as the *day residue*. Though seemingly trivial, upon analysis the day residue always turns out to be connected with something that is vitally significant to the individual. If the analysis is pushed far enough, it is invariably found that the dream attaches itself to childhood experiences. A dream is a piece of infantile mental life that has been superseded. Thus every dream in its manifest content is linked with recent experiences and in its latent content with the earliest experiences.

The usual nonpsychoanalytic assumption is that if dreams have any source at all, they come from somatic stimulation during sleep. For example, it is frequently held that if a person dreams of water it is because he has an urge to urinate. Against such an interpretation Freud raised the irrefutable argument that the same stimulus may be interpreted in any number of different ways by different people and in any number of different ways by the same person at different times during his life. Since Freud's time, this statement has been experimentally confirmed, and can be confirmed over and over again by anyone who wishes to take the trouble. Freud concluded that sensations during sleep play the same role as recent and indifferent material—they trigger off the dream which essentially derives from deeper sources in the unconscious.

In the last section of Chapter V Freud considers a number of typical dreams, such as the dream of being naked in a street, dreams of taking an examination, dreams of the death of a near relative toward whom one has consciously nothing but love feelings, etc. Such dreams Freud considers an exception to the general rule that associations have to be obtained in order to understand the meaning of dreams. Since these typical dreams are so similar in a variety of different people, they bring out deeply buried wishes which are otherwise concealed. For example, the dream of being naked brings out the exhibitionistic wish, while the dream of the death of a loved one brings out the concealed hostile feelings toward that person.

Chapter VI, "The Dream Work," is the longest chapter in the book. Inasmuch as there is both a latent and a manifest content in dreams, there must be some process by which the latent content is transformed into the manifest content. For this process Freud coined the term *dream work*, and proceeded to describe it in the greatest of detail. Inasmuch as the dream has to evade the censorship, the dream work makes use above all of extensive displacements which conceal the true meaning of the material. The thoughts have to be reproduced exclusively or predominantly in the material of visual or acoustical memory traces (primarily visual); this imposes upon the dream work considerations of representability which it meets by carrying out fresh displacements. This accounts for the fact that dreams are always dreamed in imagery; thus nobody ever dreams of justice in the abstract, but a person may dream of a judge handing down a decision. Extensive *condensation* of the dream material occurs, so that one symbol in a dream may have many different meanings. This is the principle of *overdetermination* which applies to all unconscious functioning. In general, little attention is paid to the logical relation of thoughts in dreams; those relations are ultimately given a disguised representation in certain formal characteristics in dreams. Any feeling or affect attached to the dream-thoughts undergoes less modification than their ideational content. Such affects are, as a rule, repressed; when they are retained they are detached from the ideas that properly belong to them. The dream work is cast into a form which is acceptable to consciousness by means of the process of secondary revision or secondary elaboration. This process, which is essentially the same as the thought process in waking life, is the only aspect of dreams which had been given any attention by writers before Freud.

Chapter VII, "Psychology of the Dream Processes," is the theoretical heart of the book, and sums up all the previous arguments.

In this chapter Freud asks: In the light of what has been uncovered of the nature of dreams, what kind of a mental structure can we postulate to account for the phenomena? Emphasis is placed upon the ability of the theory to account for the observations, an ability which shifts it from the sphere of speculation to that of science.

After some brief preliminary remarks pointing to the complexity of the task, the chapter is divided into a number of sections:

The Forgetting of Dreams: How does one know whether dreams are accurately remembered or not? As with memory in general, one does not know. But experience shows that the extent of forgetting is as a rule overestimated. The principle that psychic events are determined makes it certain that what is remembered is meaningful, provided one knows how to extract the meaning from it.

In analysis, forgetting serves the purpose of resistance. Similarly, in dreams to explain forgetting there is reference to the power of the censorship. *pain - block + restrain infantile*

In the light of the censorship and the resistance to which it points, the question arises: How is a dream possible at all? The answer is that the state of sleep reduces the power of censorship.

Regression. The most striking psychological characteristic of the dream is that a thought is objectified. Two features stand out: 1. Thought is represented as an immediate situation with the "perhaps" omitted; and 2. Thought is transformed into visual images and speech. In respect to the first point dreams and daydreams are similar; in respect to the second, they are not.

ego advocate

Fechner had suggested that dreams take place in a different psychic locality; this view, which Freud adopts, has nothing anatomical about it. In general, psychic processes advance from the perceptual to the motor end; this is the familiar *reflex arc concept*. A system in front of the apparatus receives perceptual stimuli but retains no trace of them and thus has no memory, while behind it lies a second system which transforms momentary excitations into permanent traces. Further considerations of this kind led Freud to describe the division of the mind into conscious (Cs), preconscious (Pcs) and unconscious (Ucs).

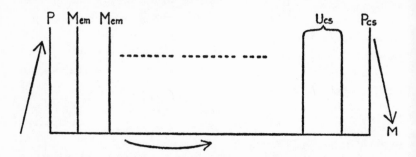

In the diagram, the left side is the perceptual end, the right side the motor end. Mem = memory. The diagram is to be read as follows: Percepts lead to memories or permanent traces, which are unconscious. The unconscious is accessible to consciousness only through the preconscious; the unconscious cannot become conscious directly. The path from the preconscious in the diagram is the road to consciousness, which must fulfill certain conditions. The perceptual end is, of course, also conscious.

Within this structure Freud then asks: Where is the impetus to the construction of dreams to be found? The answer is: In the *unconscious*.

In dreams the excitation moves in a backward direction. Instead of going from percept to motor activity, it goes from motor activity toward the sensory end and finally results in a perception. This backward movement is "regressive." It is *regression* because in a dream an idea is turned back into the sensory image from which it was originally derived.

What modification makes possible in the dream a regression which cannot occur in the waking state? The first explanation is that during the waking state there is a current from the perceptual end to the motor end, in the progressive direction. This current stops during sleep and hence facilitates the reverse, or regressive direction.

But the foregoing does not explain pathological regressions in waking states—hallucinations and visions. These turn out to be linked with repressed memories which break through in such states. This suggests that in dreams too the transformation of thoughts into visual images results from memories. Hence arises the view that the dream is a substitute for an infantile scene modified by transference to recent material. The infantile memory cannot be revived directly, and must therefore be satisfied to return as a dream. Thus dreaming is a regresson to childhood, a revival of the instinctual impulses which dominated childhood, and of the methods of expression that were then available.

Freud distinguishes three kinds of regression: topographical, in terms of the three systems, Cs, Pcs, Ucs; temporal, going back in time to older structures; formal, where archaic methods of expression and representation take the place of the more ordinary ones.

Wish-Fulfillment. It has already been shown that recent and indifferent material can appear in a dream. But such material is secondary. A wish that is represented in a dream must be an infantile one. It comes from the unconscious.

The unconscious cannot enter consciousness directly, but establishes connections with ideas which already belong to the preconscious. This is an example of *transference.* As used here "transference" is related to but is not the same as "the transference" observed in the analytic relationship. The most recent and indifferent elements are objects of this transference; furthermore, they are more likely to stand out because they have less to fear from the censorship.

Why does the unconscious offer nothing but a wish? In earliest childhood wishing ended in hallucinating the gratification, and thinking was nothing but a substitute for the hallucinatory wish. Then it becomes almost redundant to say that a dream is wish-fulfillment, since only a wish can impel the psychic apparatus to activity.

Dreaming is thus a piece of mental life that has been superseded. No matter what wishes come up, one need feel no concern—it is only a dream, and therefore now harmless. If the wishes break through the censorship in waking life, what results is a psychosis. This led Freud to say later that in his dream the normal person becomes psychotic every night.

Psychoanalysis has shown that all neurotic symptoms are to be regarded as fulfillments of unconscious wishes. From this the value of dreams for an understanding of neurosis and the close tie between dreams and neurosis become evident.

Arousal by Dreams—The Function of Dreams—Anxiety Dreams. Releases of pleasure and unpleasure automatically regulate the course of cathectic processes; this was called the *economic* factor in the metapsychological scheme (see page 37). Every dream has some arousing effect; at the same time dreams serve to get rid of the disturbance of sleep. An unconscious wish can either be left to itself and discharged in movement, or it can be influenced by the preconscious and be bound by it instead of being discharged. The second process is the one that occurs in dreams. Thus the dream is a safety valve, or the guardian of sleep.

Anxiety in dreams is no different from anxiety in general. Anxiety dreams, too, contain a hidden gratification.

The Primary and Secondary Processes—Repression. The dream work, involving extensive departures from rational thought, is a perplexing problem. To explain this and kindred phenomena, Freud postulated two basic processes: the primary and the secondary. The primary process is that which operates in the unconscious; it makes use of condensation and displacement; it easily shifts cathexes; it tolerates contradictions; it does not recognize negation; and in general it allows free mobility of cathexes. It seeks free discharge. It aims at perceptual identity. It is present from birth. The secondary process, by contrast, is man's rational self. It seeks to inhibit, rather than discharge. It can permit an idea to come to consciousness only if it can inhibit the unpleasure proceeding from it. It establishes thought identity. It is not present at birth, but develops only later. The contrast between primary- and secondary-process thinking explains the phenomena of neurosis. Hence it can be said that the psychic mechanism employed by the neuroses is already present in the normal structure of the mental apparatus. And for all people *the dream is the royal road to the unconscious.*

The Unconscious and Consciousness—Reality. Lipps, one of the leading German psychologists of the 1890's had said: The unconscious is *the* problem of psychology. With this, of course, Freud was in fullest agreement; for him, the unconscious is the true psychic reality.

There are two kinds of unconscious—one inadmissible to consciousness (the true unconscious); the other admissible, the preconscious. From this point of view, Freud describes consciousness as a sense organ for the perception of psychical qualities.

There is a close connection between censorship and consciousness. The hypercathexis or excessive concentration of desire of mobile quantities set up by consciousness leads to the thought-processes, which are a new kind of regulation of unpleasure, and constitute the superiority of men over animals.

Freud's theory of the dream was worked out with such extraordinary thoroughness and attention to detail that in its essentials it remains unaltered to the present day. The alternative to Freud is to state that dreams are meaningless aberrations. But such an alternative goes contrary to the spirit of science which assumes that everything that takes place in nature has an adequate explanation that can be ascertained if only we take the trouble to search for it.

In recent years a good deal of experimental work has been done, much of which confirms Freud's theories in many particulars. Fisher and his associates at Mt. Sinai Hospital in New York have conducted a series of investigations which tend to corroborate many of Freud's hypotheses concerning the day residue of dreams and unconscious perception.[40] Kleitman and his associates have confirmed Freud's supposition that people dream every night.[41] The apparent difference between those who dream and those who do not resolves itself into the real difference between those who remember their dreams and those who do not, which again leads to the Freudian point of view that dreams have some dynamic meaning, so that remembering them or forgetting them is a matter of considerable psychic significance to the individual.[42] Dement reports on some recent experiments in which the concept of dream deprivation has been set up.[43] In these experiments it has been shown that if a person does not dream one night, he will tend to make up for it the next night. All this material tends to support, of course, the general approach to dreams which Freud adopted, although the basic theory that a dream is a disguised form of wish-fulfillment remains a theoretical construct based primarily on clinical observation.

THE PSYCHOPATHOLOGY OF EVERYDAY LIFE

Next to *The Interpretation of Dreams* the most important work of Freud's dealing with the unconscious was *The Psychopathology of Everday Life*, issued in book form in 1904, though the material had previously been published in various journals. Undoubtedly this was the best received of all of Freud's writings. It went through ten editions in his lifetime. Illustrative material was continuously added, so that the last edition was almost four times the size of the original one.

Freud himself looked upon the work as a popular one. He made this point explicitly; in a footnote to page 173 he wrote:

> This work is of an entirely popular character; it merely aims, by an accumulation of examples, at paving the way for the necessary assumption of *unconscious yet operative* mental processes, and it avoids all theoretica' considerations on the nature of this unconscious.[44]

Nevertheless, in spite of Freud's disclaimer, the work has important theoretical implications.

On the basis of his study of dreams Freud had formulated a theory of the unconscious. In Chapter VII of that work he had elaborated this theory with extraordinary thoroughness. From now on he could use this theory to understand and to explain a variety of different phenomena.

By the "psychopathology of everyday life," as has been noted Freud referred to the variety of slips, errors, omissions, symptomatic actions, and mistakes of all kinds that occur to everybody a good deal of the time. Since then these have been given the generic name of "parapraxes." Before Freud this material simply had been ignored.

The thesis of the book is a relatively simple one. A great many errors are unconsciously motivated and a systematic analysis can reveal what these unconscious motives are. This is by no means to say that all errors are unconsciously motivated; indeed Freud was quite explicit in delineating the conditions under which there is justification in assuming that an unconscious motive is at play. Freud's theory as he envisioned it was therefore an addendum to the theory of normal remembering and forgetting, rather than a replacement of it. Thus he wrote:

Perhaps it is not superfluous to remark that the conditions which psychologists assume to be necessary for reproducing and forgetting, and which they look for in certain relations and dispositions, are not inconsistent with the above explanation. All we have done is, in certain cases, to add a _motive_ to the factors that have been recognized all along as being able to bring about the forgetting of a name; and, in addition, we have elucidated the mechanism of false recollection (paramnesia).[45]

And on the next page: "By the side of simple cases where proper names are forgotten there is a type of forgetting which is motivated by repression."[46]

Because of its strong appeal to common sense, and the way in which it can easily be confirmed by even superficial introspection, this thesis has probably been more widely accepted than any other of Freud's, although it too has met opposition. Freud himself remarked that we are always psychoanalyzing other people in this way. Customarily men do interpret other people's errors in accordance with this view, namely, that they represent some unconscious wish.

Freud's book can profitably be compared with another classic of this period, the work of Ebbinghaus.[47] Ebbinghaus conducted experiments on himself in learning and remembering, and noted meticulously the laws that seemed to govern the processes that went on in his mind. Since Ebbinghaus a variety of researchers have been able to confirm his findings and the general forms of the curves of learning and forgetting are by now reasonably well established.

In order to get away from the effects of past experience on memory, and to establish the "true laws" of memory, Ebbinghaus devised the technique of using nonsense syllables. He was trying to be as impersonal as possible. This technique obviously could ascertain only how material could be remembered that had relatively little or no meaning to the individual.

By contrast, Freud was interested in the remembering or forgetting of highly meaningful material. He went to the opposite extreme; instead of examining nonsense syllables, he looked into the accidental slips and omissions which lend themselves to observation but not to experimental investigation because they cannot be repeated at will.

Thus Freud and Ebbinghaus, or the currents which the two men represent, stand for two different approaches to the problem of human psychology. They complement one another and do not stand in any contradiction to each other.

In order to distinguish between the forgetting which is the result of normal psychological processes, and that which is motivated by repression or unconscious drives, Freud specified that a faulty psychic action must satisfy the following conditions: [48]

1. It must not exceed a certain measure, designated by the expression "within normal limits."

2. It must evince the character of a momentary and temporary disturbance. The same action must have been previously performed more correctly or we must always rely on ourselves to perform it more correctly; if we are corrected by others, we must immediately recognize the truth of the correction and the incorrectness of our psychic action.

3. If we at all perceive a faulty action, we must not perceive in ourselves any motivation of the same, but must attempt to explain it through "inattention" or attribute it to an "accident."

With the concept of the *screen memory*, a most important area was opened up by Freud. By the screen memory, Freud meant any childhood memory. It is a "screen" because theoretically it conceals a number of other earlier memories; the assumption is that it is the end-product of a long chain that has previously been repressed and is now inaccessible. Ordinary reflection on the human being's ability to remember his childhood leads to the assumption that the concept of the screen memory must have some justification to it. For of the millions of events that actually occurred in a person's lifetime, he ordinarily remembers only a selected handful. There must be some reason why this particular handful is remembered rather than some other.

The usual theoretical investigations of the memory process have not concerned themselves with this fairly obvious observation, so that once again the Freudian theory supplements the conventional approach. And again, in the investigation of screen memories, the technique of eliciting associations frequently yields fruitful results.

Freud recognized that this book was more of a contribution to normal than to abnormal psychology. The very title, which brings out the relationship to everyday life, indicates that he was here concerned with what happens to the average person.

In the analytic literature there has been relatively little follow-up of Freud's work with respect to parapraxes. No essential change in theory has been suggested; as with dreams, Freud did the work so thoroughly that it has never had to be done over again. There have, of course, been a large number of clinical observations, many of them in Freud's lifetime, along the same lines as his.

In the past few years Freud's observations on memory and other errors connected with the cognitive processes have been further investigated by a number of experimental psychologists. The term "perceptual defense" has been coined to describe the manner in which perception (and of course other cognitive processes) can be used to ward off unpleasant impressions and to facilitate the reception of pleasant impressions. It has been shown that many distortions may occur which are occasioned by the person's need to see the world in a more favorable light.

In view of the soundness and profundity of the *Psychopathology of Everyday Life* it is pertinent to examine more critically Freud's own evaluation of it as a "popular" work devoid of "theoretical" value.

The question leads at once into the nature of a scientific theory and of Freud's thinking in this area. Freud's views of science stem mainly from the teaching current during his university days, in the 1870's and 1880's. As has been noted, at that time the scientific community was still dominated by the sense of absolute certainty embodied in the Newtonian world-scheme. In this scheme a theory is something that ties together various observations with more fundamental knowledge; a theory was required only because certain facts were missing. Basic to all science was the comforting notion that mathematics at least was inherently true, and that the laws of logic represented a priori laws of the mind, again inherently true and invariable.

In the years of Freud's maturity both these positions were pretty thoroughly demolished. Relativity and quantum theory turned the world topsy-turvy. Mathematical logic could find nothing that was absolutely true, and Bertrand Russell coined his famous aphorism that mathematics is the science in which we never know what we are talking about nor whether what we say is true.* With this turnabout in the philosophy of science, the very nature of theory becomes much more elastic. Fact and theory come closer; a fact is no longer so factual and a theory is no longer so theoretical. Or as some prefer to put it, the difference between a fact and a theory becomes merely one of degree.[49]

Although modern clinical psychology is in a very real sense Freud's creation, he displayed throughout his life a most remarkable ambivalence toward it. Psychology as Freud pursued it consists of a series of observations, at first clinical, later broader in scope. How could these observations have any theoretical meaning? To explain them he had to go back to what he had been taught to believe was scientific truth—to physiology or biology or history; at best he compromised on "metapsychology" (literally: beyond psychology). At the same time he was too sound a thinker really to accept these other disciplines as absolutely secure; intuitively he rebelled against his teachers, yet he could never bring himself to make a total break. Accordingly, here, as in many other areas which will be investigated, Freud is to be found moving back and forth between psychology and biology or history or some other field.

By and large this has led to a serious misunderstanding of Freud. By taking various passages out of context it is possible to show that

* Quoted in L. Felix: *The Modern Aspect of Mathematics.* New York: Basic Books, 1960, p. 52.

he was a biologist or a physiologist or a believer in evolutionary explanations—all of which statements are partly true. But all of them only obscure the fundamental consistency of his position as a psychologist.

In *The Psychopathology of Everyday Life* Freud has made a fundamental contribution to our understanding of everyday human conduct. His theory here might be formulated in this way: In his everyday life man is governed by a variety of wishes. Under certain conditions these wishes break through and interfere with otherwise routine functioning. It is possible to specify what the conditions are and to clarify the processes involved. This theory of Freud's has remained and has stimulated much further thinking on the subject.

Available English Translations of Freud's works cited in Chapter IV

The Interpretation of Dreams. 1900.
Translated by James Strachey.
Standard Edition, Vols. IV-V.
Above translation issued as one separate volume, New York: Basic Books, 1955.

In *The Basic Writings of Sigmund Freud.* Translated and edited by A. A. Brill. New York: Modern Library Giants, Random House, 1938, pp. 181-549 (omits most of Chapter I). New York: Science Editions (paperback) New York: Macmillan, 1913 (Brill translation). 2nd ed. 1915, 1916, 1919, 1920, 1921, 1922, 1923, 1927. 3rd ed. (revised in accordance with 8th German edition) 1932, 1937, 1942, 1945, 1950.

The Psychopathology of Everyday Life. 1901.
Standard Edition, Vol. VI.

In *The Basic Writings of Sigmund Freud.* New York: Modern Library Giants, Random House, 1938, pp. 35-178. New York: New American Library of World Literature, Mentor Books (paperback). London, New York: Penguin Books.

Jokes and Their Relation to the Unconscious. 1905.
Standard Edition, Vol. VIII.
Under title: *Wit and Its Relation to the Unconscious, in The Basic Writings of Sigmund Freud.* New York: Modern Library Giants, Random House, 1938, pp. 633-803.

Five Lectures on Psychoanalysis. 1909.
Standard Edition, Vol. XI, pp. 9-55.

Under title: *Origin and Development of Psychoanalysis.* Chicago: Henry Regnery Co. (Gateway Editions paperback).

The Unconscious. 1915.
Standard Edition, Vol. XIV, pp. 166-204.
Collected Papers, Vol. IV, pp. 98-136.

A General Introduction to Psychoanalysis. 1916/1917.
New York: Boni and Liveright, 1920. Garden City, New York: Garden City Pub. Co., 1938. New York: Perma Giants, 1949. New York: Washington Square Press (paperback)
Under title: *Introductory Lectures on Psychoanalysis.* London: Allen and Unwin, 1929.

NOTES ON CHAPTER IV

For a summary of the pre-Freudian literature on the unconscious, see H. Ellenberger "The Unconscious before Freud," *Bulletin of the Menninger Clinic,* 21, 1957, 3. L. L. Whyte: *The Unconscious before Freud* (New York: Basic Books, 1960) has a good historical account but attaches much too much importance to pre-Freudian writers.

Little has been written on the theory of the unconscious since Freud, other than to state his theories in more popular language. An interesting thesis is developed in I. Matte-Blanco: "Expression in Symbolic Logic of the Characteristics of the System Ucs or the Logic of the System Ucs," *International Journal of Psychoanalysis,* XL, 1959, pp. 1-5.

Jung has an elaborate system of concepts relating to the unconscious which non-Jungians object to on the grounds that it makes too many dubious assumptions about inherent and inherited mental faculties. For a concise summary of the Jungian position, see J. Jacobi: *The Psychology of Jung* (New Haven: Yale Univ. Press, 1943) and C. G. Jung: *Psychological Types* (London: Routledge and Kegan Paul, 1923).

Enormous advances in the clinical knowledge of dreams have accumulated since Freud. A mine of information is contained in E. Gutheil: *A Handbook of Dream Analysis* (Liveright, 1951). Much useful material is summarized in R. Fliess: *The Dream: A Post-Freudian Reader* (New York: International Universities Press, 1953).

One of the most important clinical concepts since Freud is Lewin's notion of the "dream screen." See B. Lewin: "Sleep, the Mouth and the Dream Screen." *Psychoanalytic Quarterly,* XV, 1946, pp. 419-34. See also O. Issakower: "A Contribution to the Pathopsychology of Falling Asleep," *International Journal of Psychoanalysis,* XIX, 1938, pp. 331-45.

The experimental literature on dreams and unconscious perception has been systematically reported by Charles Fisher and his associates in a series of papers in the *Journal of the American Psychoanalytic Association*, 1953-date.

For a recent addition to Freud's work on the psychopathology of everyday life, see S. Feldman: *Mannerisms of Speech and Gestures in Everyday Life* (New York: International Universities Press, 1959).

Many writers have by now combined the Freudian theories of memory and perception with the more classical approaches to these problems. See: D. Rapaport: *Emotions and Memory* (Baltimore: Williams and Wilkins, 1942). G. Murphy and C. S. Solley: *Development of the Perceptual World* (New York: Basic Books, 1960). E. Hilgard: "Freud's Psychodynamics," Chapter IX in *Theories of Learning*, 2nd edition (New York: Appleton-Century-Crofts, 1956). W. N. Dember: "Motivational Effects on Perception" and "Stimulus Complexity, Motivation and Emotion," Chapters IX and X in *Psychology of Perception* (New York: Henry Holt, 1960).

Chapter V. THE LIBIDO THEORY

Freud's earliest position on sexuality has already been described above, the theory that sexual frustration is the direct cause of neurosis. It is expressed in the aphorism: No neurosis with a normal *vita sexualis*. This position was first announced around 1895, and reaffirmed several times in the next few years. However, for a long time Freud published nothing concerning sexuality, and was evidently just allowing the mass of clinical experience to be digested. He finally came out in 1905 with the more mature theory, embodied in the *Three Essays on Sexuality*. This book was revised by Freud many times throughout his lifetime, in contrast to his attitude toward some of his writings which, once published, he never looked at again.

Therapeutic experience, clinical and common observations, and self-analysis all combined to convince Freud that the sexual instinct had a long history. He had already in his earlier period started the search for the traumas in childhood which lead to hysteria or obsessional neurosis. As time went on he came to see more and more that no single trauma could be held responsible for the complexity of the clinical picture; rather, there was a biologically determined course of sexual development which could be used as a basis for further understanding.

The naïve assumption had been that the sexual instinct comes into existence full-blown at puberty. Freud rephrased this to state that at puberty the aim and the object go together.

The aim of the sexual instinct is the discharge of tension or of the sexual products. The object is the person (or substitute) who is sought out to gratify this discharge. The ordinary view can be rephrased to the effect that the average person assumes that the sexual drive consists of the wish to have sexual intercourse with a person of the opposite sex, and that this wish arises only with the maturation of the sexual organs.

Clinical experience, however, contradicted this common-sense view. Particularly significant was the connection between neurosis, perversion, and childhood. This connection was described by Freud in two formulas: The neurosis is the negative of the perversion; and The child is polymorphous perverse. *abuse*

By the first formula, Freud meant that the neurotic does in fantasy what the pervert does in actuality.* Thus sexual perversions are found in which a man defecates or urinates on a woman, or beats her or is beaten by her. Or the man may be homosexual and choose only men as love objects. Or again he may derive his main sexual pleasure from articles of clothing or other inanimate objects, known as fetishes. All these are found as unconscious wishes in the fantasies of neurotics. *shameless*

By the second, that the child is polymorphous perverse, Freud meant that all the activities that are carried out by the pervert and fantasied by the neurotic are normal to the child at some stage in childhood. It can be seen that the concepts of the unconscious and of infantile sexuality and the hypothesis of a close tie between the two have great explanatory value.

Thus it becomes apparent that the aim and the object are not always so close as popular opinion believes. This separation into aim and object Freud utilized as a basis for further investigation. The development of each of these can be traced separately.

In the course of his investigation Freud extended the concept of sexuality in two directions. On the one hand it was broadened to include all bodily pleasure; on the other it was made to cover feelings of tenderness and affection as well as the desire for genital contact. For both of these extensions there is ample ground in common observation and in clinical experience. For example, ordinary language uses the word love in many different senses. Thus, for example, I love my wife; I love to smoke; I love to listen to music; I love America; I love my alma mater; and so on.

---

* The term "pervert" does not suit the modern temper, and the concept has gradually been included in the more embracing category of "acting-out disorders."

According to Freud, the sex life of man is divided into three periods: infantile sexuality (roughly up to the age of five), the latency period, and puberty. Infantile sexuality further is subdivided into the oral, anal, and phallic stages, culminating in the Oedipus complex somewhere between the ages of three and five. Before the Oedipus stage, the aim of the sexual instinct is not tied to an object; the model for gratification is masturbation rather than intercourse with another human being. Freud did, however, recognize some so-called partial instincts in this period: sadism, voyeurism, and exhibitionism, that is, the impulses to cruelty, looking, and showing oneself, which are regularly tied to other people or objects.

Infantile sexuality culminates in the Oedipus complex, the wish to have sex relations with the parent of the opposite sex, and the corresponding antagonistic wishes toward the parent of the same sex. Freud saw the Oedipus complex as the source of all personality structure, whether neurotic or normal. By his analysis of the Oedipal situation Freud was the first to show how crucial for the formation of personality the family constellation is.

The latency period, which roughly covers the elementary-school age, Freud saw as a biologically determined stage, in which the manifestations of sexuality are either absent or reduced to a minimum.

This historical development was now made the basis for an understanding of the development at puberty. At this time in the normal person there must be a union of the tender and sexual feelings toward a person of the opposite sex; in other words, object love is reached. The object that individuals choose at puberty, that is, the person whom one wants to marry or actually marries, is a repetition of the object that had become important at the time of the Oedipus stage. Or to put it in simpler language, a person tries to find a mate who is like his parent of the opposite sex.

Thus the normal course of the development of the sexual aim is from the oral stage, when the infant derives his main pleasure from sucking at the breast, to that of genital primacy, when the major gratification is sexual intercourse.

In order to explain the manifestations of infantile sexuality Freud postulated the *libido theory*. The word "libido" comes from the Latin for lust; Freud adopted it because common language has no equivalent for sexual desire comparable to the word *hunger* for the desire to eat.

Libido is a quantitatively variable force that can serve as a measure of processes and transformations occurring in the field of sexual excitation. It is a unifying concept with many ramifications.

The "libido theory" actually consists of a number of different hypotheses that stem from different periods in Freud's development. It has changed, through Freud himself and others, more than any of Freud's other views of this period. While it is beyond the scope of this volume to attempt any systematic description of the course of psychoanalysis since Freud, some attempt will be made to indicate what the current thinking is with regard to the major hypotheses.°

The libido theory includes the following hypotheses: 1. Libido is the major source of psychic energy. 2. There is a developmental process consisting of various libidinal stages. 3. Object choice (interpersonal relations) results from the transformations of libido. 4. The libidinal drives can either be gratified, repressed, handled by a reaction formation, or sublimated. For most instinctual needs sublimation is the normal adjustment. 5. Character structure is built on the modes in which the biologically determined instincts are handled. 6. Neurosis is a fixation on or a regression to some phase of infantile sexuality. Furthermore, the earlier the fixation or the deeper the regression the greater the psychopathology.

1. LIBIDO AND PSYCHIC ENERGY

Libido is the major source of psychic energy: The sexual instincts provide the major although not the sole drive for the functioning of the individual. Freud also allowed for the ego-instincts, or drives, which are nonsexual in nature. In both practice and theory, however, the emphasis in this period was laid on the sexual drives.

In 1920 Freud revised his theory to allow for two basic drives, sexuality and aggression.

° The reader who wishes to pursue the matter further will find appropriate references in the notes and bibliography.

Since 1923, when Freud undertook a more thorough investigation of the ego, there has been much difference of opinion as to the relative role to be assigned to drives and ego-forces within the personality. This, however, should not be exaggerated, since it is a difference in emphasis rather than in basic orientation.

2. LIBIDINAL STAGES

There is a developmental process of various libidinal stages, which has already been described. This is the earliest aspect of the libido theory, which grew organically out of Freud's clinical observations of the 1890's. Nevertheless, it is vital to remember that the most important source of observation was Freud himself and his own self-analysis. Thus in 1935 he wrote:

The information about infantile sexuality was obtained from the study of men ° and the theory deduced from it was concerned with male children. It was natural enough to expect to find a complete parallel between the two sexes; but this turned out not to hold. Further investigations and reflections revealed profound differences between the sexual development of men and women.[50]

It is important as well to bear in mind that the final description of the libidinal stages evolved in Freud's mind only over a period of many years.[51] Since his explanations of the clinical data always fell back upon the libido theory, these explanations varied to some extent at different times in his thinking because the requisite libidinal stage had not yet been posited. Strachey [52] notes that the order of publication of Freud's views on the successive early organizations of the sexual instinct may be summarized as follows: auto-erotic stage, 1905 (privately described, 1899); narcissistic stage, 1911 (privately described, 1909); anal-sadistic stage, 1913; oral stage, 1915; phallic stage, 1923.

To this chronology must be added the fact that in his last years Freud gave up the idea of a rigid chronological sequence. In 1938 he wrote of the oral-anal-phallic phases:

° This can be taken to mean that Freud relied most heavily on his own self-analysis. A statement such as this from a man who spent so much of his life analyzing women is truly amazing.

It would be a mistake to suppose that these three phases succeed one another in a clear-cut fashion: one of them may appear in addition to another, they may overlap one another, they may be present simultaneously.[53]

Thus the final form in which the theory of libidinal stages comes from Freud is an approximate large-scale map rather than an exact blueprint, and still leaves much room for clarification, both generally and for any given individual.

In recent years several attempts have been made to enlarge Freud's conception of libidinal stages beyond the pubertal level. The most promising of these appears to be Erikson's epigenetic theory, which provides a framework for the full life cycle of the individual.

3. OBJECT CHOICE

Object choice results from the transformation of libido. Objects *
are required by the individual to satisfy libidinal needs. In the paper on narcissism in 1914, in which the metapsychological aspect of the libido theory was first enunciated,[54] Freud first described the stages of object choice. The earliest is the *narcissistic* stage, in which the person chooses himself or someone who is like himself. Next is the *anaclitic* stage, in which the object is someone on whom the individual becomes dependent (anaclitic: to lean on), characteristically the mother or mother-substitute. Finally comes the stage of *object love*, when the other person is regarded as an individual in his own right.

This whole scheme of object development has undergone the most extensive changes in the past thirty years. Knowledge of early object relations has increased enormously since the advent of ego psychology, so that from the present point of view Freud's description is to be looked upon as a first approximation.

---

* The use of the word "objects" is an unfortunate one. It derives from the German philosophical differentiation between subject (I, ego) and object (the other person). The term "interpersonal relations" would be clearer, but "object" is too securely entrenched. See reference 33.

4. LIBIDINAL DRIVES

The libidinal drives can be gratified, repressed, handled by a reaction-formation, or sublimated. Inasmuch as they are biologically given (though in most cases they appear in the course of maturation) they must be handled somehow. In this early period (1905) Freud saw four possibilities of such handling.

Some instinctual needs can be gratified; this, however, applies to a relative minority. They may be repressed, but this leads to neurosis since inevitably there is a *return of the repressed*, although the precise time when this takes place is uncertain. They may evoke opposing mental forces (*reaction-formations*) which lead to the mental dams of disgust, shame, and morality. Or, finally, they may be *sublimated*, which is the most normal solution. In sublimation the energy of the sexual impulses is diverted, either partly or entirely, from their sexual use and directed to socially approved ends.

To these possibilities Freud added several others in his 1915 paper "Instincts and Their Vicissitudes," particularly reversal into the opposite and turning around upon the subject. Some ten years later, in 1926, in *The Problem of Anxiety*, he reintroduced the term *defense* and distinguished the more commonly encountered defenses. Another decade later, in 1936, Anna Freud wrote her epoch-making *The Ego and the Mechanisms of Defense;* subsequently the defense mechanisms were firmly established as a central concern of the analyst. Since then the topic has been in the forefront of analytic literature.

5. CHARACTER STRUCTURE

Character structure is built on the modes in which the biologically determined instincts are handled: This proposition was added in the paper "Character and Anal Erotism" (1908), in which Freud said:

We can at any rate lay down a formula for the way in which character in its final shape is formed out of the constituent instincts: the permanent character traits are either unchanged prolongations of the original instincts, or sublimations of those instincts, or reaction-formations against them.[55]

As the knowledge of defense mechanisms and ego psychology in general grew, especially after 1923, the views of character structure were altered in many respects. The original observation of an intimate relationship between the component instincts and the ultimate character remains, but the transition from one to the other took on a far more complex cast. *deprivation. abuse*

In Freud's own work the only character type delineated with any thoroughness is the anal character in "Character and Anal Erotism" (1908). He described the traits of orderliness, parsimony, and obstinacy as typical of the anal character and traced their development to the conflicts surrounding the child's early bowel training. Later, the connection between anal erotism and obsessional neurosis was brought out, in his 1913 paper, "The Disposition to Obsessional Neurosis."

Descriptions of the anal character and obsessional neurosis dominated the analytic literature before World War I. E.g., Ferenczi described one type of homosexual as an obsessional neurotic.[56] To a considerable extent this was due to the fact that the study of the stages of libidinal development was still far from complete, and that in particular virtually nothing was known about the oral stage. As late as 1924 Abraham could write that "a retrograde transformation of character . . . in the main comes to a stop at the anal stage." [57]

When further clinical experience and information about libidinal development became available the understanding of character structure broadened considerably. Wilhelm Reich's book *Character Analysis* was a milestone in this area. However Reich was much too schematic and as the insights of ego psychology grew his work became less and less important. Today this aspect of psychoanalysis is still in a state of considerable flux.

The concept of *instinct*, so fundamental to the libido theory, merits some discussion. Freud's most usual term, *Trieb*, has variously been translated as instinct or instinctual need; it is not quite the same as the English *instinct*. At the time of the *Three Essays*, in 1905, all psychologists relied heavily on instinct theory. The best known of the American instinct theorists who wrote at that time was William McDougall. It will be recalled that William James had proposed the surprising thesis that man differs from the lower animals in that he has a broader range of instincts.

Beginning with behaviorism, the concept of instinct was exposed to considerable attack, particularly by American psychologists. It may be noted, however, that Watson, the father of behaviorism, still ended up with three instinctually determined emotions—fear, love, and hate—a formulation which does not differ essentially from Freud.

From the 1920's on many psychologists began to become more and more dubious about the value of the concept of instinct. It was argued, and much research confirmed the point, that many activities apparently instinctual were really the consequence of definable bio-chemical reactions, while others were learned. Accordingly, an extreme movement in the opposite direction set in, which attempted to do away with the term altogether. Nevertheless, what always remains is the theoretical postulate of learned and unlearned drives, difficult though these may be to disentangle in practice. In the past fifteen years a better balance has been struck, and today there would be general agreement that both native endowment and the environment must be carefully evaluated. Instinct has thus returned to its proper place in the psychological scheme of things, though most often in the form of "unlearned drives."

Particularly interesting to the psychoanalyst has been the work of the school of ethology, especially Lorenz, Tinbergen, and their co-workers. Like the analysts, the ethologists have relied most heavily on the observation of the animal in its natural habitat, and many fascinating parallels between animal and human behavior have been uncovered.

6. NEUROSIS AND INFANTILE SEXUALITY

"Neurosis is a fixation on or a regression to some phase of infantile sexuality." This proposition, first enunciated in the latter part of the *Three Essays* in 1905, has become the kernel of all modern theories of neurosis; differences crop up only with regard to detail, not to the general idea. The corollary is that the earlier the fixation or the deeper the regression the greater the psychopathology. The elaboration of these two propositions leads to a resolution of the problem of

the measure of spiritual attitude!

classical neurosis, but still leaves many questions unanswered in the broader area of character neurosis.

One particular feature of the character-neurotic problems of the general population was the subject of love, a topic which preoccupied Freud a great deal, and to which he came back again and again in his writings. In a footnote added in 1915 to the *Three Essays on Sexuality* he wrote:

The innumerable peculiarities of the erotic life of human beings as well as the compulsive character of the process of falling in love itself are quite unintelligible except by reference back to childhood and as being residual effects of childhood.[58]

Throughout his works Freud was concerned with correlating his clinical observations of love with these "residual effects of childhood." The most important instance in actual practice was that of transference love, in which the patient, unconsciously and compulsively, recapitulates with the analyst the profound feelings of love and hate he felt toward his parents when he was a child. As Freud pointed out in his essay "Transference Love," this transference love differs only in degree from ordinary love.[59] Freud saw love as essentially a fixation upon the parents. Its irrationality, its compulsiveness, its frequently self-damaging aspects were to be understood in terms of the disturbances in the child's relationship with the parents.

Two essays, one written in 1910, the other in 1912, take up two aspects of neurotic love behavior in the man. One is the need on the man's part to fall in love with some sexually promiscuous woman, often enough actually a prostitute, and to bend his every effort to rescue her. In spite of his great love he is constantly tormented by terrible feelings of jealousy. The woman in such cases is the mother, transformed through the eyes of the little boy.

The second essay deals with the most prevalent * form of degradation in the sphere of love. Here the man sets as a precondition for sexual satisfaction the debasement of the woman. She belongs to an inferior race, is inadequate, or is "bad" merely because she has sex.

* In the Standard Edition the translation reads "the universal tendency." The German text is "*Ueber die allgemeinste Erniedrigung des Liebeslebens.*" In previous translations, as, e.g., by Joan Riviere, in *Collected Papers*, IV, p. 203, "*die allgemeinste*" had been rendered by "most prevalent." The writer prefers the term "most prevalent."

The spread of Freud's teachings has done much to obliterate this distinction between the "good" and the "bad" woman, but it must be borne in mind how common it was in Freud's day and how common it still is in many parts of the world. This culturally determined taboo on sexual gratification again derives from the image of the "good" mother who would not engage in a "dirty" activity such as sex. As Freud points out in the paper, the consequences of this sharp split between "good" and "bad" women can only be psychic impotence in men and frigidity in women.

It is not, however, to be concluded from these and similar essays that Freud considered love inherently neurotic. As a clinician he was confronted with the infantile forms of love, such as the need to rescue a prostitute, or the need to degrade the woman, or love as a kind of hypnotic trance, and to these he devoted most of his attention. But he also was well aware of the constructive character of love, as, e.g., in his famous statement that the normal person is the one who can work and love.

Freud discussed love at many other points in his writings. He traced the relationship between narcissism and love, and held that, by and large, men love according to the anaclitic type of object-choice (sexual overestimation of the woman) while women love according to the narcissistic type (they wish to be loved). In these various positions his own puzzlement about women seems to have colored his vision unduly, and led him to rely too heavily on his own self-analysis; e.g., there is the strange remark that perhaps the only unambivalent love in the world is that of a mother for her son.[60]

It is still important to return to the old question: In the light of the libido theory, what becomes of sexuality proper? Since there is a long history, the simple search for sexual gratification does not solve the problem—the mere word *psychosexual* indicates that there is always a psychological component to the sexual drive. But if the childhood background is adequate, then naturally, Freud argued, a much greater degree of sexual freedom should be encouraged.

With the theory of the sexual causation of neurosis, and that of the development of the sexual instinct in general, Freud emerged upon the broader scene of social criticism. For as long as neurologists held on to the myth that mental illness was merely a variety of brain pathology, the significance for civilization in general of neurology and psychiatry was small. The job of the psychiatrist was to take care of the unfortunates crowded into mental hospitals until bio-chemical research had solved the problem.

But if sex is a source of disturbance in neurotics, and actually in all men, as Freud soon came to realize, then the whole structure of civilization is at stake, for modern society prescribes, in theory, a rigid code of sexual abstinence which very few people can tolerate and adhere to. As Kinsey discovered forty years later, laws now on the books would put 95 per cent of the population in jail if their sexual activities were uncovered and the existing laws were en-forced. The vaunted morality of the great nations, Freud said in effect, is a pack of lies and produces a world of neurotics.

Once the theoretical position was established that sexual restric-tions and disturbances lead to neurosis, it seemed inevitable that Freud should next turn his attention to the kind of society that prescribed such a harmful sexual code. Privately he left no doubt of where he stood. In a letter to James J. Putnam, a prominent Ameri-can neurologist, dated July 8, 1915, he wrote:

Sexual morality as defined by society, in its most extreme form that of America, strikes me as very contemptible. I stand for an infinitely freer sexual life, although I myself have made very little use of such freedom. Only so far as I considered myself entitled to . . .[61]

Yet publicly he showed a certain reluctance to condemn so severely the society in which he lived, even though many prominent thinkers joined in criticism of the sexual hypocrisy of that day. It was only in response to promptings from others that he committed his views to paper.

In 1906 he lectured on the subject of sexual abstinence to the Society for Education in the Social Sciences; the lecture was never published. The next year, at the request of a Hamburg colleague, he wrote a paper, "The Sexual Enlightenment of Children." Here he took up the question of whether children's sexual inquiries should be answered, and declared that they should be, and in the simplest possible manner. A curious sidelight on this advice has recently appeared in the book of his son Martin,[62] who reveals that Freud's own children had to learn the facts of life through peepholes and street gossip, just like all the other children of his day.

Freud's only open statement about the sexual reform of society was in a paper on " 'Civilized' Sexual Morality and Modern Nervousness," published in 1908. This was prompted by a book by Von Ehrenfels, entitled *Sexual Ethics,* which had appeared a year earlier.[63] Von Ehrenfels had made two main points: 1. The prevailing sexual morality of civilization is characterized by the transference of feminine demands on to the sexual life of the man, with deprecation of any sexual intercourse outside of marriage. This leads to a double standard of moral life, with evil consequences for honesty and humanity. 2. The glorifying of monogamy paralyzes the process of selection, which is the only hope of improving the human constitution, a hope which humanitarianism and hygiene had already reduced to a minimum.

Apparently Freud was in agreement with both of these points. But he went further. As the title of his paper implies, "Civilized" sexual morality is a sham and has primarily one outcome—nervous illness. A tone of considerable moral indignation at the senseless demands made on modern man runs throughout the discussion. Freud was particularly impressed by the widespread incidence of impotence in men and of frigidity in women.

If society as presently constituted creates such severe disturbances, it stands to reason that there should be a change. Freud was, of course, in favor of revolutionary changes, particularly with regard to the sexual code. However, he recognized that it is difficult to change one aspect of society without touching others, and refrained from making any specific proposals for reform.

At the same time Freud became curiously hesitant. He began to consider the other possibility, that it is not society which is necessarily at fault, but the instinct itself. As early as 1906 he had announced to the Vienna Psychoanalytic Society his intention of writing an essay or book on the love life of man. This material never appeared as a book, but several essays on the subject did, in 1910, 1912, and 1918.

In the 1912 essay he began to look more thoroughly into the instincts. There he ran into the same dilemma that was to be repeated later in the 1930 book, *Civilization and Its Discontents.* In 1912 he had written:

The fact that the curb put upon love by civilization involves a universal tendency to debase sexual objects will perhaps lead us to turn our attention from the object to the instincts themselves. The damage caused by the initial frustration of sexual pleasure is seen in the fact that the freedom later given to that pleasure in marriage does not bring full satisfaction. But at the same time, if sexual freedom is unrestricted from the outset the result is no better.[64]

And later in the same essay he said:

Thus we may perhaps be forced to become reconciled to the idea that it is quite impossible to adjust the claims of the sexual instinct to the demands of civilization; that in consequence of its cultural development renunciation and suffering, as well as the danger of extinction in the remotest future, cannot be avoided by the human race.[65]

This extreme position of 1912 is in marked contrast to the implied meliorism of 1908. At the same time even in the 1912 paper Freud qualified his views.

Even if, in some remote future, the sexual instinct and civilization must always clash, it seems a natural corollary from Freud's ideas that society as it exists can still be altered in many ways to allow modern man far more gratification than he receives. While Freud himself paid little attention to the subject, others in the psychoanalytic movement did not hesitate to make numerous suggestions about modifications of present-day social institutions, and many of these have actually been put into effect.

In comparing the civilization of today with that which existed sixty years ago, it is possible to trace a large number of consequences of the Freudian revolution in child rearing and in human relations, especially in those countries, of which the United States and England are the foremost, where psychoanalysis has had its greatest influence. Apart from a much freer attitude toward sexuality itself, today's civilized world is familiar with such practices as natural childbirth, the lying-in plan, breast-feeding, late toilet-training, a more permissive attitude toward aggression, the relaxation of the traditional tyrannical discipline of children, greater tolerance and the acceptance of sexual needs at all ages, the encouragement of fantasy productions, the greater acceptance of the body in all respects, the search for a family disturbance whenever any neurotic or social disturbance appears, and many other attitudes and phe-nomena which are attributable either directly or indirectly to Freud. Freud thought of himself as a scientist, not a revolutionary, yet his impact on the course of civilization has been enormous.

THREE ESSAYS ON SEXUALITY

Of all Freud's works dealing with the libido theory, the central one is the *Three Essays on Sexuality*, published in 1905.

The Interpretation of Dreams and the *Three Essays on Sexuality* dovetail with one another. Dreams bring out the whole world of infantile sexuality in disguised form, while infantile sexuality is repressed into the unconscious and often comes to attention only through an investigation of the dream life.

The book was the outcome of Freud's clinical experiences of the previous ten years. In an essay published a few months earlier he had described how his views had gone through a number of changes. The two foundation stones that he had held to through the years were the significance of the infantile factor and the importance of sexuality. By now, of course, sexuality had been expanded to the broader meaning, which includes both the physical and the psy-chological, which it has since occupied; hence the term psycho-sexual becomes the more common one.

The major contribution of the book is actually an exploration of the world of infantile sexuality, a whole new world which had never before even been suspected to exist. This was one reason why Freud later likened himself to one of the conquistadors, who had sailed out on uncharted seas, not really knowing what they would find when they got to the other side of the ocean. Freud himself had taken many years to reach the conclusions which he expounded in this book, and in the course of it he had found it necessary to break with Breuer, Fliess, and everyone else on the subject. Yet even in 1905 signs remained of his earlier doubts. Thus in the first two editions of *The Interpretation of Dreams* (1900 and 1909) there is a strange passage in which it is assumed that children have no sexual desires.[66] It was Jung who called Freud's attention to this passage and induced him to expunge it in the third edition (1911).[67] Even so, subsequent investigations have revealed aspects of infantile sexuality which Freud himself ignored, particularly the relationship between the infant and the mother in the first year of life.

Within the framework of this book there were many changes throughout Freud's lifetime, and there have been many since. Strachey has only recently called attention to the startling fact that the entire sections on the sexual theory of children, on the pregenital organization of the libido, and on the libido theory itself, including, especially, the new idea of ego-libido (narcissism), appeared for the first time in the third edition ten years after the original publication. The phallic stage, which is now standard theory, was not included until Freud discovered it and published a paper about it in 1923. Like so many other aspects of the libido theory, this paper on the phallic stage met with considerable dissension within the ranks of the Freudians.[68]

Nevertheless, in spite of changes and arguments that have occurred, certain essentials of the *Three Essays* remain unaltered and have been incorporated into all psychological theory. The broad outlines of psychosexual development, the need for object relationships (other people, or interpersonal relationships), the significance of the Oedipus complex, the regression and fixation on infantile sexuality as the hallmark of neurosis, the connection between neurosis and childhood—all these and much more have become part of the indispensable, theoretical outlook of every clinical psychologist.

The present-day reader finds it hard to understand why such a furor was raised about this book. Freud himself later stated that it was his destiny in life to have discovered the obvious—that children have sexual feelings and that dreams have meaning.

In fact, in the preface to the fourth edition of the *Three Essays* in 1920, he wrote:

If mankind had been able to learn from a direct observation of children, these three essays could have remained unwritten.[69]

Nevertheless, the historical fact remains that the book and the idea, particularly of infantile sexuality, aroused enormous opposition over a period of many years. The profession considered it rubbish, while there were even threats of legal prosecution against any psychiatrist or psychologist who dared to delve too freely into the sex lives of children. Ernest Jones was actually imprisoned in 1908 in England on the accusation of some children—an accusation which today would easily be recognized as a fantasy; although acquitted, he was compelled to leave England for a number of years because the incident had tarnished his reputation to such an extent.[70]

Sexual Aberrations. The book is divided into three parts. Part I is a discussion of the sexual aberrations. Here most of the material is familiar, but Freud introduces a novel descriptive approach by which the so-called aberrations or perversions can be understood. This approach involves the assumption of an aim and an object for the sexual instinct. The sexual object is the person from whom sexual attraction proceeds, while the act toward which the instinct tends he calls the underlying sexual aim. On the basis of this assumption it becomes possible to classify the observations regarding perversions in terms of the deviations in respect of both the sexual object and the sexual aim. This classification, which is quite obviously useful once it is offered, sets the framework for the remainder of the book.

First, concerning deviations in respect to the sexual object, Freud lists inversion, sexually immature persons, animals. Concerning deviations in respect to the sexual aim, he lists anatomical extensions, fixations of preliminary sexual aims (such as touching and looking), sadism, and masochism.

Next he applies these views to the perversions in general. Everyday experience has shown that these deviations are constituents which are rarely absent from the sexual life of healthy people, so that the gap between the normal and the neurotic is not so great as is popularly supposed. This implies that the perverse wishes which are present to some extent in all persons play a variable role in the development of the sexual instinct. This fact has two important consequences.

First, the perverse wishes, which come to prominence only in the clinical perversions, are present in all persons and play a variable role in the development of their actual sexual lives.

Second, it becomes clear that some of the perversions become intelligible only if they can be taken to pieces; that is, they appear to be of a composite nature. This suggests that perhaps the sexual instinct itself may be no simple thing, but made up of various components that have come apart again in the perversons. If this is so, the clinical observation of these abnormalities will have drawn attention to composites which have been lost to view in the more uniform behavior of normal people.

In the following section Freud considers the sexual instinct in neurotics, as it has been investigated through psychoanalysis. He emphasizes that psychoanalysis is the only method of investigation which will show that these factors exist in neurosis. The results of psychoanalytic investigation in neurosis may be summed up in two statements. First, the symptoms of neurosis express the sexual life of the neurotic; it is to be emphasized, however, that by "sexual" he already includes infantile sexuality and abnormal sexuality. Second, this means that the neuroses are the negative of the perversions. That is, the pervert actually *does* what the neurotic *fantasies*. Freud particularly emphasizes three aspects of this relationship:

1. The unconscious mental life of all neurotics (without exception) shows inverted impulses, fixation of their libido upon persons of their own sex.

2. It is possible to trace in the unconscious of neurotics tendencies to every kind of anatomical extension of sexual activity and to show that these tendencies are factors in the formation of symptoms.

3. An especially prominent part is played, as factors in the formation of symptoms in neuroses, by the component instincts, which emerge for the most part as pairs of opposites, such as the instincts of looking and of being looked at and the active and passive forms of the instinct for cruelty.

Freud then turns to component instincts and erotogenic zones. Component instincts involve other people as objects—scopophilia, the wish to see, exhibitionism, and cruelty. These also exist in the early period of infantile sexuality. The erotogenic zones relate particularly to the sexual significance which is assigned by neurotics and perverts to the oral and anal openings. Other erotogenic zones exist as well. Thus a further parallel is drawn between the zones which are particularly susceptible to symptom formation in neurotics and the zones which are susceptible to activity in perverts.

In the next section Freud considers the reasons for the apparent preponderance of perverse sexuality in the psychoneuroses. He assumes that a particularly strongly developed tendency to perversion is among the characteristics of the psychoneurotic constitution, and is then able to distinguish a number of such constitutions according to the innate preponderance of one or the other of the erotic zones or one or the other of the component instincts.

The final section of this part is at once a summary of what has gone before and an introduction to the rest of the book. In it Freud provides an intimation of the infantile character of sexuality. If perversions and neuroses are complementary, and if both perverts and neurotics are so numerous, it must also be considered that an unbroken chain bridges the gap between neuroses and normality. If then these symptoms and symptom formations are so common, it follows that there must be something innate which is connected with these manifestations. He concludes:

A formula begins to take shape which lays it down that the sexuality of neurotics has remained in, or been brought back to, an infantile state. Thus our interest turns to the sexual life of children, and we will now proceed to trace the play of influences which govern the evolution of infantile sexuality till its outcome in perversion, neurosis, or normal sexual life.[71]

Infantile Sexuality. In Part II Freud turns to infantile sexuality, the most original section of the work. He considers first why all other writers have overlooked the existence of sexuality in childhood, and ascribes it to the amnesia that ordinarily blocks the childhood memories of most people from reaching consciousness.

Sexuality is divided into three main periods: 1. From birth to its first flowering around the ages of three to five. 2. The latency period from five to puberty, when sexual manifestations are by and large quiescent. 3. Puberty, when sexuality reaches its final adult form.

In the first period sexual manifestations are auto-erotic, attached to some biologically important area, and dominated by an erotogenic zone. Freud uses the example of thumb-sucking. The aim of the infantile sexual wish is satisfaction by self-stimulation, or the discharge of tension; it has no object (though this statement is qualified to some extent by other considerations). Thumb-sucking is akin to masturbation. All the infantile instincts are similar to thumb-sucking and masturbation; once one is understood there is little to learn about the others.

Children are seen to be *polymorphous perverse;* they can be led to derive pleasure from any bodily activity. Further consideration shows that this disposition is a general human characteristic.

During the first flowering of the sex life, from three to five, the child engages in extensive *sexual exploration.* The first problem he tries to solve is the riddle of where babies come from. Birth theories frequently lead to the idea that babies are conceived by eating and are born via the rectum. Fantasies about the penis arise: in boys there is castration anxiety, in girls penis envy. Sexual intercourse is regarded as an act of sadism. Two elements, however, remain undiscovered by children—the role of the sexual products and the existence of the vagina. The sexual explorations are carried out in solitude and alienate the child from the people in his environment.

Noteworthy here is Freud's point that the child who is uninformed about sexual matters will begin to have fantasies about them. Such matters never remain a subject of indifference, as is popularly supposed.

There are two phases in the choice of object: one comes in the period from two to five, the other at puberty. These two phases may not be in harmony, and this leads to trouble for the individual.

In enumerating the various factors which lead to sexual excitation Freud includes—besides the usual outer and inner erotic stimuli— mechanical excitations, muscular activity, affective processes, and intellectual work. This list seems so inclusive that he writes:

It may well be that nothing of considerable importance can occur in the organism without contributing some component to the excitation of the sexual instinct.[72]

The many sources that lead to sexual excitation can also be reversed, so that sexuality can affect, say, other feelings or intellectual work. This reversal explains a good part of the symptomatology of the neuroses.

Infantile Sexuality and Pubertal Change. In Part III Freud applies his findings about infantile sexuality to the changes at puberty. Now a new sexual aim appears, the discharge of the sexual products; all the other aims become subordinated to this one. An object must be chosen toward whom there is a combination of tender and sexual impulses.

The sexual characteristic of adulthood is the primacy of the genitals. Gratifications of the pregenital instincts and of the component instincts serve to give *fore-pleasure* to the normal individual; only sexual intercourse gives full or *end pleasure*. If fore-pleasure is overaccentuated there results an inhibition in development, and this is what happens in many perversions.

About the chemistry of sexual excitation Freud confesses ignorance. He assumes only that substances of a peculiar kind arise from the sexual metabolism. (In other words, he says that the biochemical knowledge of his day did not explain the clinical findings; even today unsolved problems in this area still exist.)

At puberty, males and females begin to diverge markedly from each other. The woman must shift her principal erogenous zone, or major source of sexual gratification, from the clitoris to the vagina, a shift which often creates problems. The man's principal erogenous zone is the penis; it requires no change at puberty.

The *finding of an object* at puberty is a complicated process. The infant sucking at the mother's breast becomes the prototype of every love relationship, so that the finding of an object is actually a re-finding. The early objects are the parents; this creates the *incestuous object-choice*. Adolescent and adult love relationships are strongly dominated by the vicissitudes of the problem of incest and the whole Oedipus complex.

Neurosis can now be understood better; for every disorder represents an inhibition in development. The neurotic does have a disturbed sex life, but "sex life" now refers to infantile sexuality as well as adult.

CRITICISM OF THE LIBIDO THEORY

The libido theory has been more vigorously criticized than any other of Freud's theories, especially by the culturalist school which has been prominent since the 1930's. In evaluating these and similar criticisms, some essential distinctions must first be made.

To begin with, a number of statements about Freud are simply incorrect; he never made the remark or held the view attributed to him. Thus, for example, in a paper entitled "A Methodological Study of Freudian Theory" Kardiner, Karush and Ovesey state: "The accumulation of clinical data eventually led Freud to abandon his environmental theory of neurosis in favor of a constitutional one." [73] For this statement no quotation from Freud is given; and one can only say that it does not represent Freud's view of neurosis accurately.

Second, Freud's remarks are frequently taken out of context. At times insufficient attention is paid to the fact that on numerous occasions he changed his mind over the years. It has already been pointed out above, and will be documented further, how the early probings of the 1890's were considerably recast, and in many instances totally repudiated, in the period under discussion.

Third, authors sometimes pick out for strong criticism hypotheses of Freud's which are peripheral or irrelevant to the main body of his thought. It is a fact that Freud rather stubbornly maintained the Lamarckian belief in the inheritance of acquired characteristics, in spite of the accumulation of scientific evidence against it and its repudiation by virtually all reputable biologists. But whether Lamarckism is true or not is really of no consequence in an evaluation of Freud's total position.

ANALYSIS OF THE LIBIDO THEORY

After these preliminaries, here is a critical analysis of the issues involved in the libido theory. To understand Freud's arguments properly the total historical development must be taken into consideration.

It is only in relatively recent times that the treatment of the mentally ill has become the province of the medical profession. As Zilboorg has so ably shown, "from about the middle of the fifteenth century medical psychology became a part of codified demonology and the darkest ages of psychiatry set in." [74] It is to be recalled that persecution for witchcraft continued until nearly the end of the eighteenth century. The whole matter was in fact still so recent that in one of his papers (1886) Freud wrote:

> During the last few decades a hysterical woman would have been almost as certain to be treated as a malingerer, as in earlier centuries she would have been certain to be judged and condemned as a witch or as possessed of the devil.[75]

Historically psychotics and neurotics were rescued from persecution by the Church only by the introduction of a medical assumption: They were not possessed by the devil or by demons; they were sick, and research would eventually show the nature of the brain damage which led to their aberrant behavior. Since about the beginning of the nineteenth century this conviction has dominated a large segment of psychiatry. It was shaken first by the consistent inability to find any organic brain damage in the great majority of psychiatric conditions, and second by the enormous mass of evidence accumulated by psychoanalysis which supports not an organic but a psychological explanation.

With such a background it can readily be understood that at the time when Freud came upon the scene only the one orientation—the biological, the organic—was available. Several versions of this orientation were current. One school (Pierre Janet) held that the neurotic suffered from hereditary degeneracy. Another, the American psychiatrist Beard, saw the neurotic as suffering from nerve weakness, and accordingly coined the diagnosis "neurasthenia." This school, however, also held that outside influences could excite the nerves of the neurasthenic; Beard himself ascribed some of the increase in American nervousness to the hectic pace of life after the Civil War. Here, however, a therapeutic possibility suggested itself, namely, remove the neurasthenic from excessive stimulation by putting him to bed. Thus was born the Weir Mitchell rest-cure which Freud himself made use of for a while, and which still plays a role in the thinking of that group in the medical profession which is not psychoanalytically oriented. Beard's theory could be considered a cultural one, since he attributed the exacerbation of the illness, if not the illness itself, to cultural forces.

Thus Freud had two theories of neurosis from which to choose—one biological, the other cultural. To both of these he rightly objected that they were not specific enough and could be used to explain anything at all. It was necessary to show why some people developed nervous symptoms while others did not. His first answer was, as has been seen, a *psychological* one: Neurosis is an inner conflict that stems from the need to defend against unbearable ideas. From the very beginning, then, Freud was psychologically oriented, although he attached weight to both the biological and the cultural factors.

For a long time he sought to put his psychological findings on some "firm basis in physiology." (See above, pp. 10-11.) The great change in his thinking, as has been shown, came about with his self-analysis, and henceforth he always regarded his system as a pure psychology without a clear-cut physiological basis, though from time to time he again tried to find such a basis, always unsuccessfully.

Freud published nothing really new on the subject of sexuality in the ten years from the *Studies on Hysteria* in 1895, which marked the culmination of his early views, to the *Three Essays on Sexuality* in 1905, which set forth his mature position. During this decade he was preoccupied with his self-analysis, his practise and his work on dreams and its sequelae.

When a second edition of the *Studies on Hysteria* was issued in 1908 Freud wrote in the preface:

The developments and changes in my views during the course of thirteen years of work have been too far-reaching for it to be possible to attach them to my earlier exposition without entirely destroying its essential character. Nor have I any reason for wishing to eliminate this evidence of my initial views. Even today I regard them not as errors but as valuable first approximations to knowledge. . . .[76]

The changes were indeed far-reaching. As Freud said in the paper, "My Views on the Part Played by Sexuality in the Etiology of the Neuroses," written at about the same time as the *Three Essays*, only two positions remained which were never repudiated or abandoned—the importance of sexuality and of infantilism.[77]

However, Freud had the personal peculiarity of being reluctant to state that he had abandoned an old position completely. Although he changed his mind many times in the course of his life, there are few occasions on which he actually said so. The casual reader (and some experts) thus get the erroneous impression that one can freely equate writings from different stages in Freud's work. Such is not the case.

What happened between 1895 and 1905 was the accumulation of a vast mass of clinical psychological observations. These were unified on the one hand by the concept of the unconscious, and on the other by the concept of infantile sexuality,

Freud never really left any doubt that his system was a psychological one. (See above, pp. 9-12.) He even objected to Adler's theory of organ inferiority on the grounds that "it amounts to replacing the psychological by the biological. . . . All this is quite wrong." [78]

At the same time, Freud was caught up in his own curious ambivalence about psychology. There was the incontrovertible fact that psychology must be related to physiology in some way. The answer to this he at first found in his hypothesis of a biologically determined sequence of libidinal stages.

But this epoch-making discovery, which might do very well for most men, was not enough for him. He always longed for the surer knowledge of his youth. As he put it some years later in *Beyond the Pleasure Principle:*

> The deficiencies in our description would probably vanish if we were already in a position to replace the psychological terms by physiological or chemical ones. . . .
> Biology is truly a land of unlimited possibilities. . . .[79]

It was under the pressure of this kind of thinking * that Freud formulated what is undoubtedly the most dubious of the numerous hypotheses contained in the libido theory: Libido is a quantitatively variable force which can serve as a measure of processes and transformations occurring in the field of sexual excitation. This theory of the libido as a quantity was added in 1915, when he was attempting

---

* In the *Three Essays* Freud even wrote:
My aim has rather been to discover how far psychological investigation can throw light upon the biology of the sexual life of man.[80]

a theoretical integration of all his thinking, an integration which evidently was not achieved; it was never published.[81]

What is meant by Freud's "biological orientation" thus has various meanings at different periods in his career. In the period under discussion (1900-1914) his emphasis was on infantile sexuality, and the opposition to Freud, which was exceptionally vicious then, concentrated on that idea. By now the theory of infantile sexuality has become such an integral part of all psychology that the whole controversy has receded into the background, if it is not forgotten entirely.

In theory, Freud never maintained that sexuality was the only motive force of human behavior. He always recognized the existence of ego-instincts, though for a long time he did not probe further into them. Thus (see above, p. 46) at a number of points in *The Interpretation of Dreams* he denied that he had ever made the assertion that all dreams have a sexual meaning.

In a sense it was because of the opposition that he himself often stressed the vital truths contained in his sexual theories. "Mankind has always known that it possesses spirit; I had to show it that there are also instincts." [82]

After World War I psychoanalysis became much more popular and a new argument about the libido theory and Freud's biological orientation arose. This time the question came up in connection with anthropological research. Among those who were stimulated by Freud was the Polish-British anthropologist Bronislaw Malinowski. At first Malinowski was strongly drawn to psychoanalysis and acknowledged his deep indebtedness to it; later he came to feel that some of its statements were too far reaching. It was widely maintained that Freud had assumed the Oedipus complex to be universal. However, Malinowski in his research on the matrilineal Trobrianders had shown on the contrary that the form of the Oedipus complex varies with the nuclear family complex, and is thus not universal, and that his (Malinowski's) findings prove Freud's biological orientation to be wrong. Freud's observations, it was held, were correct (at least for the most part) but they should be explained on the basis of cultural conditioning rather than of innate biological drives.

A review of the history of the controversy and of the available evidence shows once again that the arguments of this culturalist school are misleading and do not do justice to all the facts.

The supposition that the Oedipus complex is universal was stated by Freud in *Totem and Taboo* in 1913 after he had examined all the anthropological material then known. Though the book was officially excoriated by anthropologists (see below, pp. 144-151) it nevertheless had the effect of stimulating field workers first to check Freud's hypotheses and second to use the new research tools he had discovered (dreams, myths, later projective techniques and even psychoanalysis).

As so often happens, this argument stresses one point to the exclusion of all others and distorts the total picture. Meyer Fortes has recently reviewed the influence Freud had on Malinowski and the controversies centering around this influence and contends that far from being in opposition to Freud by and large Malinowski was stimulated to his most useful ideas by psychoanalysis.[83]

Malinowski himself describes his work as an "attempt at a collaboration between anthropology and psychoanalysis." [84] While he is in disagreement with Freud and Jones on the Oedipus complex, on many other points he is in full agreement. Thus he says:

In Melanesia, we find an altogether different type of sexual development in the child. *That the biological impulses do not essentially differ, seems beyond doubt.*[85] (Italics mine)

Freud himself had no a priori opinion on what anthropologists would find in the field once they set out to look. When he heard of Malinowski's research he expressed pleasure at the thought.[86] And when Roheim in 1928 set off on a similar field trip he wrote:

Roheim is burning with eagerness to "analyze" his primitive natives. I think it would be more urgent to make observations concerning the sexual freedom and the latency period of the children, on any signs of the Oedipus complex, and on any indications of a masculine complex among the primitive women. But we agreed that the program would in the end follow the opportunities that presented themselves.[87]

Since 1925 or thereabouts, the particular questions around which the disputes concerning Freud's biological orientation revolve are whether any given trait or characteristic is determined by the culture or by biological forces (innate). A review of the historical development shows that this is actually a new problem; before then Freud had simply never gotten around to it. When he did consider it he appeared to adopt the common-sense view that while physiology (or biology) determines the drives themselves, culture will determine how these drives are molded. Thus in a footnote to his *Autobiography* in 1935 he wrote:

The period of latency is a physiological phenomenon. It can, however, only give rise to a complete interruption of sexual life in cultural organizations which have made the suppression of infantile sexuality a part of their system. This is not the case with the majority of primitive peoples.[88]

Compare this statement with one by Kardiner, one of the leaders of the culturalist school:

The study of psychology must begin with the biological characteristics of man. These biological characteristics delimit the field in which psychological processes take place.[89]

It becomes clear that the two men are actually saying pretty much the same thing. In general, the difference between the biological and the cultural orientations is one of emphasis rather than of fundamental position.

It thus appears that the attacks on the libido theory and on Freud's biological orientation, which have been so frequent since the 1930's, are just another red herring which misconstrues the historical development and does not accurately portray the present situation. Freud was both biologically and culturally oriented; but more basically he was first and always a psychologist.

Turning now to the six major hypotheses involved in the libido theory (and the numerous subsidiary ones which there has not been space to consider) and trying to evaluate them critically (see pages 65-70) difficulties similar to those sketched above again arise. Each of these propositions has a long history, both before it was enunciated by Freud and after. All have changed in many ways in the course of Freud's development and since.

Consider, for example, the first proposition (see p. 65) that libido is the major source of psychic energy. This is the theoretical basis of many clinical observations, such as the discharge phenomenon which leads to dreams, hysteria, and many other neurotic symptoms. Libido was never the only source of psychic energy; it always existed side-by-side with the ego-instincts, but Freud never clarified the relationship between the two, so that we are never sure of just what Freud himself meant when he said on occasion that sexuality is the prime motivating force of mankind. Furthermore, in 1920 this theory was replaced by the dual-instinct theory, of Eros and Thanatos, sexuality and aggression. It is obvious, then, that aggression is also a source of psychic energy. How the energy deriving from the sexual instinct is related to that arising from the aggressive requires clarification, which it never received from Freud in any adequate way. By 1923 Freud had defined the ego, and so a new element was introduced, again requiring integration into the system, an integration, however, which was never satisfactorily achieved.

Through all these changes, however, one essential proposition stands out: Much of human behavior and a considerable portion of man's mental life is concerned with bodily gratification in one form or another. To this there is a corollary: If the libidinal frustrations are too great, they tend to supersede every other concern. Put in this form, it becomes clear that, although it was at first vigorously denied, it has since become part of the thinking of every dynamic psychologist. The issues involved in it are quantitative ones. When do the major libidinal areas mature? How much frustration in each libidinal area can a human being tolerate? How much aggression can be held back? Looked at in this way, it becomes obvious that there are as many differences of opinion among the Freudians as there are among the non-Freudians. To take but a few examples: Freud himself held for a long time to his theory of actual neurosis, namely, that lack of sexual satisfaction causes pathologic symptoms. His colleagues did not go along with him. Freud's views on the phallic stage and the psychology of women were vigorously disputed by Jones in the 1920's, and in some respects Freud changed his mind. The influential school of Melanie Klein has placed the maturational age for the levels of psychosexual development much earlier than any other Freudian group, and this, too, has led to much controversy.

The list of disagreements could be multiplied almost indefinitely. The same holds true as regards all the other aspects of the libido theory—the stages of libinidal development, the relationship between object-choice and libido, the defenses against impulses, the development of character structure out of libidinal traits, neurosis as a regression. As a first approximation all of these are accepted as correct and incorporated by all schools of psychoanalysis and dynamic psychology today. The real issues are quantitative ones, for example, what infantile fixations lie at the basis of the various neurotic manifestations? Why do some neurotic problems lead to a conscious inner conflict, while others do not? Here, too, disagreements are legion among Freudians as well as non-Freudians.

Thus in its broad form the libido theory and its attendant hypotheses are seen as the basis of all dynamic psychology today. It has given rise, and still does, to many real issues which are essentially of a quantitative nature. These can only be settled by empirical research. Freud himself, as the historical record clearly shows, welcomed all such research, whether it resulted in confirming his specific hypotheses or not.

Available English Translations of Freud's Works Cited in Chapter V.

Three Essays on the Theory of Sexuality. 1905.
  Standard Edition, Vol. VII, pp. 130-243.
  Under title: "Three Contributions to the Theory of Sex." In *The Basic Writings of Sigmund Freud.* New York: Modern Library Giants, Random House, 1938, pp. 553-629.

My Views on the Part Played by Sexuality in the Etiology of the Neuroses. 1905.
  Standard Edition, Vol. VII, pp. 269-279.
  Collected Papers, Vol. I, pp. 272-283.

The Sexual Enlightenment of Children. 1907.
  Standard Edition, Vol. IX, pp. 131-139.
  Collected Papers, Vol. II, pp. 36-44.

Character and Anal Erotism. 1908.
  Standard Edition, Vol. IX, pp. 169-175.
  Collected Papers, Vol. II, pp. 45-50.

"Civilized" Sexual Morality and Modern Nervous Illness. 1908.
Standard Edition, Vol. IX, pp. 181-204.
Under title: " 'Civilized' Sexual Morality and Modern Nervousness."
Collected Papers, Vol. II, pp. 76-99.

Contributions to the Psychology of Love. 1910-1918.
Standard Edition, Vol. XI, pp. 165-208.
Collected Papers, Vol., IV, pp. 192-235.
Above contains the following three papers: "A Special Type of Object Choice Made by Men." 1910. "On the Universal Tendency to Debasement in the Sphere of Love." 1912. (Translated in Collected Papers as: "The Most Prevalent Form of Degradation in Erotic Life.") "The Taboo of Virginity." 1918.

Formulations on the Two Principles of Mental Functioning. 1911.
Standard Edition, Vol. XII, pp. 218-226.
Under title: "Formulations Regarding the Two Principles in Mental Functioning." Collected Papers, Vol. IV, pp. 13-21.

The Disposition to Obsessional Neurosis. 1913.
Standard Edition, Vol. XII, pp. 317-326.
Under title: "The Predisposition to Obsessional Neurosis." Collected Papers, Vol. II, pp. 122-132.

On Narcissism: An Introduction. 1914.
Standard Edition, Vol. XIV, pp. 73-102.
Collected Papers, Vol. IV, pp. 30-59.

Instincts and Their Vicissitudes. 1915.
Standard Edition, Vol. XIV, pp. 117-140.
Collected Papers, Vol. IV, pp. 60-83.
In *A General Selection from the Works of Sigmund Freud,* Edited by John Rickman. New York: Doubleday Anchor Books, paperback, pp. 70-86.

Observations on Transference-Love. 1915.
Standard Edition, Vol. XII, pp. 159-171.
Collected Papers, Vol. II, pp. 377-391.

NOTES ON CHAPTER V

General reviews of the various aspects of *libido theory* in the light of experience since Freud may be found in a number of papers. See particularly: N. Reider (reporter): "Re-Evaluation of the Libido Theory," *Journal of the American Psychoanalytic Association,* III, 1955, pp. 299-308. C. Brenner: "Re-Evaluation of the Libido Theory," *Journal of the*

American Psychoanalytic Association, IV, 1956, pp. 162-9. R. Loewenstein (ed.): *Drives, Affects, Behavior* (New York: International Universities Press, 1953). L. Kaywin: "An Epigenetic Approach to the Psychoanalytic Theory of Instincts and Affects," *Journal of the American Psychoanalytic Association*, VIII, 1960, pp. 613-58. D. Rapaport: "On the Psychoanalytic Theory of Affect." *International Journal of Psychoanalysis*, XXXIV, 1953, pp. 177-98.

For more recent material on *identity* and *character formation*, see E. Erikson, "Identity and the Life Cycle," *Psychological Issues*, I, 1959, No. 1. This is probably the most important extension of the chronological scheme of development since Freud. W. Reich: *Character Analysis* (New York: Orgone Institute, 1949) is historically important, but much too over-schematized. For summary papers see D. Rubinfine (reporter): "The Problem of Identity," *Journal of the American Psychoanalytic Association*, VI, 1958, pp. 131-42, and A. Valenstein (reporter): "The Psychoanalytic Concept of Character," *Ibid.*, pp. 567-75.

On the topic of *instinct* the best summary reference is R. Fletcher: *Instinct in Man* (New York: International Universities Press, 1957). A scholarly review by an anthropologist is S. Posinsky: "Instincts, Culture and Science," *Psychoanalytic Quarterly*, XXVII, 1958, pp. 1-37. For a description of how several behavioristic psychologists have returned to the concept of instinct see K. Breland and M. Breland: "The Misbehavior of Organisms," *American Psychologist*, XVI, 1961, pp. 681-4.

The psychoanalytic interest in *ethology* is reflected in M. Ostow: "Psychoanalysis and Ethology," *Journal of the American Psychoanalytic Association*, VIII, 1960, pp. 526-34, and I. L. Kaufman: "Some Ethological Studies of Social Relationships and Conflict Situations," *Ibid.*, pp. 671-85.

The *psychoanalytic view of nosology* still rests most heavily on O. Fenichel: *The Psychoanalytic Theory of Neurosis* (New York: Norton, 1945). Much dissatisfaction continues to be expressed with the traditional concepts, but no new scheme has found wide acceptance.

See N. Ross (reporter): "An Examination of Nosology According to Psychoanalytic Concepts," *Journal of the American Psychoanalytic Association*, VIII, 1960, pp. 535-51, and L. L. Robbins (reporter): "The Borderline Case," *Ibid.*, IV, 1956, pp. 550-62.

Freud's views on *love* are scattered throughout his writings. For an over-all review see E. Hitschmann: "Freud's Conception of Love," *International Journal of Psychoanalysis*, XXXIII, 1952, pp. 421-8.

The *cultural critique* of Freud is summarized mainly in two books: Clara Thompson: *Psychoanalysis: Its Evolution and Development* (New York: Hermitage House, 1950), and Karen Horney: *New Ways in Psychoanalysis* (New York: Norton, 1939). A more recent paper by Kardiner and his associates does not add to the traditional arguments (A. Kardiner, A. Karush and L. Ovesey: "A Methodological Study of Freudian Theory,"

Journal of Nervous and Mental Disease, CXXIX, 1959, Nos. 1-4, 1.) In general these works misstate the Freudian position by oversimplifying it and giving insufficient weight to the many historical changes which took place and are still going on. For some discussions of these misrepresentations of Freud see R. Fine, "Review of E. S. Tauber and M. R. Green: "Prelogical Experience," *Contemporary Psychology,* V, 1960, No. 3, and R. Fine: "Review of E. Fromm: 'Sigmund Freud's Mission,'" *Psychoanalysis and the Psychoanalytic Review,* XLVI, 1959-1960, pp. 119-25.

Chapter VI. TRANSFERENCE AND RESISTANCE

Anyone who has ever undertaken the task of helping another human being by means of psychotherapy, and even any patient who is perceptive about what happens during the course of his psychotherapy, is immediately aware of the fact that purely rational procedures do not get one very far. There is, instead, the development of an emotional relationship with the therapist that varies in intensity with the personality of the patient; there is also a strong fight on the part of the patient against the possibility of improvement. The emotional relationship is known as the "transference"; the fight is known as "resistance." Freud always attached the greatest importance to these two phenomena. Thus, for example, in *The History of the Psychoanalytic Movement* (1914) he wrote:

It may thus be said that the theory of psychoanalysis is an attempt to account for two striking and unexpected facts of observation which emerge whenever an attempt is made to trace the symptoms of a neurotic back to their sources in his past life: the facts of transference and of resistance. Any line of investigation which recognizes these two facts and takes them as the starting point of its work may call itself psychoanalysis, though it arrives at results other than my own.[90]

Unfortunately, Freud never set out to give a systematic account of these two phenomena, fundamental as they are to the whole theory and practice of psychoanalysis. In all his writings there is not a single paper devoted exclusively to resistance in the psychoanalytic process. From 1910 on, when he began to have a number of followers and noticed that some of them did not grasp what he was teaching, he began to write a series of papers on transference. Even these papers, however, are rather sketchy and scarcely satisfactory for the purpose. His rather casual handling of the topics of transference and resistance is in sharp contrast to his meticulous discussion of the unconscious in *The Interpretation of Dreams* and of sexuality in the *Three Essays*. There are, of course, many references to the subject scattered throughout all his works, and many of his students later put down in much more detail just what Freud meant.

Nevertheless, all analysts since Freud have been unanimous in the belief that the observations of transference and resistance are the most profound ever made about psychotherapy, and help to explain at one stroke the whole gamut of baffling phenomena which occur in the process of trying to help another human being.

TRANSFERENCE

"Transference" may be described as the observation that the patient in psychoanalysis does not submit to a dispassionate consideration of his difficulties, but rather enters at an early stage of the analysis into an intense relationship with the therapist. As could be predicted from theory, this relationship centers primarily around the two aspects of the Oedipus complex, the sexual attraction for the parent of the opposite sex, and the antagonism toward the parent of the same sex. As in life in general, the individual finds it extremely difficult to recognize his unconscious emotional drives and so he represses them. In the psychoanalytic treatment process the repression becomes a resistance, a refusal, unconscious, of course, to see the real nature of the ties to the therapist, of the instinctual drives which motivate the individual, and of the ties to other people in general.

The interconnectedness of the three cornerstones of Freud's first psychoanalytic system now becomes apparent. The unconscious deals mainly with the remains of infantile sexuality; conversely, infantile sexuality is unacceptable to the individual and is repressed into the unconscious. The total process causes the person to be driven by a mass of irrational urges which he can neither fathom nor adequately control. Under the impulse of these urges he comes as a patient into analytic treatment and poses the same kind of resistance to the uncovering of his wishes that he opposes in real life to their recognition. Consequently, therapy which attempts to proceed in a completely rational manner—for instance, by pointing out to a patient with a subway phobia that after all millions of people do ride unharmed in the subway every day, and that this fear on his part is unwarranted—must necessarily fail because it does not take into consideration the nature of the illness. To be successful, therapy must to a greater or lesser extent make use of the principles of transference and resistance.

For the layman, the doctrines of transference and resistance are the hardest of all the Freudian theories to grasp. On the other hand, they are the most fundamental to the practice and theory of psychotherapy. There is no easy way of bridging this gap. As in many other fields the considerations which dominate the professional in his thinking are reached only after many years of painful experience, and it is quite difficult, as Freud realized, to communicate this to someone who has not had the same experiences. Freud himself actually felt that the process of psychotherapy was one that could not readily be taught. At one point he likened it to chess, where one can learn the opening moves and the end game moves, while the middle game can be acquired only by actual practice and contact with the games of great masters. Others since Freud have made many attempts to systematize the teaching of psychoanalytic therapy more thoroughly, yet there always remains a highly personal element in psychoanalysis which makes it in a sense more of an art than an exact science.

PSYCHOANALYTIC TECHNIQUE

The development of Freud's ideas about technique is somewhat difficult to trace because he wrote so little about it. Nevertheless, the broad outlines are reasonably clear. In the 1890's the cathartic method was gradually replaced by psychoanalysis. After the long discussion of the technique of psychotherapy in the *Studies on Hysteria* (1895), Freud wrote nothing at all on the subject until 1904, and that only because he was prompted to do so by his friend Loewenfeld. In this paper, entitled "Freud's Psychoanalytic Procedure," Freud states with regard to the cathartic method of treatment that new findings have necessitated a different though not contradictory concept of the therapeutic process. Looking back, however, it would have to be said that the changes are considerably greater than Freud seemed to think; as has been noted, Freud had a certain aversion to renouncing any old idea completely, and usually tried to hold on to it in one form or another.

Freud also says in this paper that the "technique of psychoanalysis is much easier in practice, when once one has learned it, than any description of it would indicate," [91] an opinion which undoubtedly arouses a feeling of despair in the contemporary analyst!

Lifting the Amnesias. At this time, as his case histories and papers describe, Freud tried, by the study of free associations, dreams, and life-history data (anamnesis) to *lift the amnesias of childhood.* This was a departure from the cathartic method in two respects: First, the therapeutic role of abreaction was relegated to the background, to be eventually discarded. Making the unconscious conscious became the major technical tool. And second, the concept of the unconscious was considerably broadened and deepened, so that it ultimately came to have little resemblance to the unconscious of the 1890's.

For a long while lifting the amnesias remained the goal of analysis. In the paper "Freud's Psychoanalytic Procedure" (1904) he wrote:

... the task of the treatment is to remove the amnesias. When all gaps in memory have been filled in, all the enigmatic products of mental life elucidated, the continuance and even a renewal of the morbid condition are made impossible. Or the formula may be expressed in this fashion: all repressions must be undone. The mental condition is then the same as one in which all amnesias have been removed. Another formulation reaches further: the task consists in making the unconscious accessible to consciousness, which is done by overcoming the resistances. But it must be remembered that an ideal condition such as this is not present even in the normal, and further that it is only rarely possible to carry the treatment to a point approaching it. Just as health and sickness are not different from each other in essence but are only separated by a quantitative line of demarcation which can be determined in practice, so the aim of the treatment will never be anything else but the *practical* recovery of the patient, the restoration of his ability to lead an active life, and of his capacity for enjoyment.[92]

In the *Three Essays* Freud had made the observation that the sexual life of children usually emerges in a form accessible to observation around the third or fourth year of life.[93] Since it was precisely this period which in his view lay at the root of the neurosis (the Oedipus complex), ideally analysis should remove the amnesias of these early years and make the memories accessible.

Such an ideal led to a new concept, that of *analyzability* as distinguished from accessibility to help, or psychotherapy. Clearly only those persons who were in a position to remember their early years could be analyzed, and it was only in such cases that one could justifiably speak of psychoanalysis as distinct from psychotherapy. Freud set up limitations on the choice of patients—they must be capable of a psychically normal condition, must have a certain measure of natural intelligence and ethical development, must be neither too old (past fifty) nor too young (he did not analyze children). This difference between psychoanalysis and psychotherapy and the proper evaluation of who is suitable for each has ever since remained one of the central concerns of psychoanalysis. It has, of course, had to be recast at various periods throughout the history of psychoanalysis.[94]

The process of restoring the gaps in memory could easily become a kind of intellectual game. As long as the emphasis was on the memory, it did not matter where the memory came from. As in the old cathartic method, this likewise soon led to many disappointments. In the 1913 paper "On Beginning the Treatment," Freud wrote:

It is true that in the earliest days of analytic technique we took an intellectualist view of the situation. We set a high value on the patient's knowledge of what he had forgotten, and in this we made hardly any distinction between our knowledge of it and his. We thought it a special piece of good luck if we were able to obtain information about the forgotten childhood trauma from other sources—for instance, from parents or nurses or the seducer himself—as in some cases it was possible to do; and we hastened to convey the information and the proofs of its correctness to the patient, in the certain expectation of thus bringing the neurosis and the treatment to a rapid end. It was a severe disappointment when the expected success was not forthcoming.[95]

In reflecting on why "the expected success was not forthcoming" Freud came to stress the transference more and more. In *The Case of Dora*, which was originally written in 1901, he said:

If the theory of psychoanalytic technique is gone into, it becomes evident that transference is an inevitable necessity. Practical experience, at all events, shows conclusively that there is no means of avoiding it, and that this latest creation of the disease must be combated like all the earlier ones. This happens, however, to be by far the hardest part of the whole task.[96]

In the Dora case history Freud took himself to task for missing some transference manifestations, which led to an abrupt and premature termination of the psychoanalytic treatment. Evidently he continued to hope that merely pressing for memories would resolve the neurosis, and it was not until 1912 in the paper "*The Dynamics of Transference*" that he said flatly: ". . . finally every conflict has to be fought out in the sphere of transference." [97]

No doubt it was because of this uncertainty and the fluctuating positions that he took that Freud did not publish more on technique. As early as 1908 he announced that he was thinking of writing a general account of psychoanalytic technique. Of its planned fifty pages, thirty-six were already written. In 1909 he told Jones that he was proposing to write a little memorandum of maxims and rules of technique which he intended to distribute privately among only those analysts nearest to him. At the International Psychoanalytic Congress in Nuremberg in 1910 he announced in his paper that he was planning a book that would systematically explain analytic technique. Of all these projects nothing came to fruition.

"*On the Technique of Psychoanalysis.*" Instead, he wrote a series of six papers between December, 1911 and July, 1914 which he reprinted in 1918 in his fourth collection of shorter papers under the heading "On the Technique of Psychoanalysis." In spite of the wealth of clinical wisdom which they contain, they are still a far cry from a fully systematic consideration of the topic. Often Freud felt that it was impossible to describe technique adequately in any written form, that most of it had to be learned from experience. At one point he expressed the idea that the technique he described was the one best suited to him; that another analyst might find another approach more congenial.[98]

Nevertheless, the six papers all have one unifying theme. With greater or lesser intensity they all focus on the phenomena of transference and resistance. By this time the theory was clear to him, namely that psychoanalysis succeeds to the extent that the transference and the concomitant resistances are properly handled by the analyst.

After the publication of these papers every rule with regard to analysis had to be evaluated in relation to the transference. The avoidance of social relations between patient and analyst, of replies to personal questions about the analyst's life, of more intimate contacts with relatives or even close friends of the patient, the timing of interpretations, the handling of time and fees, the principle of abstinence during analysis, and many other matters which have since become part of standard analytic technique, all derive from Freud's need to keep the transference uncontaminated and therefore subject to analysis.

However, within this general framework much leeway is left to the analyst's initiative. In a study in 1938 of the members of the British Psychoanalytic Association, Glover found considerable differences in specific day-to-day practices, even though all the analysts involved had had similar training.[99]

Transference Neurosis. The stress on transference led Freud to the recognition of the *transference neurosis*. In the transference neurosis, a transitional stage between illness and health, the patient recapitulates with the analyst the pathological aspects of his relationship with his parents. Transference neuroses appear in all kinds of interpersonal situations, but it is only in analysis that they are worked through so that they may be fully understood. Many of the features of the psychoanalytic setup serve the purpose of facilitating the appearance of this transference neurosis and of making it accessible to psychoanalytic understanding.

Transference, although uncovered in the analytic situation, is not confined to it. Transference, Freud wrote, is a universal phenomenon of the human mind, it decides the success of all medical influence, and in fact dominates the whole of each person's relations to his human environment.[100]

It is this wider meaning of transference which makes it a basis of general psychology rather than merely of psychopathology. This theme was elaborated more fully in some of Freud's later works, particularly *Group Psychology and the Analysis of the Ego* (1921).

The analysis of the transference is met by a strong resistance on the part of the patient. In practice this transference resistance, part of the transference neurosis, becomes the focal point of the therapeutic process in analysis.

Working-Through. Increasingly, then, in Freud's view, resistance comes more and more into the forefront. It is in a sense even more important than the understanding of the transference. The resistances, however, do not disappear as soon as they come up. They continue to appear, and must be analyzed every time they do. To this process Freud gave the name of *working-through.* Essentially this working-through does not differ from the repetition of difficult material which is part of every learning procedure. It is only by persistent and repeated analysis of the pathological transference productions that the patient gradually comes to see the true nature of his neurosis and to overcome it.

By 1914, in the important paper "Remembering, Repeating, and Working-Through," Freud had shifted his position to the view that this kind of working-through is the most essential part of analysis. There he wrote:

> This working-through of the resistances may in practice turn out to be an arduous task for the subject of the analysis and a trial of patience for the analyst. Nevertheless, it is a part of the work which effects the greatest changes in the patient and which distinguishes analytic treatment from any kind of treatment by suggestion.[101]

What now becomes of the lifting of childhood amnesias? Here Freud's theories underwent a curious change. In the 1890's he had been misled into thinking that the seduction stories of his hysterical patients related to actual events; they turned out to be fantasies. Ever since he had been preoccupied with trying to determine the differential effects on personality growth of, say, a fantasy of seduction and an actual seduction. He took this or a similar question up a number of times: In *Leonardo da Vinci* (1910), the man who claimed to have remembered how a kite put its beak between his lips while he was still in his cradle; in *Totem and Taboo* (1913), where Freud postulated the murder of the father by the sons at some remote time in history; and in the Wolf Man case (1918), where he felt he had reconstructed the patient's memory of witnessing the primal scene (parental intercourse) when he was eighteen months old. In all these instances he debated at considerable length whether he was dealing with a fantasy or a reality. Finally, he came to the rather remarkable conclusion that it makes no difference. In *A General Introduction to Psychoanalysis*, 1916–17, he wrote:

All this [discussion of fantasy] seems to lead to but one impression, that childhood experiences of this kind are in some way necessarily required by the neurosis, that they belong to its unvarying inventory. If they can be found in real events, well and good; but if reality has not supplied them, they will be evolved out of hints and elaborated by phantasy. The effect is the same, and even today we have not succeeded in tracing any variations in the results according as phantasy or reality plays the greater part in these experiences.[102]

In spite of the significance of these contributions to technique, Freud was eternally dissatisfied with them, and looked forward to a thorough revision. In a letter to Ferenczi in 1928 he wrote:

... the "Recommendations on Technique" I wrote long ago were essentially of a negative nature. I considered the most important thing was to emphasize what one should *not* do, and to point out the temptations in directions contrary to analysis. Almost everything positive that one *should* do I have left to "tact," the discussion of which you are introducing. The result was that the docile analysts did not perceive the elasticity of the rules I had laid down, and submitted to them as if they were taboos. Some time all that must be revised, without, it is true, doing away with the obligations I had mentioned.[103]

Freud did not come back to the theory of technique again until 1937, in his paper "Analysis Terminable and Interminable" (see below, pp. 234-238). There, of course, he had to consider the far-reaching changes brought about by the newer ego-psychological formulations.

Available English Translations of Freud's Works Cited in Chapter VI.

The Handling of Dream Interpretation in Psychoanalysis. 1911.
Standard Edition, Vol. XII, pp. 91-96.
Under title: "The Employment of Dream Interpretation in Psychoanalysis." Collected Papers, Vol. II, pp. 305-311.

The Dynamics of Transference. 1912.
Standard Edition, Vol. XII, pp. 99-108.
Under title: "The Dynamics of the Transference." Collected Papers, Vol. II, pp. 312-322.

Recommendations to Physicians Practising Psychoanalysis. 1912.
Standard Edition, Vol. XII, pp. 111-120.
Under title: "Recommendations to Physicians on the Psychoanalytic Method of Treatment." Collected Papers, Vol. II, pp. 323-333.

On Beginning the Treatment (Further Recommendations on the Technique of Psychoanalysis. I.) 1913.
Standard Edition, Vol. XII, pp. 123-144.
Under title: "Further Recommendations on the Technique of Psychoanalysis." "On Beginning the Treatment." "The Question of the First Communications." "The Dynamics of the Cure." Collected Papers, Vol. II, pp. 342-365.

Remembering, Repeating and Working-Through. (Further Recommendations on the Technique of Psychoanalysis. II.) 1914.
Standard Edition, Vol. XII, pp. 147-156.
Under title "Further Recommendations on the Technique of Psychoanalysis." "Recollection, Repetition and Working-Through." Collected Papers, Vol. II, pp. 366-376.

Observations on Transference-Love. 1915.
See bibliographic note to Chapter V.

NOTES ON CHAPTER VI

For an excellent historical review of the topic of *transference,* see D. W. Orr: "Transference and Counter-Transference: A Historical Survey," *Journal of the American Psychoanalytic Association,* II, 1954, pp. 621-70.

The literature on *psychoanalytic technique* to 1936 is summarized in Chapter VII of O. Fenichel: *Problems of Psychoanalytic Technique* (The Psychoanalytic Quarterly, 1941). Particularly important for the expansion of psychoanalytic technique are S. Ferenczi and O. Rank: *The Development of Psychoanalysis* (New York and Washington, D.C.: Nervous and Mental Disease Publishing Co., 1925). W. Reich: *Character Analysis*

(New York: Orgone Institute, 1945). A. Freud: *The Ego and The Mechanisms of Defense* (London: Hogarth Press, 1936).

Just as Freud never wrote a full-length paper on resistances, the subsequent writers, in spite of their voluminous contributions, have not tackled the problem systematically either. Reich's "resistance analysis" is merely an approach to one kind of resistance. For a further understanding of the classical technique, the reader is best advised to consult the appropriate chapters on transference and resistance in standard works on technique, particularly: O. Fenichel: *Problems of Psychoanalytic Technique, op. cit.* E. Glover: *The Technique of Psychoanalysis* (New York: International Universities Press, 1955); S. Lorand: *The Technique of Psychoanalytic Therapy* (New York: International Universities Press, 1946); K. Menninger: *Theory of Psychoanalytic Technique* (New York: Basic Books, 1958).

For a review of developments since 1937 see notes at the end of Chapter XII.

Chapter VII.   THE RESOLUTION OF
THE PROBLEM OF THE
CLASSICAL NEUROSES

Freud's practice was devoted very largely to neurotics, and it is in this area of dealing with neurosis that he made his most enduring clinical contributions. His work in this period, from 1900 to 1914, provided a resolution of the problem which then became an integral part of the framework of psychoanalytic theory.

NATURE OF NEUROSIS

The degree to which all psychotherapists today are indebted to Freud for clarification of the nature of neurosis is still not too well recognized. First, he established that neurosis was a psychological problem worthy of study, and not a form of malingering or a sign of hereditary degeneracy as had been hitherto believed. Second, he reformulated the disparate symptoms which his predecessors and colleagues had described, dividing them into two major clinical entities—obsessional neurosis (the term itself stems from Freud) and hysteria. Hysteria was further subdivided into conversion hysteria and anxiety hysteria; both designations were coined by Freud. Third, in terms of the libido theory, he established what could be regarded as the normal course of development and showed how neurosis could be made intelligible by reference to such normal development. Fourth, he demonstrated that neurosis and normality differ only in degree, not in kind, and thereby restored the neurotic, [and even more so the psychotic,] to a place in society. Fifth, he established that these neuroses are amenable to psychoanalysis, and that analysis is the treatment of choice for them. The analyzability of these patients rests on the fact that they form transferences, which can then be worked through.

It is well to remember that the term "neurosis" is still only vaguely defined. When Freud began he wrote of the "neuropsychoses," a designation which would be unthinkable today. As late as 1913 he spoke of schizophrenia as one of the major neuroses. The sharp dividing line between neurosis and psychosis postulated by Krae-pelinian psychiatry has not been borne out by more careful psycho-analytic research, and even today the dividing line remains rather unclear. Even the more recent category of so-called "borderline states" has not resolved the impasse. Furthermore, the growth of psychoanalysis in general and ego psychology in particular has led to the recognition that there are all kinds of disturbances that can-not be subsumed under the more traditional categories.

Differentiation of the Neuroses. In the light of this historical back-ground it is useful to differentiate hysteria and obsessional neurosis from the broader categories of character neurosis, borderline condi-tions, psychoses, and other diagnoses. A term which has been pro-posed and used from time to time is the *classical neuroses,* and, for the sake of clarity, these classical neuroses will here be differentiated from the other disorders.

In the 1890's Freud had distinguished the psychoneuroses from the actual neuroses.[104] Although he held on to the idea of the actual neurosis [until 1932] this idea recedes more and more into the back-ground in his writings. From then on when he writes of neuroses he means primarily the psychoneuroses. Eventually the prefix *psycho* was dropped, and he spoke simply of the neuroses.

Once it appeared that some neuroses were amenable to analytic treatment, while others were not, a new classification on a thera-peutic basis suggested itself. This was the division into the *transfer-ence* neuroses and the *narcissistic* neuroses. The transference neu-roses are those where the patient establishes a transference to the analyst; the narcissistic neuroses are those where he does not, because he is too narcissistic or self-centered. The fact that Freud switched from a descriptive to a therapeutic division is one more proof of the close tie that always existed in his mind between theory and therapy.

The libido theory provided Freud with a novel basis for the theory of neurosis. From general pathology he borrowed the observation that every developmental process leaves in its wake certain weak spots, which vary from individual to individual, and which form the basis for future difficulties or retrogressions. The weak spots he called fixations, and he postulated that the neurotic in time of stress *regresses* to these fixation points which lie in the world of infantile sexuality, roughly the first five years of life. The Oedipal fixations Freud considered to be most important, and he looked upon the Oedipus complex as the core of all neurotic difficulties.

Neurosis and Fixation. It was always Freud's conviction that the specific neuroses could be differentiated from one another in terms of the different levels of fixation. In trying to apply the theory, however, to Freud's work at this time there is the difficulty that the final schema of the libidinal stages was clarified only over a period of many years. (See above, p. 66.)

Freud's various correlations of neurosis with a particular fixation point should be viewed against the light of this historical background. In his 1913 paper "The Disposition to Obsessional Neurosis" he enumerated four main forms of neurosis—hysteria, obsessional neurosis, paranoia, dementia praecox, and postulated that the fixation points occur in reverse order: hysteria at the genital stage (the phallic stage had not yet been described); obsessional neurosis at the anal-sadistic; paranoia and dementia praecox somewhere between auto-erotism and narcissism (the oral stage had only barely been mentioned). Although the general idea has been generally accepted that the more severe the illness the earlier the fixation, specific details of the scheme were altered by Freud and other writers.

Freud held that neurosis involves a fixation on the world of infantile sexuality. This view allowed him to give a relatively simple explanation of the symptoms of classical neurosis. Most often the symptom is the unconscious sexual activity of the patient. It may be a defense against such sexual activity, or else some compromise formation may result.

So much for the general characteristics of neurosis. The question now arises: Within this fixation on, and regression to, infantile sexuality, what differentiates the various neuroses from one another? Freud considered this question a number of times, and at different times in his development came to somewhat different conclusions. After the discovery of the significance of the sexual factor in the 1890's, he tried to locate the difference in the types of traumatic sexual experiences. When this had to be abandoned, he ventured on a more detailed clinical description of each illness, particularly of the classical neuroses.

He had begun with the investigation of the nature of unbearable ideas. As time went on, he came to feel that these were basically similar in all neurotics and in the normal individual as well. What created the difference was what he called the psychological factor, or, as it eventually was phrased, the defenses. Thus the foundation for the transition to ego psychology was established.

Neurosis and Psychosis. Freud himself could not treat psychosis and made no fundamental contribution to the therapy of the psychoses. Such therapy was offered only after he had ended the major portion of his intellectual work, beginning around the 1930's. It is somewhat paradoxical that the advances which have come since 1930 in the understanding and treatment of the psychoses have all been based on Freudian principles, and particularly on the more thorough understanding of the nature of the transference relationship which the psychotic is able to build up. For experience has shown that, if properly approached, the psychotic does establish some relationship with the therapist and that just as in the analogous case of the neurotic, this relationship can be used to therapeutic advantage. Thus Freud's initial observation of a narcissistic neurosis, in which no transference is effected, was really one in which he merely followed his psychiatric colleagues without attempting to probe more deeply into the nature of the observed phenomena. When his own views were later adopted and applied more systematically to the study of psychoses, it turned out that they, too, could in many cases yield to psychotherapy, although the nature of the therapy had to be different, and the outcome of the therapy was always far more dubious.

Qualitative Classification of Neurosis. A further qualification must be added. The classification of the neuroses along the transference-narcissistic lines, or in terms of the major clinical entities of hysteria, obsessional neurosis, paranoia, and schizophrenia, is a qualitative one. Many psychiatrists have argued and still argue that the presence of one such illness excludes the presence of another; that is, that these are mutually exclusive entities. This is the qualitative point of view. By contrast, there is the quantitative point of view, which holds that a person may be afflicted with any one of these or all of them in varying degrees. While Freud seems to speak in a qualitative manner, he also emphatically asserts the significance of the quantitative. Thus in the paper "Types of Onset of Neurosis," he says:

It remains to say a few words on the relation of these types to the facts of observation. If I survey the set of patients on whose analysis I am now engaged, I must record that not one of them is a pure example of any of the four types of onset. In each of them, rather, I find a portion of frustration operating alongside a portion of incapacity to adapt to the demands of realities; inhibition in development, which coincides, of course, with inflexibility of fixations, has to be reckoned with in all of them, and, as I already said, the importance of quantity of libido must never be neglected. I find, indeed, that in several of these patients their illness has appeared in successive waves, between which there have been healthy intervals, and that each of these waves has been traceable to a different type of precipitating cause. Thus, the erection of these four types cannot lay claims to any high theoretical value; they are merely different ways of establishing a particular pathogenic constellation in the mental economy —namely the damming-up of libido, which the ego cannot with the means at its command ward off without damage. But this situation itself only becomes pathogenic as a result of a quantitative factor; it does not come as a novelty to mental life and is not created by the impact of what is spoken of as a "cause of illness." [105]

Again in this paper he points out that it is not a question of an absolute quantity but the relationship between the quantity of libido released and the capacity of the ego to handle it. He says:

We may assume that it is not a question of an *absolute* quantity, but of the relation between the quota of libido in operation and the quantity of libido which the individual ego is able to deal with—that is, to hold under tension, to sublimate or to employ directly. For this reason, a *relative* increase in the quantity of libido may have the same effect as an absolute one. An enfeeblement of the ego owing to organic illness or owing to some special demand upon its energy will be able to cause the emergence of neuroses which would otherwise have remained latent in spite of any disposition which might have been present.

The importance in the causation of illness which must be ascribed to *quantity* of libido is in satisfactory agreement with two main theses of the theory of the neuroses to which psychoanalysis has led us: First, the thesis that the neuroses are derived from the conflict between the ego and the libido, and secondly, that there is no *qualitative* distinction between the determinants of health and those of neurosis, and that, on the contrary, healthy people have to contend with the same tasks of mastering their libido—they have simply succeeded better in them.[106]

HYSTERIA AND OBSESSIONAL NEUROSIS

The two major clinical entities with which Freud was concerned most of his life were hysteria and obsessional neurosis. It was originally for these and these only that classical psychoanalysis was considered applicable. He mastered both the theoretical and practical problems connected with them so thoroughly that his work has not had to be redone; it has merely been fitted into a larger framework.

Hysteria. The paper "Hysterical Phantasies and Their Relation to Bisexuality" (1908) contains the most comprehensive discussion of hysteria since the 1890's. Earlier, Freud dealt only with genital sexuality; now he could consider the whole range of infantile sexuality. Although superficially some of his statements are the same as before (e.g., those concerning conversion) actually they have a different meaning in the light of the altered theory.

Around this time Freud suggested the classification of anxiety hysteria to Stekel, who included it in his book on anxiety states. This led to a division of hysteria into two types, conversion and anxiety, which in turn meant that there were now three classical neuroses (the third is obsessional neurosis) instead of the previous two. In the Hysterical Fantasies paper, however, he confined himself to conversion hysteria, although the only difference between it and anxiety hysteria is that where the former develops a somatic conversion the latter reacts with anxiety or a phobia.

Freud summarized his revised views on conversion hysteria in a number of formulas. According to these, hysterical symptoms are (1) memory symbols of certain operative (traumatic) impressions and experiences; (2) substitutes, produced by "conversion," for the associative return of these traumatic experiences; (3) like other psychical structures—an expression of the fulfillment of a wish; (4) the realization of an unconscious fantasy which serves the fulfillment of a wish.

Further, hysterical symptoms (5) serve the purpose of sexual satisfaction and represent a portion of the subject's sexual life (a portion that corresponds to one of the constituents of his sexual instinct); (6) correspond to a return of a mode of sexual satisfaction which was a real one in infantile life and has since been repressed; (7) arise as a compromise between two opposite affective and instinctual impulses, of which one is attempting to bring to expression a component instinct or a constituent of the sexual constitution, and the other is attempting to suppress it; (8) may take over the representation of various unconscious impulses which are not sexual, but they can never be without a sexual significance.

Finally, (9) these conversion symptoms are the expression, on the one hand, of a masculine unconscious sexual fantasy, and, on the other hand, of a feminine one.

The next year Freud wrote a paper on hysterical attacks. Here he was able to confirm in terms of the new theory what had proved to be true in terms of the old, namely that acute attacks and chronic symptoms have the same underlying basis. He found he could bring to light many of the unconscious fantasies which are acted out in these attacks.

Obsessional Neurosis. The most complete description of the structure of obsessional neurosis is found in the theoretical portion of the case history entitled *Notes upon a Case of Obsessional Neurosis* (1909), which has come to be known in the literature as the Rat Man (see pp. 120-123).

Freud begins by saying that in the year 1896 he had defined obsessional ideas as "transformed self-reproaches which have re-emerged from repression and which always relate to some sexual act that was performed with pleasure in childhood." This he now considered to be much too narrow a statement, although the position taken was inherently correct. He went on to describe in much broader detail what is today called the character structure of the obsessional neurotic.

In the obsessional neurotic, repression proceeds by the isolation of the affects from the ideation, rather than, as in hysteria, by total amnesia or repression of entire events. Later he used the formulation: "The obsessional (neurotic) separates the feeling from the idea, while the hysteric simply represses." When he came to describe defense mechanisms more formally, he stated that the obsessional (neurotic) uses isolation, while the hysteric uses repression, so that this was the beginning of the thinking that led eventually to the idea that repression was only one of many defense mechanisms.

The obsessional individual suffers from a deep ambivalence between love and hate. This ambivalence was one of the factors that led Freud later to see the anal-sadistic phase as the fixation point for the obsessional neurotic. The two opposite feelings are split apart in childhood and one, usually the hatred, is repressed. Such a repression leads to a reaction-formation in which the surface feeling is the exact opposite of what lies underneath.

Particularly significant in the psychic make-up of the obsessional neurotic is the holding on to infantile masturbatory wishes, dating from the period roughly from three to five. These wishes may be generalized to include many forms of touching, a point which Freud elaborated at considerable detail in *Totem and Taboo*. The infantile masturbatory wishes are repressed, but the obsessional act tends to approximate more and more to it.

Obsessional thinking uses a secondary defensive process against the primary obsessional ideas. Freud described many features of this type of thinking. There is a considerable distortion in the use of language, which involves substitutions, abbreviations, distortions, ellipses (omissions and condensations) of all kinds. The obsessional individual tends to be very superstitious, even though he may be of high intelligence. Uncertainty and doubt, which appear together with all-pervading procrastination and indecision, are typical. There is a preoccupation with death and a peculiar attitude toward it.

One explanation of many of these peculiarities of the thinking process in the obsessional neurotic is that there is "an omnipotence of thoughts," a phrase which Freud ascribed to one of his obsessional patients. The patient treats thoughts as if they were real, rather than something in his mind. This leads to many varieties of magical thinking. It was again this omnipotence of thought and the prevalence of magical thinking that led Freud to see many similarities between the obsessional neurotic and the taboo prohibitions of primitive societies.

In obsessional neurotics feelings are frequently displaced; this is related to the process of isolation of the affect from the idea. Regressions of all kinds also occur. Thinking replaces action. An obsessive or compulsive thought is one, the function of which is to represent an act regressively.

Already early in his work, Freud was concerned with the question of the difference between the neurotic and the normal, a problem that has remained in the forefront of psychoanalytic thinking, and is still the subject of a great deal of controversy. It did not take Freud long to observe that the difference between the neurotic and the normal is only one of degree and that very often this degree is slight. In sexual matters he had discovered fairly early that the majority of modern men and women suffer from some kind of sexual disturbance. Unconscious factors, of course, play a role in everybody's personality. Transferences and resistances are virtually universal. Accordingly, as time went on, Freud came to see that he had, as he put it, all the world as his patient.

Psychoanalytic psychology provides a basis for a broader understanding of personality. For, since there is a normal course of development, any deviation from this normal development can in a certain sense be described as a neurotic problem, even though it does not lead to any symptom that is technically "neurotic." Here for the first time psychiatry had an opportunity to describe the underlying illness, rather than merely the external symptoms.

CHARACTER NEUROSIS

In terms of the developmental process it eventually became apparent to Freud and to his followers that the classical neuroses are only a small part of the total symptom picture. Thus sexual difficulties form no part of the classical neuroses, although they are virtually universal. Disturbances in the dream life are found in everyone, as are slips and parapraxes of all kinds. Fixations and regressions of varying degrees of severity are also everyday occurrences.

When all these and similar phenomena are included, the concept of neurosis is considerably broadened. In modern parlance, there has been a shift from the symptom neurosis to the character neurosis. If today psychiatrists deal primarily with character neuroses, it is not because men have changed, but because advances in psychoanalytic theory and technique have led to the recognition of the existence of character neuroses, and to a consistent therapy which can handle them.

In one sense it can be said that Freud resolved the problem of classical neurosis. He classified the clinical material, correlated the symptom picture with infantile sexuality, and created the therapeutic technique of psychoanalysis which has in the main been quite successful with this type of patient.

In character neurosis, however, the situation is much less clear. Freud did not explore this field to any appreciable degree, although he provided the conceptual tools which allowed others to do so.

In Freud's writings, as in much other psychoanalytic literature, the word "neurosis" is often used ambiguously. Most often Freud in using it referred to the classical neuroses to which he had devoted so much of his life. At times, however, he uses it to refer to what would now be called psychoses or character neuroses. To attain precision in thinking it is necessary to specify in Freud, as in others, exactly what kind of neurosis is being referred to.

Available English Translations of Freud's Works Cited in Chapter VII.

Hysterical Phantasies and Their Relation to Bisexuality. 1908.
    Standard Edition, Vol. IX, pp. 159-166.
    Collected Papers, Vol. II, pp. 51-58.

Some General Remarks on Hysterical Attacks. 1909.
    Standard Edition, Vol. IX, pp. 229-234.
    Under title: "General Remarks on Hysterical Attacks." Collected Papers, Vol. II, pp. 100-104.

Types of Onset of Neurosis. 1912.
   Standard Edition, Vol. XII, pp. 231-238.
   Under title: "Types of Neurotic Nosogenesis." Collected Papers, Vol. II, pp. 113-121.
   In *A General Selection from the Works of Sigmund Freud.* Edited by J. Rickman. New York: Doubleday Anchor Books, paperback, pp. 62-69.

The Disposition to Obsessional Neurosis. 1913.
   See bibliographic note at end of Chapter V.

Notes upon a Case of Obsessional Neurosis (The Rat Man). 1909.
   See bibliographic note at end of Chapter VIII.

NOTES ON CHAPTER VII

The clinical descriptions of *hysteria* and *obsessional neurosis* are still largely unchanged from where Freud left them. For more recent discussions of these entities, see J. Marmor: "Orality in the Hysterical Personality," *Journal of the American Psychoanalytic Association,* I, 1953, pp. 656-71. G. Gero and D. Rubinfine: "On Obsessive Thoughts," *Ibid.,* III, 1955, pp. 222-43. For a Sullivanian view see Chapters XI, XII in H. S. Sullivan: *Clinical Studies in Psychiatry* (Washington: William Alanson White Psychiatric Foundation, 1956.)

For a stimulating discussion of the whole problem of *diagnosis,* see T. S. Szasz: "The Myth of Mental Illness," *The American Psychologist,* XV, 1960, pp. 113-18.

The psychoanalytic view of *normality* is well presented in a number of sources. See especially E. Jones: "The Concept of a Normal Mind," in *Papers on Psychoanalysis,* 5th edition (London: Bailliere, Tindall and Cox, 1948), L. S. Kubie: "The Concept of Normality and the Neurotic Process," in *Practical and Theoretical Aspects of Psychoanalysis,* Chapter III (New York: International Universities Press, 1950). E. Fromm: *The Sane Society* (New York: Rinehart, 1955).

Chapter VIII.   CASE HISTORIES

The case histories which Freud published were in themselves a unique achievement in psychiatric history. Never before had the neurotic individual been described in such intimate and human terms. It was not his fault, Freud urged rather apologetically, if the histories read like novels; it was the heart of his doctrine that the human and social circumstances of the patient were in the forefront of the causes of his neurosis, and accordingly they had to be described in the greatest of detail.

It is not easy to write up a psychoanalytic case history. In his entire life Freud published only five of major consequence. These cases all date from the period, 1905–14, although the last, written in 1914, was not published until 1918. They are so interesting in their own right, and have become such an integral part of the analytic literature that they will be reviewed here in some detail.

THE CASE OF DORA

This, the first case Freud published after the *Studies on Hysteria* in 1895, had as its full title "Fragment of an Analysis of a Case of Hysteria." Originally, it was to be entitled Dreams and Hysteria, and its purpose was to show the role which dreams play in the analysis of hysteria. As Freud presents this case history, it centers around two dreams produced by the patient and their detailed analysis.

Freud displayed considerable ambivalence about the publication of this particular case history. In 1901 he offered the paper to the *Monatsschrift fuer Psychiatrie und Neurologie*, in which it was ultimately published. It had been immediately accepted, but Freud asked to have the manuscript returned and kept it for another four years before he could bring himself to allow it to see the light of day. Furthermore, although the analysis itself came to an end actually at the end of 1900, Freud several times erroneously gave the date as 1899.

Dora was the younger of two children; her brother was a year and a half older. Their father was in his late forties, and had suffered from a number of illnesses throughout his life. He had been a patient of Freud's, who had treated him for the consequences of a syphilitic infection; his symptoms had cleared up entirely. Four years later he brought his daughter to Freud, and psychotherapy had been recommended. At that time, it was rejected by the girl. Two years later, however, she returned and stayed in treatment with Freud for three months.

When treatment began, Dora was eighteen years old. She had been suffering from a variety of hysterical symptoms since the age of eight. Freud says that she suffered from the commonest of all somatic and mental symptoms—breathing difficulties, nervous cough, loss of voice (sometimes for five weeks at a time), possible migraine, depression, hysterical unsociability, suicidal ideas, and a general dissatisfaction with life.

Dora's mother was described by Freud as a woman suffering from what he called "housewife psychosis"—that is, a woman who was so wrapped up in the details of housekeeping chores that she was unable to relate to any of her family.

Dora's parents had become friendly with another family, the K's. As compensation for the coldness of his wife, Dora's father had begun an affair with Mrs. K, as soon appeared in the course of Dora's analysis. Mr. K had made sexual advances to Dora and had wanted to marry her. Dora's illness was connected with her love for her father, the proposals of Mr. K, and her homosexual love for Mrs. K, as well. All this, in turn, was tied up with her own family situation, that is, her Oedipal conflict. It is to be noted, however, that at this time (1901) Freud did not trace the conflict back to the childhood Oedipal period, between three and five, but contented himself with working out the difficulties that had arisen in the period of Dora's adolescence.

As already noted, Dora remained in treatment for three months.

at the end of which time she abruptly broke off without explanation. Fifteen months later, however, she returned for a consultation. It appeared that she had made some symptomatic improvement, although hysterical symptoms of one kind or another continued to crop up.

Many years later, in 1922, Dora was referred for treatment to Dr. Felix Deutsch, a Viennese practicing psychoanalyst. After Dora's death some years ago, Dr. Deutsch wrote up his experiences.[107] Deutsch's paper is of particular interest because he had an opportunity to compare what actually happened to the patient with what Freud had predicted would happen. A number of Freud's interpretations could be confirmed in the patient's later life. For example, her attitude toward marital life, her frigidity, and her disgust with heterosexuality, bore out Freud's concept of displacement. The improvement which Freud had noted in Dora did not last very long. The same kind of rapid improvement occurred when she was under treatment by Dr. Deutsch, and again failed to last. Freud, in the latter part of his paper on Dora, had discussed his omission of an analysis of various important transference phenomena. Dora, like so many hysterical women, was obviously capable of transference improvement, but had not been completely analyzed.

THE CASE OF LITTLE HANS

Little Hans was a five-year-old boy who developed such a fear that a horse would bite him that he refused to go out of doors. The child's father was an adherent of Freud's and came to him with the problem. Freud treated the child through the father, and saw the boy only once. The case was written up in 1909 in a paper entitled "Analysis of a Phobia in a Five-Year-old Boy."

The dynamics of the phobia were traced by Freud and tied up with the Oedipal situation. The father brought the various productions of the child to Freud, who interpreted them, and these interpretations were then given back to the child by the father. It turned out that the phobia had started after the birth of a sister when Little Hans was three and one-half years old. This started the child on a train of thought about where babies come from, the difference between the sexes, and related questions. Hans was much pre-occupied with his penis, which he called his "widdler," and with castration fears. These eventually led to the horse phobia. The phobia was directly derived from the Oedipus complex: the horse was equated with the father who, Hans thought, would castrate him for wanting mother. For protection Hans stayed home with mother.

The therapeutic result was excellent. The child got over the phobia completely. His interest turned to music, which was his father's profession, and he later pursued a musical career. According to all reports, he has led a comparatively normal life since.

Fourteen years after the therapy, little Hans, then nineteen years old, appeared in Freud's office and announced himself: "I am little Hans." He had forgotten the whole incident completely and no longer recalled anything, either of his phobia or of his treatments.[108]

The case is important because it is the first time that infantile sexuality was demonstrated to exist in a child. As Freud says, strictly speaking, the case taught him nothing new, but he was able to show directly in a child the suppositions which he had derived from the analyses of adults. It is surprising that Freud saw it only as an exception, and did not utilize the opportunity to make this the beginning of child analysis. Evidently here Freud still retained traces of hesitation about getting too far into the sex life of the child. Since then, of course, especially since the 1920's, child analysis has become a full-fledged specialty, and cases such as those of little Hans are now everyday occurrences.

THE CASE OF THE RAT MAN

This is the only complete successful analysis which Freud ever published. The case of Dora cannot be considered a complete analysis, since she broke off treatment prematurely; furthermore it was not really successful. Other cases which Freud published were only fragmentary.

The official title of the paper is "Notes upon a Case of Obsessional Neurosis." Freud's main purpose in publishing the case was to how the structure of an obsessional neurosis. This he did admirably in the theoretical portion.

The analysis began on October 1, 1907, and lasted eleven months. The treatment ended very successfully. The symptoms cleared up, he man re-established himself in his vocation and in his love life. Unfortunately, he died in World War I.

The nickname "The Rat Man" derives from the great obsessive fear which brought the patient into analysis. The patient was a lawyer of almost thirty, who had been drafted into the army. During maneuvers, he had had various obsessional ideas, all of which, however, had passed off rather quickly. On one occasion, however, during a march, he lost his pince-nez and wired to his optician in Vienna to send him another pair by the next mail. During the same stop, he sat between two officers, one of whom, a captain with a Czech name, was obviously fond of cruelty. This captain defended the introduction of corporal punishment and in this connection told of an especially horrible punishment used in the East. This punishment consisted of tying the criminal up, turning a pot full of rats upside down on his buttocks, and allowing the rats to bore their way into his anus.

As soon as the patient heard the captain tell of this punishment, the idea flashed through his mind that this was happening to a person who was very dear to him. This person was the woman he loved. At the same time, he was afraid that the punishment would be visited upon his father, despite the fact that his father had died many years previously. Whenever he thought that a punishment would be carried out, there always appeared a "sanction," that is, a defensive measure which he was obliged to adopt in order to prevent the fantasy from being fulfilled. In this way, many obsessional maneuvers had been built up.

The case history reveals many features which are seen over and over again in similar patients today. For example, in the earliest sessions the patient began to relate details of his sex life. He remembered, from his fourth or fifth year, a scene where he had some sex play with a pretty young governess, which left him with burning and tormenting curiosity to see the female body. At six he had erections and once went to his mother to complain about them. He used to have a morbid idea that his parents knew his thoughts; he explained this to himself by supposing that he had spoken them out loud without having heard himself do it.

The theoretical explanation which Freud gives of the obsessional neurosis on the basis of this case, is still essentially true today, although it would be expanded in a number of directions in terms of present-day concepts. Although at that time ego psychology had not yet been explicitly formulated, Freud's description of the illness is really much more in terms of the ego structure of the patient than in terms of the id (see pp. 112-115).

By chance, Freud's daily notes of the first four months of treatment have been found posthumously among his papers. The first third, roughly, of these notes was published by Freud in the case history. The remainder appeared for the first time in the Standard Edition. They give a vivid picture of how Freud worked.

The notes on a few of the sessions are reproduced here.

Nov. 8.—When he was a child he suffered much from worms. He probably used to put his fingers up his behind and was an awful pig, he said, like his brother. Now carries cleanliness to excess.

Phantasy before sleep:—He was married to his cousin (the lady). He kissed her feet; but they weren't clean. They had black marks on them, which horrified him. During the day he had not been able to wash very carefully and had noticed the same thing on his own feet. He was displacing this on to his lady. During the night he dreamt that he was licking her feet, which were clean, however. This last element is a dream-wish. The perversion here is exactly the same as the one we are familiar with in its undistorted form.

That the behind was particularly exciting to him is shown by the fact that when his sister asked him what it was that he liked about his cousin he replied jokingly "her behind." The dressmaker whom he kissed today first excited his libido when she bent down and showed the curves of her buttocks especially clearly.

Postscript to the rat-adventure. Captain Novak said that this torture ought to be applied to some members of Parliament. The idea then came to him, that he must not mention Gisa, and to his horror immediately afterwards he did mention Dr. Hertz, which once more seemed to him a fateful occurrence. His cousin is actually called Hertz and he at once thought that the name Hertz would make him think of his cousin, and he sees the point of this. He tries to isolate his cousin from everything dirty.

He suffers from sacrilegious compulsions, like nuns. A dream had to do with joking terms of abuse used by his friend V.—"son of a whore," "son of a one-eyed monkey" (*Arabian Nights*).

When he was eleven he was initiated into the secrets of sexual life by his [*male*] cousin, whom he now detests, and who made out to him that all women were whores, including his mother and sisters. He countered this with the question, "Do you think the same of *your* mother?"

Nov. 11.—During an illness of his [female] cousin's (throat trouble and disturbances of sleep), at the time when his affection and sympathy were at their greatest, she was lying on a sofa and he suddenly thought "may she lie like this for ever." He interpreted this as a wish that she should be permanently ill, for his own relief, so that he could be freed from his dread of her being ill. An over-clever misunderstanding! What he has already told me shows that this was connected with a wish to see her defenseless, because of her having resisted him by rejecting his love; and it corresponds crudely to a necrophilic phantasy which he once had consciously but which did not venture beyond the point of looking at the whole body.

He is made up of three personalities—one humorous and normal, another ascetic and religious, and a third immoral and perverse.

Inevitable misunderstanding of the Ucs by the Cs, or rather, distortion of the shape of the Ucs wish.

The hybrid thoughts resulting from these.[109]

THE SCHREBER CASE

The fourth of Freud's case histories was actually not a case of his at all; it was based on the published account of a paranoid illness by Dr. Daniel Paul Schreber, who in 1903 had written a book, *Memoirs of My Nervous Illness*. As justification for the choice of the publication of a case from the literature rather than one from his own practice, Freud cited the fact that the practicing analyst who is not attached to institutions rarely has the opportunity to see a case of paranoia at first hand. As a result of Freud's pioneering efforts, the situation today is of course quite different, and there are many analytically oriented psychiatrists who have done detailed studies of paranoid and other psychotic illnesses.

The full title of the paper is "Psycho-Analytic Notes on an Autobiographical Account of a Case of Paranoia (Dementia Paranoides)."

It is one of the anomalies of history that Freud, who in many respects is the founder of modern psychiatry, was not a practicing psychiatrist at all in our present-day sense. As has been noted he did not treat psychosis, and his only concern with it, apart from the theoretical one, was to make sure in the beginning of analysis that he was not dealing with an underlying or incipient psychotic. The conflict between the organic and the psychological points of view in psychiatry is still being waged in some respects, although it is by now generally agreed, at least among American psychiatrists that psychoanalysis furnishes the basis for all dynamic understanding in psychiatry, even though in many cases its therapeutic effort may have to be modified in many important ways before the technique can be adapted to the psychotic.

Freud himself spoke of the Schreber case as the boldest adventure into psychiatry that he had yet undertaken. He wrote that he expected either scornful laughter or immortality, or both.[110]

Daniel Paul Schreber was a judge presiding over a division of an appeals court in Saxony. He was by profession a lawyer; the title of doctor is customarily used by European lawyers. His first attack of nervous illness was recorded in 1885, and at that time was called "hypochondria." He spent six months in Flechsig's clinic in Leipzig the attack lasted in all about fifteen months and he recovered from it.

He was apparently well until the summer of 1893 when he was notified of his prospective appointment as a judge, an appointment that was to start in October, 1893. Between these dates he had a number of bad dreams. One morning he woke up with the thought that, after all, it really must be very nice to be a woman submitting to the act of copulation.

The second illness set in at the end of October, 1893, with a torturing bout of sleeplessness. He went back to Flechsig's clinic where he got worse. He had hypochondriacal ideas (apparently what today would be called somatic delusions), ideas of persecution and suicidal ideas. He gradually developed a complete delusional system, although in other respects he was quite rational. The worst of the illness disappeared, but he never got over his belief in much of his delusional system. His civil rights were restored in July, 1902 and his book, *Memoirs of My Nervous Illness,* on which Freud based his analysis, was published in 1903.

The two principal elements in Schreber's delusional system were his transformation into a woman and his favored relationship to God. One of his delusions was:

He believed that he had a mission to redeem the world and to restore it to its lost state of bliss. This, however, he could only bring about if he were first transformed from a man into a woman.[111]

Schreber had a variety of other delusions which fitted in with the two main ones. Thus he believed that his nerves were in a condition of great excitement, and nerves such as this had precisely the property of exerting an attraction upon God. Further, inasmuch as he is the only object upon which divine miracles are worked, he believed himself the most remarkable man who ever lived on earth. During the first years of his illness certain of his bodily organs suffered such destructive injuries as would inevitably have led to the death of any other man: he lived for a long time without a stomach, without intestines, almost without lungs, with a torn esophagus, without a bladder, and with shattered ribs; he used sometimes to swallow part of his own larynx with his food, and so on. But divine miracles ("rays") always restored what had been destroyed and therefore as long as he remains a man he is not in any way mortal. These alarming phenomena stopped a long time ago and instead his "femaleness" became prominent. This involved a process of development which will probably require decades, if not centuries, for its completion, and it is unlikely that anyone now living will survive to see the end of it. He had a feeling that great numbers of "female nerves" have already passed over into his body, and out of them a new race of men will proceed, through a process of direct impregnation by God. He held that God had played a part in a plot in which his soul was to be murdered and his body was to be used like a strumpet's.

The delusion of the transformation into a woman readily lends itself to the interpretation of a homosexual panic, and to the theoretical delineation of a relationship between homosexuality and paranoia.

In fact, the dynamic character of all of Schreber's delusions is so obvious that it is most remarkable that it escaped the attention of previous psychiatrists. Of course we can readily understand this difficulty of Freud's predecessors, in that they were always looking for some kind of organic explanation of the phenomena and totally ignored the psychological material which was so readily at hand.

Freud used the material to elucidate the nature of libidinal development and the relationship between the various neuroses and the psychoses, the distinction between which had at that time not yet been clarified. Freud himself did suggest a diagnostic category, paraphrenia, to take the place of Bleuler's schizophrenia, but the suggestion never caught on.

Freud based his analysis of paranoia on its close connection with homosexuality. The paranoiac begins with the statement, I love a man. He then can deny this statement in one of four different ways, by denying the subject, the predicate, the object, or by denying the sentence altogether, and each of these denials leads to a different clinical picture.

1. *Delusions of persecution,* which say: "I do not *love* him—I *hate* him." Such a delusion then becomes transformed by *projection* into another one: "He hates (persecutes) me, which will justify me in hating him."

2. The predicate is contradicted in *erotomania.* Here the man says first: "I do not love *him*—I love *her.*" By projection, this is transformed into: "I observe that *she* loves *me.*" Then it is enlarged into: "I do not love *him*—I love *her,* because she loves *me.*" (It is in this way that many apparent Don Juans cover up their homosexual desires.)

3. The third way in which the proposition can be contradicted is by contradicting the subject, which leads to *delusions of jealousy.* Here the man says: "It is not *I* who loves the man—*she* loves him." And he suspects the woman in relation to all the men whom he himself is tempted to love. Projection does not play a role here.

4. A fourth kind of contradiction is possible, namely one which rejects the proposition altogether. Here the man says: "I do not love *at all*—I do not love *anyone.*" In this case, something must

be done with the libido, which then turns back upon itself and the man says: "I love only *myself*." This leads to *megalomania*.

A very significant factor in the mechanism of symptom formation in paranoia is the use of *projection*. Projection is the process by virtue of which internal perceptions of feelings which are unacceptable to the individual are projected to an outsider or to some outside force.

The illness in the paranoiac is precipitated by a profound inner change, which Freud sees as a detachment of libido from persons in the paranoiac's environment and from the external world generally. The end of the world, which is so frequently part of paranoid delusion formation, is the projection of this internal catastrophe; the individual's subjective world has come to an end since his withdrawal of his love from it. The delusional formation, which psychiatrists had previously taken to be the pathological product, is now seen to be in reality an attempt at recovery, a process of reconstruction.

Freud's illuminating insights concerning paranoia and psychosis in general have stood the test of time. However, as clinical experience with the psychoses has grown, it has become particularly evident that these disorders are intimately tied up with the oral stage, and the image of the bad mother, a concept which Freud did not have.[112]

The Schreber case in itself has become the hub of a considerable literature, and there have been many subsequent re-evaluations of the material.

THE CASE OF THE WOLF MAN

The last of Freud's great case histories, "The Wolf Man," is in many respects the best. It has the most exhaustive analysis to be found in any of Freud's writings of the development in childhood of a neurosis in an adult. The full title of the work is "From the History of an Infantile Neurosis." It was finished in 1914, several months after the patient terminated treatment, but was not published until 1918 because of conditions created by World War I.

The nickname of the patient derives from his childhood phobia of wolves, which he knew only from stories and picture books.

The patient was a wealthy Russian who was completely incapacitated by his neurotic illness. At the time he came to Freud he was twenty-three years old. For years he had traveled around accompanied by a private doctor and a valet, unable even to dress himself or face any aspect of life.

The bizarre character of his ideation is sufficiently indicated by his offer in the first hour of treatment with Freud to have rectal intercourse with him and then to defecate on his head.

The Wolf Man was in treatment with Freud for five years, from 1909 to 1914, at the end of which time he was fully recovered. The revolution in Russia left him penniless, and in 1919, he escaped from Russia and managed to find his way once again to Vienna. There Freud analyzed him for another four months (November, 1919 to February, 1920) because of a symptom of constipation, which then finally disappeared entirely. In this period Freud not only treated him free of charge, but regularly for the next six years collected money for the patient and his invalid wife.

For twelve years after Freud's first treatment, the patient remained free of any serious neurosis, and then developed an entirely different illness, a paranoiac psychosis. This time Ruth Mack Brunswick treated him for four or five months (October, 1926 to February, 1927) and he once more recovered. Two years later he again came back to her and she treated him at various times for several years. Her last report of him was in 1940 when he was in excellent health; a similar report has been published more recently by Muriel Gardner. At the time that Jones wrote his biography of Freud, he stated that he (Jones) was still in correspondence with the patient.

Because of the unusual interest that attaches to this case, it has been possible to follow it up for a period of almost fifty years. The patient is still (1961) alive, now in his seventies, and apparently in good health. This is one case where there is certainly an adequate and intensive follow-up of Freud's original treatment! The patient is a highly intelligent man and has written a number of papers about his contacts with Freud which have been published in psychoanalytic journals.

One of the Wolf Man's most recent communications, "How I Came into Analysis with Freud," was published in 1958 and gives an unusually perceptive account of the problems facing a psychiatric patient in those early days of psychoanalysis. A portion of this paper is worth quoting here. The Wolf Man says:

I first met Freud in the year 1910. At that time psychoanalysis and the name of its founder were practically unknown beyond the borders of Austria. Before I report on how I came into analysis with Freud, however, I should like to recall to you the desolate situation in which a neurotic found himself at that period before psychoanalysis. A sufferer from neurosis is trying to find his way back into normal life, as he has come into conflict with his environment and then lost contact with it. His emotional life has become "inadequate," inappropriate to outer reality. His goal is not a real, known object, but rather some other object, hidden in his unconscious, unknown to himself. His affect by-passes the real object, accessible to his consciousness. As long as nothing is known of this state of affairs, only two explanations were possible: one, that of the layman, concerned itself with the increase in intensity of affect, which was out of proportion to the real situation; it was said that the neurotic exaggerated everything. The other explanation, that of the neurologist or psychiatrist, derived the mental and emotional from the physical, and sought to persuade the patient that his trouble was due to a disease of the nervous system. The neurotic went to a physician with the wish to pour out his heart to him, and was bitterly disappointed when the physician would scarcely listen to his problems, much less try to understand them. But that which to the doctor was only a superficial manifestation of the illness was for the neurotic himself a profound inner experience. So there could be no real contact between patient and physician. The treatment of emotional illness seemed to have got into a dead-end street. . . .

It was a revelation to me to hear the fundamental concepts of a completely new science of the human psyche from the mouth of its founder. I perceived at once that Freud had succeeded in discovering an unexplored region of the human soul, and that if I could follow him along this path, a new world would open for me. The error of "classical" psychiatry had been that, ignorant of the existence and laws of the unconscious, it derived everything from the physical. A further consequence of this error was a too sharp distinction between healthy and sick. Everything the neurotic undertook was considered sick. If, for example, he fell in love with a woman, this was described as "manic," or as a "compulsion." But for Freud the "break-through to the woman" would under certain circumstances be considered a healthy achievement, a sign of the neurotic's will to live, an attempt at restitution. This followed from the psychoanalytic point of view that there was no sharp division between sick and healthy, that in the healthy person also the unconscious may dominate. Although Freud certainly did not underestimate the neurotic in his patients, he attempted always to support and strengthen the kernel of health, separated from the chaff of neurosis.

It will be easy to imagine the sense of relief I now felt, when Freud asked me various questions about my childhood and about the relationships in my family, and listened with the greatest attention to all I had to say. Occasionally he let fall some remark which was witness to his complete understanding of everything I had experienced. My new knowledge, the feeling that I had, so to speak, "discovered" Freud, and the hope of regaining my health, made my condition rapidly improve. But now Freud warned me against overoptimism, foreseeing quite rightly that resistance and its attendant difficulties were still to come.[113]

Freud did not publish the entire history of the case, as he had done with the Rat Man, just the reconstruction of the patient's infantile neurosis, as the title of the paper indicates. His main theoretical interest in publishing the case was to show how it is possible from an exhaustive analysis to reconstruct the infantile history of a patient. It is this reconstruction which particularly captured the imagination of the psychoanalytic world and became the model which many analysts aimed to imitate for a long time to come.

Freud maintained that the adult neurosis was understandable only in the light of the infantile material, which in such a person would necessarily have to be regarded as neurotic. He declared:

I am ready to assert that every neurosis in an adult is built upon a neurosis which has occurred in his childhood but has not invariably been severe enough to strike the eye and be recognized as such.[114]

In 1923 Freud added a footnote to the case in which he set out the chronology of the main events listed in the case history. This chronology gives those events which Freud considered of particular significance in the formation of the patient's personality. It is reproduced here with some explanation of the events to which Freud makes reference.

Born on Christmas Day. The fact that the patient was born on Christmas Day was significant because it helped to date some of the other events in his life.

1-½ years old: Malaria. Observation of his parents copulating; or observation of them when they were together, into which he later introduced a phantasy of them copulating.

The question of whether an infant a year and a half old can recognize that his parents are having sexual intercourse has been much discussed among psychoanalysts since this publication of Freud's. It is to be noted that Freud himself specifically maintains that he is not sure whether the recollection is a phantasy or an actual event, and in any case, does not feel that it really makes any difference so far as the formation of the personality is concerned. Since Freud, there has been much more direct observation of children. While it is clear enough that infants often do see their parents having sexual intercourse, the precise meaning of this to them is still not at all clear.

Just before 2-½: scene with Grusha, a maid in his parents' household.

This scene with the maid Grusha was finally worked out as follows: Grusha was kneeling on the floor, and beside her were a pail and a short broom made of a bundle of twigs; he was also there and she was teasing him or scolding him. When he had seen the girl scrubbing the floor, he had urinated in the room, and she had rejoined, no doubt jokingly, with a threat of castration.

When he saw the girl upon the floor engaged in scrubbing it, and kneeling down, with her buttocks projecting and her back horizontal, he was faced once again with the attitude which his mother had assumed in the coitus scene. She became his mother to him; he was seized with sexual excitement owing to the activation of this picture; and like his father (whose action he can only have regarded at the time as urination) he behaved in a masculine way towards her. His urinating on the floor was in reality an attempt at a seduction and the girl replied to it with a threat of castration, just as though she had understood what he meant.

It was to this scene that Freud traced a peculiar love-compulsion which the patient showed later on in life. Whenever he saw a girl leaning over washing clothes he was seized by an irresistible sexual desire or an irresistible love feeling toward her. From one such girl whom he met in his eighteenth year he had contracted gonorrhea which incapacitated him for some time.

2-½: Screen memory of his parents' departure with his sister. This showed him along with his Nanya (nurse) and so disowned Grusha and his sister. His sister was two years older.

Before 3-¼: His mother's laments to the doctor. This refers to the following: His mother had once taken him with her when she was walking down to the station with a doctor who had come to visit her. During this walk she had lamented over her pains and hemorrhages and had broken out into the words, "I cannot go on living like this," without imagining that the child whose hand she was holding would keep these words in his memory. The patient repeated this lament on innumerable occasions during his later illness; this lament thus has the significance of an identification with his mother.

3-¼: Beginning of his seduction by his sister. Soon afterward, the threat of castration from his Nanya.

The patient suddenly called to mind the fact that when he was still very small his sister had seduced him into sexual practices. First came a recollection that in the lavatory which the children frequently used to visit together she had made this proposal: "Let's show our bottoms," and had proceeded from words to deeds. Subsequently the more essential part of this seduction came to light and there were full particulars as to time and place. It was in spring, at a time when his father was away; the children were in one room playing on the floor while the mother was working in the next room. His sister had taken hold of his penis and played with it, at the same time telling him incomprehensible stories about his Nanya, as though by way of explanation. His Nanya, she said, used to do the same thing with all kinds of people—for instance, with the gardener. She used to stand him on his head and then take hold of his genitals.

In reaction to the seduction by his sister, the boy refused her, and her solicitations soon ceased, but he tried to win instead of her another person whom he was fond of; the information which his sister herself had given him—and in which his Nanya was a model—turned his choice in that direction. He therefore began to play with his penis in his Nanya's presence, and this must be regarded as an attempt at seduction. His Nanya disillusioned him; she made a serious face and explained that that wasn't good. Children who did that, she said, got a wound in that place.

With this new frustration he secretly began to look about for another sexual object. His sexual researches began, and he soon came upon the problem of castration. He succeeded in observing two girls, his sister and a friend of hers, while they were urinating. This gave rise to all kinds of thoughts about the body.

Soon after the refusal of his Nanya and the threat of castration he gave up masturbation. His sexual life, therefore, which was beginning to come under the sway of the genital zone * gave way before an external obstacle, and was thrown back by its influence into an earlier phase of pregenital organization. The boy regressed to the sadistic anal stage.

Eventually, he again became attached to his father in a passive way.

3-½: The English governess. Beginning of the change in his character. When the child was 3½ the family engaged an English governess for him. At roughly the same time a decided change in his character took place. Where before he was sweet and gentle, now he entered a phase of naughtiness and perversity. Freud traced this to the regression to the sadistic anal stage. The boy became irritable and a tormenter, and gratified himself in this way at the expense of animals and humans. His principal object was his beloved Nanya and he knew how to torment her so she would burst into tears. He began to be cruel to small animals, to catch flies and pull off their wings, and to crush beetles underfoot. In his imagination he liked beating large animals (horses) as well. There were also masochistic phantasies which came to light. The content of these was of boys being chastised and beaten, and especially being beaten on the penis. This kind of constant ambivalence was peculiarly characteristic of the patient and is, as is well known, quite characteristic of the obsessional individual. Freud generalized from here to say that a child who behaves in such an

* (Today it would be called the phallic phase, but at this time (1914) Freud had not yet postulated this phase of development; that came only in 1923.)

unmanageable way is making a concession and trying to provoke punishment. He hopes for a beating as a simultaneous means of setting at rest his sense of guilt and of satisfying his masochistic sexual urge.

4: The wolf dream. Origin of the phobia.

Freud traced this dream to a precise age in the patient's childhood because of the accidental fact that he was born on Christmas Day. The dream, which came when the child was four, was:

I dreamt that it was night and that I was lying in my bed. (My bed stood with its foot toward the window; in front of the window there was a row of old walnut trees. I know it was winter when I had the dream, and night-time.) Suddenly the window opened of its own accord and I was terrified to see that some white wolves were sitting on a big walnut tree in front of the window. There were six or seven of them. The wolves were quite white, and more like foxes or sheep dogs, for they had big tails like foxes and they had their ears pricked like dogs when they pay attention to something. In great terror, evidently of being eaten up by the wolves, I screamed and woke up.

Freud, through the analysis, traced this as the first anxiety dream which the boy had in the course of his life, stemming from the fear of his father which from that time forward was to dominate his life.

The form taken by the fear of his father, the fear of being eaten by the wolf, was only the regressive transposition of the wish to be copulated with by his father, that is, to be given sexual satisfaction in the same way as his mother. This explained why the dream ended in a state of anxiety from which he did not recover until he had his nurse with him. He therefore fled from his father to her.

To understand this anxiety, Freud hypothesized that what sprang into activity the night of the dream out of the chaos of the dream as unconscious memory traces, was the picture of copulation between his parents, copulation in circumstances which were not entirely usual and were especially favorable for observation. This *primal scene* (the term is here used for the first time in this paper, although it had been mentioned earlier by Freud in one of his letters to Fliess) occurred when the infant was a year and a half old.

Freud himself considered the tracing of the infantile neurosis back to a primal scene at the age of one and a half years to be a reconstruction which required extraordinary documentation. He expressed the fear that at that point the reader's belief would abandon him. He said:

I have now reached the point at which I must abandon the support which I have hitherto had from the course of analysis. I am afraid it will also be the point at which the reader's belief will abandon me.[115]

He considered the doubts as to the probability of such an occurrence in considerable detail. He fell back upon his theory of deferred action, which he had already put forward in the *Studies on Hysteria*. This was the idea that a sexual scene in childhood in itself has no pathogenic effect, but at some later date when the child becomes more mature sexually he suddenly remembers the earlier sexual experience and it then has a traumatic effect on him. In the *Studies on Hysteria*, however, the primal scenes were considered to be of a much later date, and the effects of them were deferred at least until the age of puberty. Here Freud proposed that the primal scene trauma occurred at the age of one and a half and that its activation which led to the neurotic transformation occurred at the age of four.

4-½: Influence of the Bible story. Appearance of the obsessional symptoms.

At the age of about four and a half occurred his initiation into religion and from then onward the period of the obsessional neurosis up to a time later than his tenth year. His mother told him the sacred story herself and also made his nurse read aloud to him about it from a book adorned with illustrations. The chief stress in the story was laid upon the story of the Passion. His Nanya, who was very pious and superstitious, added her own comments on it, but was obliged to listen to all the little critic's objections and doubts.

Freud had already, in a paper published in 1907 (see below, p. 145), called attention to the close connection between obsessional actions and religious practices. Here he produced more evidence along the same lines. For example, the little boy had no sooner heard the Bible story than he began to add illuminations and doubts of all kinds. One of the first questions which he addressed to his nurse was whether Christ had a behind too. Nanya informed him that He had been a God and also a man, and as a man had had all the same things as other men. This did not satisfy him, but he succeeded in reconciling himself to the situation by telling himself that the behind is really only a continuation of the legs. But then came another question, whether Christ used to shit. He did not venture to put this question to his pious nurse, but he himself found a way out. Since Christ had made wine out of nothing, he could also make food out of nothing and in this way have avoided defecating. (It is to be noted that serious difficulties connected with defecation were part of the patient's neurotic symptomatology when he came to Freud and that severe constipation was the reason for the re-analysis by Freud from 1919 to 1920.)

Marked ambivalence toward God took the place of the marked ambivalence toward his father, and was part of the obsessional neurosis. One of the last flickerings of his neurosis was the obsession of having to think of The Holy Trinity whenever he saw three heaps of dung lying together on the road.

Just before 5: hallucination of the loss of his finger.

The patient described the following experience at the age of five:

When I was five years old, I was playing in the garden near my nurse, and was carving with my pocket-knife in the bark of one of the walnut trees that had come into my dream as well. Suddenly, to my unspeakable terror, I noticed that I had cut through the little finger of my (right or left?) hand, so that it was only hanging on by its skin. I felt no pain, but great fear. I did not venture to say anything to my nurse, who was only a few paces distant, but I sank down on a near seat and sat there, incapable of casting another glance at my finger. At last I calmed down, took a look at the finger, and saw that it was entirely uninjured.[116]

It turned out that this hallucination was instigated by a story that a female relative of his had been born with six toes, and that the extra toe had immediately afterwards been chopped off with an axe. Women, then, had no penis because it was taken away from them at birth. The hallucination of the severed finger was an obvious substitute for a castration fear.

5: *Departure from the first estate.*

The family's move from one estate to another helped to date a number of events in the patient's life. It was shortly after this move that the father became mentally ill and had to be confined to a sanitarium.

After 6: Visits to his sick father.

The patient had developed a pious ritual by means of which he eventually atoned for his blasphemies. Part of this was to breathe in a ceremonious manner under certain conditions. Each time he made the sign of the Cross he was obliged to breathe in deeply or to exhale forcibly. In his native tongue "breath" is the same as "spirit" so that here the Holy Ghost came in. He was obliged to breathe in the Holy Spirit, to breathe out the evil spirits which he had heard and read about. He ascribed to these evil spirits the blasphemous thoughts for which he had to inflict such heavy penance upon himself. He was also obliged to exhale when he saw beggars or cripples; ugly, old, or wretched-looking people, but he could think of no way of connecting this obsession with the spirits. The only account he could give to himself was that he did it so as not to become like such people.

Eventually, the analysis showed that this breathing out at the sight of pitiable-looking people had begun only after his sixth year and was related to his father. Shortly after he was six, when he had not seen his father for some time, his mother took the children to a sanitarium where they saw their father again; he looked sick and the boy felt very sorry for him. His father was thus the prototype of all the cripples, beggars, and poor people in whose presence he was obliged to breathe out. And thus his determination not to become like cripples (which was the motive of his breathing out in their presence) was his old identification with his father, transformed into the negative. But in this he was also imitating his father in the positive sense, for the heavy breathing was an imitation of the noise which he had heard coming from his father during the intercourse.

8-10: *Final outbreaks of the obsessional neurosis.*

The obsessional neurosis came to an end when he was given a German tutor when he was ten years old. This German tutor very soon exerted a great influence over him. The whole of his strict piety faded away, never to be revived, after he had noticed and learned from enlightening conversations with his tutor that this father substitute attached no importance to piety and set no store by the truth of religion. His religion sank away along with his dependence upon his father who was now replaced by a new and more sociable father.

Under the influence of the German tutor there arose a new and better sublimation of the patient's sadism, which then gained the upper hand over his masochism. He developed an enthusiasm for military affairs, for uniforms, weapons and horses, and used them as food for continual daydreams. Thus, for the first time, he found himself, for the time being at any rate, on fairly normal lines.

17: Breakdown, precipitated by gonorrhea.

23: Beginning of treatment.

SUMMARY

In reviewing these case histories, one is struck above all by Freud's incredible capacity to master an enormous number of details and to organize them in a coherent fashion. It is this very difficulty in handling the tremendous complexity of a case history that has stopped others from writing up their cases. None of Freud's contemporaries or successors has ever provided anything remotely comparable. One result is that while one has a reasonably good idea of how Freud analyzed, the same cannot be said for other analysts.

Freud's emphasis was on tracing the precise connections between the symptoms and the infantile sexuality, as reconstructed in the course of the analysis. By this meticulous attention to the actual events of the patient's life Freud was able to draw the necessary connections and effect the disappearance of symptoms. When others began to philosophize or introduce social or moral questions he objected on the grounds that this did not help the patient. This was one of his objections to both Adler and Jung—they did not explain the specific neurotic conflict with which they were dealing, but resorted rather to broad generalities.[117]

Once Freud described his manner of work as follows:

> When I recollect isolated cases from the history of my work, I find that my working hypothesis invariably came about as a direct result of a great number of impressions based on experience. Later on, whenever I had the ~pportunity of recognizing an hypothesis of this kind to be erroneous, it was always replaced—and I hope improved—by another idea which occurred to me (based on the former as well as new experiences) and to which I then submitted the material.[118]

It is this painstaking attention to the specific genetic development of any symptom or character pattern that makes Freud's case histories so unique in the analytic literature.

Each case history that he wrote had a specific purpose, and is to be evaluated with that in mind. The case of Dora was written to show how dreams can be used in therapy. Little Hans was analyzed to show that the Oedipal conflict inferred from the analyses of adults could be directly observed in children. The Rat Man demonstrates the intricate structure of an obsessional neurosis. The Schreber case casts light on paranoid mechanisms which are so severe that they require hospitalization; in his office practise Freud did not encounter such cases, and few hospital psychiatrists of that day were alive to the teachings of psychoanalysis. The Wolf Man was in part a reply to Jung and his more general theory of the libido; Freud was here trying to show exactly how the reconstruction of the patient's childhood confirmed his hypotheses of psychosexual development.

At the same time careful perusal of the cases discloses some weaknesses in Freud's approach, some of which have since been corrected. Actually, as already noted, Freud published only one really complete history of a psychoanalysis, that of the Rat Man. Dora interrupted treatment prematurely, and later relapsed. It is odd that Freud never described a really successful analysis of a woman. Of the five case histories, that of Dora, the only female, was a partial failure. The other four were all men, including the spontaneous recovery in Schreber.

Perhaps the major lack in these early case histories is the absence of systematic character analysis. It was still mainly the symptom that concerned Freud here; understanding of the total personality came only later, in the 1920's. Even then, however, as the many autobiographical accounts of his students show, Freud frequently did not practice the strict classical technique he himself had devised. He would interrupt, engage in general conversations, at times conduct analysis for only a few months, and so on.

As with his self-analysis, in some ways Freud was too modest about his achievements. The careful unravelling of the patient's childhood, as described particularly in the Wolf Man, was something that Freud could do, but few others. The attempt to imitate this particular achievement of Freud's led in the 1920's to many disappointments and many attempts to revise analytic technique.

Available English Translations of Freud's Works Cited in Chapter VIII.

Fragment of an Analysis of a Case of Hysteria (Dora). 1905.
  Standard Edition, Vol. VII, pp. 7-122.
  Collected Papers, Vol. III, pp. 13-146.
  The Case of Dora and Other Papers. New York: Norton, 1952.

Analysis of a Phobia in a Five-Year Old Boy (Little Hans). 1909.
  Standard Edition, Vol. X, pp. 5-149.
  Collected Papers, Vol. III, pp. 149-287.

Notes upon a Case of Obsessional Neurosis (The Rat Man). 1909.
  Standard Edition, Vol. X, pp. 155-318.
  Collected Papers, Vol. III, pp. 293-383.
  The Standard Edition contains the invaluable daily notes which were discovered posthumously; they are not included in the Collected Papers.

Psycho-Analytic Notes on an Autobiographical Account of a Case of Paranoia (Dementia Paranoides) (The Schreber Case). 1911.
  Standard Edition, Vol. XII, pp. 9-82.
  Collected Papers, Vol. III, pp. 387-470.

From the History of an Infantile Neurosis (The Wolf Man). 1918.
  Standard Edition, Vol. XVII, pp. 7-122.
  Collected Papers, Vol. III, pp. 473-605.

NOTES ON CHAPTER VIII

Some subsequent literature is available on four of the case histories. On *Little Hans,* Freud himself wrote a paper in 1922: "Postscript," *Standard Edition,* X, pp. 148-9.

For *Dora,* see F. Deutsch: "A Footnote to Freud's 'Fragment of an Analysis of a Case of Hysteria,'" *Psychoanalytic Quarterly,* XXVI, 1957, pp. 159-67.

Most extensive attention has been devoted to the *Schreber case.* Dr. William Niederland has uncovered much new material and shed a good deal of light on the history. See W. Niederland: "Schreber's Father," *Journal of the American Psychoanalytic Association,* VIII, 1960, pp. 492-9. W. Niederland, "The 'Miracled-up' World of Schreber's Childhood." *Psychoanalytic Study of the Child,* XIV, 1959, pp. 383-413. W. Niederland: "Three Notes on the Schreber Case," *Psychoanalytic Quarterly,* XX, 1951, pp. 579-91. F. Baumeyer: "The Schreber Case," *International Journal of Psychoanalysis,* XXXVII, 1956, pp. 61-74. I. MacAlpine and R. A. Hunter: *Daniel Paul Schreber: Memoirs of My Nervous Illness* (Cambridge: Robert Bentley, 1955). M. Katan: "Schreber's Hereafter," *Psychoanalytic Study of the Child,* XV, 1959, pp. 314-82.

On the *Wolf Man,* see The Wolf Man: "How I Came Into Analysis with Freud," *Journal of the American Psychoanalytic Association,* VI, 1958, pp. 348-52.

For accounts of *personal analyses with Freud* after World War I, see: C. P. Oberndorf: *A History of Psychoanalysis in America* (New York: Grune and Stratton, 1953), Chapter VIII. H. D.: *Tribute to Freud* (New York: Pantheon, 1956). J. Wortis: *Fragments of an Analysis with Freud* (New York: Simon and Schuster, 1954). A. Kardiner: "Freud—the Man I Knew, the Scientist and His Influence," in B. Nelson (ed.): *Freud and the 20th Century* (New York: Meridian, 1957), paperback, Chapter V. R. R. Grinker: "Reminiscences of a Personal Contact with Freud," *American Journal of Orthopsychiatry,* X, 1940, pp. 850-55.

Chapter IX. THE BROADER SCOPE
OF PSYCHOANALYSIS

Numerous allusions have been made to the fact that from a very early date Freud began to become aware of the broader implications of his discoveries. Psychology is indeed basic, not merely to psychiatry but to all the sciences that deal with man, and so any fundamental contribution to psychology must necessarily have a wide range of applicability. In a paper he wrote in 1913, called "The Claims of Psychoanalysis to Scientific Interest," Freud showed that psychoanalysis had already been applied to a variety of different fields, including psychology, philology, philosophy, biology, child development, the history of civilization, esthetics, sociology, and education.

While Freud never wrote about society in any fully systematic sense, it was soon clear why he belonged to "those who have disturbed men's sleep." In terms of the cornerstones of the first psychoanalytic system, the contrast between the neurotic and the normal seems very limited, and the picture that psychoanalysis presented of the normal individual was so unflattering in many respects that the intense resistance to psychoanalysis was readily understandable. In effect, Freud said, most men are fixated at an Oedipal level.

Much of what goes on in normal life has the same characteristics as what goes on in the neurotic. Dreams are the embodiment of wishes for everyone. Jokes and other forms of humor release tensions which are acutely and widely felt. Religion is very similar to an obsessional neurosis, and the rituals of the religious person are not essentially different from those of the obsessional neurotic. Even in the world of art wish-fulfillment plays a predominant role.

The artist can allow himself to portray forbidden wishes because they come out in disguised form or are permitted in the medium which he is using, while the spectator who enjoys the artistic production also finds in it an outlet for his forbidden wishes.

It has been argued that in the early twentieth century psychoanalysis was too concerned to find the neurotic in everything. In one sense this criticism is justified, since in the days before World War I it was a major concern of Freud and his followers to show that instincts and their derivatives played an overwhelming role in human life. Ego psychology, the next stage in the history of psychoanalysis, tended to correct this one-sided emphasis. On the other hand, psychoanalysis could be said to have destroyed the comforting illusion which men held before Freud that modern civilization was essentially good and that evil was on its way out. Certainly the experiences of two world wars and their aftermath have amply confirmed Freud's thesis that man is driven by irrational, unconscious primitive urges of which he has far less control than he thinks.

From a scientific point of view, Freud's applications of psychoanalysis were especially significant in two fields, namely anthropology and art.

ANTHROPOLOGY

At the outset, an important question arises: In what way is psychoanalysis relevant to anthropology? Essentially in that it provides the basis for a psychological understanding of the individuals in any society. This does not mean that one psychoanalytic factor, such as the Oedipus complex, explains everything. In *Totem and Taboo* Freud twice entered a disclaimer to that effect, insisting that the psychoanalytic aspect is only one of many, all of which must be taken into account in a broader synthesis. Thus at one point he says:

There are no grounds for fearing that psychoanalysis, which first discovered that psychical acts and structures are invariably overdetermined, will be tempted to trace the origin of anything so complicated as religion to a single source. If psychoanalysis is compelled—and is, indeed, in duty bound—to lay all the emphasis upon one particular source, that does not mean it is claiming either that the source is the only one or that it occupies first place among the numerous contributory factors. Only when we can synthesize the findings in the different fields of research will it become possible to arrive at the relative importance of the part played in the genesis of religion by the mechanism discussed in these pages. Such a task lies beyond the means as well as beyond the purposes of a psychoanalyst.[119]

Totem and Taboo. Freud's central thesis, and the one which has in the long run had the deepest impact on anthropological science, is that contained in the original title of *Totem and Taboo*, when it appeared in *Imago:* "Some Points of Agreement between the Mental Lives of Savages and Neurotics." There is a certain essential psychological unity in all men in all societies, and psychoanalysis is best equipped to show us what this unity is.

At the conclusion of his paper on the Schreber case Freud had already mentioned the thesis worked out in detail in *Totem and Taboo* two years later. He wrote:

"In dreams and in neuroses," so our thesis has run, "we come once more upon the *child,* and the peculiarities which characterize his modes of thought and his emotional life." "And we come upon the *savage* too" we may now add, "upon the *primitive* man as he stands revealed to us in the light of the researches of archaeology and ethnology." [120]

Totem and Taboo, published in book form in 1913, is Freud's major contribution to anthropology in this period. In embarking on it, Freud was well aware that he was undertaking a work of the greatest importance. In one of many letters of the period he wrote:

I am now slowly composing the fourth of the *Uebereinstimmungen,* that on totemism, which is to close the series. It is the most daring enterprise I have ever ventured . . .

I am writing TOTEM, at present, with the feeling that it is my greatest, best, perhaps my last good work . . .

I have not written anything with such conviction since *The Interpretation of Dreams,* so I can't predict the fate of the essay.[121]

Totem and Taboo is divided into four parts or essays. The first is entitled "The Horror of Incest." Here Freud reviews the anthropological literature on incest, and shows that, surprisingly, it is a stronger taboo among primitive people than among the more civilized, and that this incest taboo extends much further among primitive men than it does among others. It is a well-known fact that this incest taboo may be so extensive as to lead to a system of exogamy, in which both men and women are compelled to seek their sexual and marital partners from groups far outside their immediate range. Exogamy is closely related to totemism, that is, wherever totems are to be found, there is also to be found a law against persons of the same totem having sexual relations with one another and consequently against their marrying.

Part II is entitled "Taboo and Emotional Ambivalence." In this essay, Freud continues the arguments of his previous paper on obsessive acts and religious practices (1907). There he had confined himself to pointing to similarities and differences between the religions known in Western civilization and obsessional neurosis. Now he ranged much further afield, and tried to understand the more primitive religions which are still found in many parts of the world. He is able to point to far-reaching similarities between taboo and obsessional neurosis; in fact he says if the term "obsessional neurosis" had not been invented, the illness which is seen in the modern neurotic could just as well have been called "taboo sickness." [122]

This thesis is elaborated in considerable detail, and Freud was able to show that many of the practices which had hitherto been unintelligible could be grasped in terms of the psychological principles which had been discovered in the investigation of the neuroses, particularly of the obsessional neurosis. He shows in particular how the psychological characteristics of ambivalence and the defense mechanism which is known as projection are peculiarly significant in the mental lives of primitive peoples. At the same time he recognizes the essential difference between taboo and neurosis, in that the one is socially approved while the other is not, and he tries to explain this difference. The fact that characterizes the neurosis, in his opinion, is the preponderance of the sexual over the social instinctual element; in taboo the reverse is true.

The third essay is entitled "Animism, Magic and the Omnipotence of Thoughts." Here, Freud accepted the account which was the standard one in his day of the evolution of the human views of the universe: first, an animistic phase; second, a religious phase; and finally, a scientific phase. These three phases he could explain in terms of the vicissitudes of the omnipotence of thoughts, a phrase which he had borrowed from a highly intelligent patient (the Rat Man. See pages 120-123 above). In the stage of animism, men consider themselves omnipotent. At the stage of religion, they transfer this omnipotence to the gods, but do not seriously abandon it themselves, since they reserve the power of influencing the gods in a variety of ways, according to their own wishes. Finally, in the scientific stage, there is no longer any room for the omnipotence of thoughts. Men deal with reality, and give up the belief in magic and in the power of their thoughts to influence the real world. Nevertheless, some of this primitive belief in omnipotence and in magic still survives, in childhood, in neurosis, and in dreams.

The fourth essay is entitled: "The Return of Totemism in Childhood." This is the historical section containing the famous primal horde theory, which has usually been the target of anthropological attacks on the whole work, although it is only one small element in the work.

Freud begins with Darwin's hypothesis that primitive man, like the higher apes, lived in hordes, with a father, many wives, and a large number of children. This was known as the primal horde. The theory, which was perfectly consistent with the evolutionary thinking of the latter half of the nineteenth and the early part of the twentieth century, was further developed by Atkinson. To it Freud added a hypothesis of Robertson Smith's that the sacramental killing and communal eating of the totem animal, the consumption of which was forbidden on all other occasions, constituted an important feature of totemic religion.

Freud now hypothesized that in this situation the children would grow up and the boys would eventually become men. For a while the father would be able to chase the sons out of the community, in order to keep the women to himself. Eventually, however, the sons would be able to band together and kill the father. This murder would, however, leave in its wake the absence of the father's authority which had previously prevailed. As a substitute for it the sons would then set up a totem, which would, in all psychological respects, be similar to the father whom they had slain. Furthermore, in order to avoid disastrous competition with one another, they would have to institute a law against incest, by which they all alike renounced the women whom they desired and who had been their chief motive for dispatching their father. In this way the murder of the father of the primal horde led to the two main taboos of totemic religions—totemism and exogamy. A variety of subsidiary features of totemic and historical religions could be deduced from this situation.

In his over-all summing-up Freud says that with regard to the motives that impel men to behave as they do he finds that the Oedipus complex is universal. Everywhere men are enjoined not to have sex with their mothers and not to kill their fathers. He puts it in this way:

At the conclusion, then, of this exceedingly condensed inquiry, I should like to insist that its outcome shows that the beginnings of religion, morals, society, and art converge in the Oedipus complex. This is in complete agreement with the psychoanalytic finding that the same complex constitutes the nucleus of all neuroses, insofar as our present knowledge goes. It seems to me a most surprising discovery that the problems of social psychology, too, should prove soluble on the basis of one single concrete point—man's relation to his father.[123]

The question has often been raised whether Freud really believed that at some point in history the sons actually banded together and slew the father, and that the whole process which he described was one which corresponded to historical reality. The answer to this is "Yes, but." At the conclusion of the fourth essay, on the return of totemism in childhood, Freud takes up the question of whether it is necessary to regard the crime as one which had actually been committed, since the mere existence of a wishful fantasy of killing and devouring the father would have been enough to produce the moral reaction that created totemism and taboo. He then says that it must be confessed that the distinction between the thought and the action, which may seem fundamental to others does not, in his judgment, affect the heart of the matter. At the same time he argues that primitive man is by and large uninhibited, and that with him thought passes directly into action (although earlier he had pointed to the greater inhibitions which exist in primitive men). He concludes that it may safely be assumed that "in the beginning was the deed." Yet earlier in the work he states:

Our assertion that taboo originated in a primeval prohibition imposed at one time or another by some external authority is obviously incapable of demonstration.[124]

Thus Freud is himself quite obviously ambivalent about whether the crime actually occurred. On the one hand, he says that it is a speculation which cannot possibly be confirmed. Then, again, he argues that the distinction between the thought of killing the father and the action of killing the father is an unessential one, and that thought could just as well have led to the whole historical development. Finally, however, he insists that the crime did actually occur. A similar type of ambivalence is to be found with regard to childhood memories. (See pp. 102-103.)

For a long time the reaction of the great majority of anthropologists to *Totem and Taboo* was an extremely negative one. Kroeber in an early review of the book, when it appeared in English translation, probably summed up the views of most of his colleagues when he said that the mere presentation of the Freudian hypothesis on the origin of socio-religious civilization was probably sufficient to prevent its acceptance.[125] Some twenty years later in another review Kroeber reasserted his initial position.

There is no indication that the consensus of anthropologists during these twenty years has moved even an inch nearer acceptance of Freud's central thesis.[126]

Nevertheless, in this second review Kroeber did pay tribute to what he called "one of the great minds of our day."

To a certain extent the reaction of the anthropologists was due to an overemphasis on certain aspects of the Freudian thesis and an ignoring of others. Generally, as in Kroeber's review, major attention was focused on the primal horde theory, which Freud himself had admitted was speculation. The broader and more

nportant thesis that there is an essential psychic unity in all man-
ind was underplayed. At the same time, again it can be seen in
Kroeber the repudiation of Freud's historical speculation went along
ith the repudiation of the historical speculations of several genera-
ons of anthropologists who had, up to World War I, been con-
idered the leading authorities in the field. They included such men
s Reinach, Wundt, Spencer and Gillen, Lang, Robertson Smith,
Durkheim and his school, Keane, Avebury, and Frazer. For a long
me anthropologists felt that any kind of psychological or historical
peculation was not a suitable subject for scientific inquiry, and,
stead, preferred to concentrate on a description of the functioning
f different societies. In this respect the development of anthropol-
gy in the 1920's parallels the behavioristic approach in psychology
uring the same period.

However, among the anthropologists, as among the psychologists,
ere were many who recognized the bold sweep and imagination
f Freud's thinking, and who paid tribute to his ability to offer
lausible explanations for data which otherwise made little or no
nse. In England particularly Malinowski, as already noted, made
everal valiant attempts to reconcile psychoanalysis and anthro-
ology.

Once enough societies or cultures had been described in sufficient
etail by enough field workers, there still remained the task of
ying to find a unifying thread running through them. Here psy-
hoanalysis came back into its own. Beginning in the 1930's, and
temming particularly from the work of Kardiner and Erikson in
ie late 1930's, it was shown over and over again how the psycho-
nalytic frame of reference could be applied to a large number
f different cultures. Just as psychologists came to see increasingly
iat the total repudiation of instinct as an explanatory concept was
ot feasible, anthropologists came to recognize that in spite of the
lmost limitless diversity of human cultures there were still certain
iings which they had in common. These they called "cultural
niversals." The cultural universals certainly include a good many
f the psychic mechanisms which were described by Freud and the
sychoanalysts. Kluckhohn has recently summed up this develop-
ient as follows:

I still believe that some of the cautions uttered by Boas and others o
the possible extravagances of interpretations in terms of universal sym
bolisms, completely or largely divorced from minute examination of cu
tural context, are sound. But the facts uncovered in my own field wor
and that of my collaborators have forced me to the conclusion that Freu
and other psychoanalysts have depicted with astonishing correctnes
many central themes in motivational life which are universal. The styl
of expression of these themes and much of the manifest content are cu
turally determined; however, the underlying psychological drama tran
scends cultural difference.

This should not be too surprising—except to an anthropologist ove
indoctrinated with a theory of cultural relativism—for many of the in
escapable givens of human life are also universal. Human anatomy an
human physiology are, in the large, about the same the world over. The
are two sexes with palpably visible differences in external genitalia an
secondary sexual characteristics. All human infants, regardless of cultur
know the psychological experience of helplessness and dependency. Situ
tions making for competition for the affections of one or both parents, fc
sibling rivalry can be to some extent channeled this way or that way by
culture, but they cannot be eliminated, given the universality of fami
life. The trouble has been—because of accidents of intellectual and poli
ical history—that the anthropologist for two generations has been obsesse
with the differences between peoples, neglecting the equally real similar
ties—upon which the "universal culture pattern" as well as the psycholo
ical uniformities are clearly built.[127]

In a letter to Jones in 1955 Kluckhohn wrote:

I am convinced that the essential universality of the Oedipus comple
and of sibling rivalry are now established by the anthropological record.[1]

With regard to the particular issues which Freud took up i
Totem and Taboo, the question of the origins of totemism and i
psychological explanation are still as much in dispute today as the
were fifty years ago. Anthropologists are no longer as intereste
in historical reconstructions as they were in the early part of th
century. Nevertheless, the data are still there, and they will requi
some kind of theory to account for them. It is to be noted that tl
1958 edition of the Encyclopaedia Britannica, in the article c
totemism (Volume XXII, page 318), states that while Freud's pa
ticular presentation may or may not be adequate, he does appe
to have indicated the direction in which an explanation of totemis
and exogamy is to be sought.

In the postwar years Freud came back to anthropological topics number of times from the vantage point of ego psychology.

To sum up, whatever the future may hold in store for particular heories, the main contributions of psychoanalysis have become an ntegral part of the science of anthropology.

ART

In his approach to art Freud saw a number of ways in which the ndings of psychoanalysis are applicable. The artist is a human eing who is trying to say something, to himself or to other human eings. What the work of art is about is often a puzzle; psycho- nalysis can try to uncover its hidden meaning. Why the work of rt has such a compelling effect on others (if it has) is likewise a ruitful subject for psychological inquiry. Such an inquiry leads o an investigation both of the artist and of the audience or spectator. Finally the symbolism which the artist employs must necessarily e related to the symbolism which the analyst deals with in his veryday work.

Art is an exercise of imagination or fantasy. This world of fantasy s familiar to the psychoanalyst—it is the basis of his understanding f neurosis and personality in general. Hence fantasy supplies the onnecting link between the artist and his audience.

In *A General Introduction to Psychoanalysis* (1916–17) Freud ;ave a concise summary of his views on art and the artist:

There is, in fact, a path from fantasy back again to reality, and that is— rt. The artist has also an introverted disposition and has not far to go o become neurotic. He is one who is urged on by instinctual needs which re too clamorous; he longs to attain to honor, power, riches, fame, and he love of women; but he lacks the means of achieving these gratifica- ions. So, like any other with an unsatisfied longing, he turns away from eality and transfers all his interest, and all his libido, too, on to the reation of his wishes in the life of fantasy, from which the way might eadily lead to neurosis. There must be many factors in combination to revent this becoming the whole outcome of his development; it is well nown how often artists in particular suffer from partial inhibition of their apacities through neurosis. Probably their constitution is endowed with powerful capacity for sublimation and with a certain flexibility in the epressions determining the conflict. But the way back to reality is found by the artist thus: He is not the only one who has a life of fantasy: the intermediate world of fantasy is sanctioned by general human consent and every hungry soul looks to it for comfort and consolation. But to those who are not artists the gratification that can be drawn from the springs of fantasy is very limited; their inexorable repressions prevent the enjoyment of all but the meager daydreams which can become conscious. A true artist has more at his disposal. First of all, he understands how to elaborate his daydreams, so that they lose that personal note which grates upon strange ears and become enjoyable to others; he knows, too, how to modify them sufficiently so that their origin in prohibited sources is not easily detected. Further, he possesses the mysterious ability to mould his particular material until it expresses the ideas of his fantasy faithfully; and then he knows how to attach to this reflection of his fantasy life so strong a stream of pleasure that, for a time at least, the repressions are outbalanced and dispelled by it. When he can do all this, he opens out to others the way back to the comfort and consolation of their own unconscious sources of pleasure, and so reaps their gratitude and admiration; then he has won—through his fantasy—what before he could only win in fantasy: honor, power, and the love of women.[129]

The artist, then, puts into artistic form the fantasies which the ordinary mortal daydreams about. These fantasies are the universal strivings: "It's still the same old story, a fight for love and glory." The artist derives his gratification from the permissible release of his fantasies, the audience from the tolerated viewing or reading of them. It is also clear that since fantasies are being dealt with that are otherwise forbidden but that are now allowed to come out within certain limits, these limits can easily be exceeded and neurosis can result.

Freud's first formal paper on art was "Psychopathic Characters on the Stage." It was written in 1904 and published posthumously. In it he raises the question of how it is that an audience can view psychopathic behavior on the stage which it could not tolerate in real life. The reason is, of course, that it is a "play," and so does not make the viewer aware that these are really his wishes.

In his book on Jokes, published in 1905, Freud made a major contribution to the psychology of humor. In order to understand jokes and humor in general, Freud considered two aspects of humor —the technique of humor, and the purposes which it serves. With regard to the techniques which humor employs to create something nny, Freud was intrigued by finding that there was a marked imilarity between the techniques which he could see in jokes and hose which he had already elucidated in dreams. With regard to he purposes which jokes serve, it was readily apparent that they llow for the discharge of some pleasure which is otherwise not ermitted to the individual, particularly erotic and aggressive pleasure. Jokes in general are another instance of the fact that conomy in the expenditure of psychic energy gives pleasure to he individual.

Freud noted a difference between jokes and dreams in that the oke seeks to give pleasure while the dream seeks to ward off un-leasure. Put another way, one can say that in the joke the gratifica-ion is obvious, while in the dream it is concealed. At the same time he mechanisms of condensation, displacement, distortion, repre-entation through the opposite, and so on, which he could enumerate or dreams, he could also find illustrated in jokes.

People tell jokes to make others laugh. This laughter derives from he discharge of certain pleasures which would otherwise be for-idden. Thus in jokes one is permitted sexual allusions, or outbursts f anger, contempt, sarcasm, which would otherwise have to be uppressed.

Some examples will make clearer the process of analysis which 'reud used. He quotes a joke that Heine makes with regard to a haracter in one of his books. This character, Hirsch-Hyacinth, oasts to the poet of his relations with the wealthy Baron Roth-child, and finally says:

And, as true as God shall grant me all good things, Doctor, I sat beside olomon Rothschild and he treated me quite as his equal—quite famil-onairely.[130]

The word "famillionairely" is obviously an abbreviation. It can e described as a composite structure, a condensation accom-anied by the formation of a substitute, which in this case consists f a composite word. The tension that is released through the joke is he feeling of unmistakable bitterness, understandable in a poor man rought face to face with great wealth.

Another example: "How are you getting along?" the blind man

asks the lame man. "As you see," the lame man replies to the blind man.

In this joke there are double meanings attached to the word "getting along" and "as you see," each of which has one meaning in ordinary usage and another in terms of the other man's handicap. Clearly the joke releases the feelings of spite which each feel toward the other.

A particularly important feature of jokes is that they provide *fore-pleasure*. This is similar to the fore-pleasure in sex play, which is preliminary to the final consummation. The fore-pleasure mechanism holds for other types of artistic productions as well.

It may seem surprising that the psychoanalytic literature includes jokes in a discussion of art. The reason is that the analyst is interested in the psychological mechanisms involved, in contrast to the artist, who is primarily concerned with standards of beauty. The psychology of jokes and humor does not differ essentially from that of more conventional art forms.

CREATIVE WRITING

In a paper "Creative Writers and Daydreaming," (1908) Freud turned to the psychology of the writer. He asks first whether there is anything in the ordinary person which corresponds to the writer's gift, and finds it in daydreams or fantasies. These fantasies are for the adult what play was in childhood. Freud's main thesis is that a piece of creative writing, like a daydream, is a continuation of and a substitute for, what was once the play of childhood.

Leonardo da Vinci. Freud's best-known contribution to the psychology of the artist was his study of Leonardo da Vinci (1910). This may be regarded as the first psychoanalytic biography. The figure of Leonardo, one of the most universal of men in a period of history which produced many universal men, had long intrigued Freud. The translation into German of a psychological novel about Leonardo by the Russian, Merezhkovsky, provided an impetus for him to examine the subject more fully.

Freud's study has two aspects—first, an examination of Leonardo's personality and its relationship to his work and achievements, and

econd, the search for the roots of this pattern in an infantile experience of the artist.

The most striking feature in Leonardo's life, and one which was
obviously of particular interest to Freud, was the complete absence
of a sex life. He never married, never related to women sexually,
and although accused of some homosexual practices in his ado-
escence (the accusation forced him to leave his native Florence)
was evidently never an overt homosexual. Despite his acknowledged
genius, his work was notoriously slow and frequently remained
unfinished. He was dominated by an insatiable desire to know,
specially the desire to understand the secrets of nature, which
meant more to him than actively doing anything.

These and other features of his life and work Freud traced to
Leonardo's relationship to his mother and father. He was an il-
egitimate child, in itself by no means unusual in that epoch, but
he was taken from his mother when he was about five and brought
up by a stepmother; he did not see his mother again for many
years. Under these circumstances it is understandable that the
onging for his mother, normally a highly powerful motive in any
man, would become the paramount unconscious drive in Leonardo
and would provide a unifying thread to both his life and his work.
This thesis Freud elaborates in considerable detail.

It has been argued that the psychoanalytic biography, or "pathog-
aphy," as it has come to be called does not explain Leonardo's
greatness. With this, Freud was in fullest agreement. He said:

Since artistic talent and capacity are intimately connected with sub-
mation we must admit that the nature of the artistic function is also
inaccessible to us along psychoanalytic lines.[131]

The major weakness of the analytic pathography, as Freud himself commented, is that it generally, as with Leonardo, rests upon
insufficient historical data. Nevertheless the analytic point of view
is an invaluable addition to the other techniques of the biographer,
and from Freud's pioneering work an enormous literature has since
grown up.

James Strachey, the general editor of the Standard Edition, has
unearthed the fact that a part of Freud's argument is affected by a

mistranslation. Leonardo had a memory or fantasy from childhood that a vulture came to him when he was in his cradle, opened his mouth with its tail, and struck him many times with its tail against his lips. This is the memory referred to in Freud's title, and Freud devoted much time to it. Unfortunately, it has since been shown that the word is not "vulture" but "kite," which makes some of Freud's mythological parallels worthless. Nevertheless, on careful examination it still appears that Freud's essential argument is not affected by this mistake.[132]

SUMMARY

Freud's work had an enormous impact on art and artists. In fact, they recognized its significance long before the psychoanalytic profession did. Equally the psychoanalytic approach to art and the artist which Freud initiated has become almost an independent discipline. Here, too, Freud opened up a new chapter in man's intellectual development.

Available English Translations of Freud's Works Cited in Chapter IX

Obsessive Acts and Religious Practises. 1907.
　　Standard Edition, Vol. IX, pp. 115-127.
　　Collected Papers, Vol. II, pp. 25-35.

Totem and Taboo. 1912-1913.
　　Standard Edition, Vol. XIII, pp. 1-161.
　　Above issued separately: New York, Norton, 1952.
　　In *The Basic Writings of Sigmund Freud,* Modern Library Giants Random House, 1938, pp. 807-930. New York: Penguin Books, 1938 New York: Vintage Books, Random House (paperback).

The Claims of Psychoanalysis to Scientific Interest. 1913.
　　Standard Edition, Vol. XIII, pp. 165-190.

Psychopathic Characters on the Stage. 1904.
　　Standard Edition, Vol. VII, pp. 303-310.

Jokes and Their Relation to the Unconscious. 1905.
　　See bibliographic note to Chapter IV.

Creative Writers and Daydreaming. 1908.
  Standard Edition, Vol. IX, pp. 143-153.
  Under title: *The Relation of the Poet to Daydreaming.* Collected
  Papers, Vol. IV, pp. 172-183.

Leonardo da Vinci and a Memory of His Childhood. 1910.
  Standard Edition, Vol. XI, pp. 63-137.
  Under title: *Leonardo da Vinci: A Psychosexual Study of Infantile
  Reminiscence.* New York: Moffat, Yard. New York: Dodd Mead, 1932.
  Under title: *Leonardo da Vinci: A Study in Psychosexuality.* New York:
  Vintage Books, Random House (paperback).

Various papers on art are included in the following two collections:

On Creativity and the Unconscious. Edited by B. Nelson. New York:
  Harper Bros. (paperback).

Delusion and Dream and Other Essays. Edited by P. Rieff. Boston:
  Beacon Press (paperback).

NOTES ON CHAPTER IX

For the traditional *anthropological appraisal* of *Totem and Taboo*, see
two papers by A. L. Kroeber: "Totem and Taboo, An Ethnologic Psychoanalysis," *American Anthropologist*, XXII, 1920, pp. 48-55. A. L. Kroeber,
"Totem and Taboo in Retrospect," *American Journal of Sociology*, XLV,
1939, pp. 446-51.

The interrelationship between *psychoanalysis and anthropology* is now
so intimate that only a few landmarks can be cited. See especially
E. Erikson: *Childhood and Society* (New York: Norton, 1950). G. Ro-
heim: *Psychoanalysis and Anthropology* (New York: International Uni-
versities Press, 1950). A. Kardiner: *The Individual and His Society* (New
York: Columbia University Press, 1939). A. Kardiner: *The Psychological
Frontiers of Society* (New York: Columbia University Press, 1945).
E. Fromm: *The Sane Society* (New York: Rinehart, 1955). C. Kluckhohn:
"Universal Categories of Culture," in A. L. Kroeber (ed): *Anthropology
Today* (Chicago: University of Chicago Press, 1953). J. M. Whiting
and I. L. Child: *Child Training and Personality* (New Haven: Yale Uni-
versity Press, 1953). For a critical review of a number of works, see
S. Axelrad: "On Some Uses of Psychoanalysis," *Journal of the American
Psychoanalytic Association*, VIII, 1960, pp. 175-218.

See also below: Notes on Chapter XIII.

On *psychoanalysis and art*, some important reference works which summarize a good deal of the literature are: E. Kris: *Psychoanalytic Explorations in Art* (New York: International Universities Press, 1952). O. Rank:

Art and the Artist (New York: Tudor Publishing Company, 1932). H. Sachs: *The Creative Unconscious* (Cambridge: Sci-Art Publishers, 1942). F. J. Hoffman: *Freudianism and the Literary Mind* (Baton Rouge: Louisiana State University Press, 1945). H. Slochower: "Psychoanalysis and Literature," in D. Brower and L. Abt (eds.): *Progress in Clinical Psychology* (New York: Grune and Stratton, 1960).

Chapter X. THE REACTION TO FREUD

Freud's early work was almost completely ignored—to such an extent that he later referred to "a ten-year period of splendid isolation." Of *The Interpretation of Dreams*, as has been noted, it took eight years to sell the six hundred copies that had been printed. Eighteen months after the publication of the book Freud wrote that not a single scientific periodical and only a few others had mentioned it. His other major work, *Three Essays on Sexuality*, fared slighly better: one thousand copies were printed and sold within four years. Obviously at this time the world was paying little attention to Freud.

The situation began to change during the first decade of the present century. By 1908 Freud had enough followers to call an informal meeting of the psychoanalytic association at Salzburg in Austria, and by 1910 there were enough psychoanalysts in the world to arrange a formal meeting at Nuremberg in Germany.

The theories of the unconscious and of infantile sexuality produced a fantastic storm of opposition and gross misunderstanding, which has by no means fully abated today, although it is far more subdued in tone. Jones in Volume II of his Freud biography has a whole chapter devoted to reports of the opposition. These can scarcely inspire one with respect for either the honesty or the competence of Freud's medical colleagues.

A few examples will serve to illustrate the irrational prejudice which greeted Freud. At a Congress of German Neurologists and Psychiatrists in Hamburg in 1910 Professor Wilhelm Weygandt, when Freud's theories were mentioned, banged his fist on the table and shouted: "This is not a topic for discussion at a scientific meeting; it is a matter for the police." When Ferenczi in 1911 read a paper before the medical society at Budapest he was informed that Freud's work was nothing but pornography and that the proper place for psychoanalysts was prison. In 1910 Professor Oppenheim, author of a leading German textbook on neurology, proposed that a boycott be established against any institution where Freud's writings were tolerated. This met with an immediate response from the audience, and all the directors of sanatoriums present stood up to declare their innocence.

The fantastic lengths to which neurologists could go to deny the evidence of their senses in illustrated by the following story about Ziehen, the German director of the Berlin Psychiatric Clinic. In 1911 a patient came to the clinic, complaining of an obsessional impulse to lift women's skirts in the streets. Ziehen said to his students: "This is an opportunity to test the supposed sexual nature of such obsessions. I will ask the patient if this applies to old women as well, in which case it obviously cannot be erotic." The patient's reply was, "Oh, yes, to all women, even to my mother and sister." Upon which Ziehen triumphantly ordered the entry in the protocol to describe the case as definitely "nonsexual."

Psychologists at first were more receptive than the medical profession to the new ideas. William James declared to Jones: "The future of psychology belongs to your work." [133] G. Stanley Hall, president of Clark University in Massachusetts invited Freud to give lectures on psychoanalysis at the university in 1909, the first public presentation of the theories of psychoanalysis. Freud's own University of Vienna would not do as much for him, even though he was a professor there. Unfortunately, however, soon the attitude of the psychologists changed and became similar to that of psychiatrists. For many years psychoanalysis was pooh-poohed as "unscientific," "pure speculation," and the presentation of its doctrines was seriously hampered by the attitude of official authorities. Actually, the situation in both psychiatry and psychology began to change only after the horror-inspiring experiences of World War II.

Freud was not only unperturbed by the opposition; he tried to understand it. His explanation derived from and re-enforced the observations he made about his patients. The psychiatrists and psychologists were fighting a ferocious battle, in simple terms, because their own inadequacies were being exposed and because in their own personal lives they were having to repress the impulses which Freud had described in such detail. The opposition could not be handled by intellectual argument; it was of an emotional, irrational character, and represented primarily a resistance to unpleasant observations.

History has certainly borne Freud out.

The effects of the rabid opposition to Freud and psychoanalysis were far-reaching. Looked at in retrospect, the first psychoanalytic system, built on the unconscious, psychosexual development and transference-resistance, has become the basis of all dynamic theories of personality in existence today. Yet it was shunted to one side, attacked or at best ignored. Freud once said that it was his fate to discover the obvious, that children have sexual feelings and that dreams have meaning; one can only wonder at the capacity of mankind, including the learned professions of psychiatry and psychology, to ignore these obvious truths.

Psychoanalysis, rejected by both the medical profession and the universities, was perforce pushed into an independent position. The institutes which were set up after World War I to train psychoanalysts had no official status. Prerequisites for admission to these institutes became a thorny problem and still remain so. Groups sprang up around charismatic individuals and tended to follow the new discoveries of their leaders because they were denied the freer possibilities for discussion that exist in other fields. Facilities for research were strictly limited. At the same time the major professions stigmatized psychoanalysis as scientific rubbish for a long time, so that the number of qualified persons who were attracted to psychoanalysis remained small.

If this pre-World War I period is re-examined from today's vantage point it becomes clear that the development of the science of man was seriously hindered by the neglect of Freud and his teachings. The psychiatrist was for many years virtually at the lowest rung of the medical ladder. He spent his time primarily as a custodian for the hopelessly sick in mental hospitals. He lacked any dynamic understanding of his patients and at best could give them only whatever human kindness he might have as a person.

Enormous time, energy and money were spent on physiological research, spurred on by the vain illusion that some day a physiological cause for all these peculiar mental aberrations would be found. The discovery of the malaria cure for general paresis by Wagner-Jauregg in 1918 spurred the hope that similar findings would be obtained in other illnesses. Until World War II the orientation of psychiatry remained essentially physiological, and even today a considerable proportion of the psychiatric profession is dubious of the psychodynamic position espoused by psychoanalysis. Psychological research into the nature of mental illness was virtually non-existent before World War II.

The essential nature of psychiatry was misunderstood. Sullivan once said that the psychiatry of his day was neither science nor art but sheer confusion. Freud said in *The Question of Lay Analysis* that the non-analytic psychiatrist was basically untrained. Psychiatry kept on looking for some medical revelation and bogged down in a state of therapeutic pessimism. Analysis sought to understand the psychological mechanisms involved in people and became steadily more optimistic therapeutically. Today probably the majority of psychiatrists see psychoanalysis and its formulations as the basis for the dynamic understanding of all people, but it took many years and bitter struggles to reach that conclusion. And even today there are many parts of the United States and many countries of the world where there are virtually no trained analysts, and the psychiatrist is still practicing on the basis of theories which were discarded fifty years ago.

The rejection of psychoanalysis by academic psychology led to a serious neglect of the theory of personality. Such questions as instinct, motivation, defenses, anxieties, psychotherapy and many others related to personality were virtually ignored by the main body of the psychological profession. As a result those who wished to study these problems were forced into psychiatry or psychoanalytic training institutes. Psychology before World War II was in many ways a sterile discipline which tended to neglect the functioning human being. Its main achievements were in perception and intelligence, where the emotional conflicts of the individual could be relegated to a subordinate role.

With the upsurge of clinical psychology after World War II, the human being again became a focal concern for the psychologist. Defenses, anxieties, developmental questions, the self and many other concepts taken from psychoanalysis were intensively studied.

At the same time the other tradition in psychology, that of the laboratory experiment, which later concentrated more and more on learning theory, continued to be strong. The result was a bifurcation of the field of psychology, with one group strongly interested in learning, especially in the laboratory animal, and another attracted mainly by problems of personality functioning. It is only in recent years that some meeting of the minds between these two groups is taking place.

One unfortunate result of this rejection of psychoanalysis has been that for many years few psychologists were trained to do psychotherapy. They were brought up in the tradition of experimentation, and tended to look upon psychotherapy as a crude hit-or-miss affair with no real scientific status. Again this attitude has been changing only in recent years.

The enormous potential inherent in psychoanalysis and psychoanalytic psychotherapy was neglected for a long time. People who went to psychoanalysts were tarred with the stigma of "psychiatric patients." It was a matter of shame to go, and accordingly a great deal of public opposition to the idea always persisted. It has taken many years of public education to make some dent in this attitude.

The contribution of psychoanalysis to the prevention of emotional disorder could not be properly utilized. There were too few practitioners and its doctrines were too widely denied. Freud himself believed that the preventive potential of psychoanalysis could be greater than its therapeutic potential, and perhaps eventually this position will come to prevail.

Available English Translations of Freud's Works Cited in Chapter X.

The Resistances to Psychoanalysis. 1925.
  Standard Edition, Vol. XIX, pp. 213-222.
  Collected Papers, Vol. V, pp. 163-174.

NOTES ON CHAPTER X

The intensive opposition to Freud which prevailed before World War I and persisted until roughly World War II is full of the grossest misunderstandings and misinterpretations. Most of it has already passed into the limbo of history. The student who is interested in unravelling the course of error can consult a variety of works. E. Jones: *The Life and Work of Sigmund Freud* (New York: Basic Books, 1955), II, Chapter IV has some juicy quotations from pre-World War I psychiatrists. J. Jastrow: *Freud: His Dream and Sex Theories* (Cleveland: World Publishing Co., 1932) is typical of the psychologists of that day, and their inability to comprehend Freud's psychological system. R. S. Woodworth: *Psychology* (New York: Henry Holt, 1921) in spite of his enormous erudition, could not even present psychoanalysis properly. G. Seldes: *Can These Things Be?* (New York: Brewer, Warren and Putnam, 1931) talks, as did so many works of that day, of the tremendous "harm" done by psychoanalysis. R. M. Dorcus and G. W. Shaffer: *A Textbook of Abnormal Psychology* (Baltimore: Williams and Wilkins, 1934), write (2nd ed., p. 12): "Freud's Oedipus and Electra complexes are typical examples of abnormal behavior . . ." Apart from the gross misconception that the Oedipus complex is "abnormal" the authors are not even aware that Freud never postulated an Electra complex; it has indeed been suggested by other psychoanalytic writers, but the concept has not caught on and is almost never used. Equally characteristic is H. H. Hollingsworth: *Abnormal Psychology: Its Concepts and Theories* (New York: Ronald Press, 1920) who "refutes" Freud by "showing that he is nothing but a repetition of Herbart."

Kris, Herma and Shor: "Freud's Theory of the Dream in American Textbooks," *Journal of Abnormal and Social Psychology*, XXXVIII, 1943, pp. 319-34, have much interesting historical material showing how more and more of Freud has been accepted by psychology in spite of opposition and misunderstandings.

F. Wittels: *Freud and His Time* (New York: Liveright, 1931) is an account by an "in-again out-again" adherent-antagonist of Freud.

The attitude of professionals in the 1930's is summed up in A. Myerson: "The Attitude of Neurologists, Psychiatrists and Psychologists toward Psychoanalysis," *American Journal of Psychiatry*, XCVI, 1939, pp. 623-41.

For recent collections of absurdities about psychoanalysis see R. LaPiere: *The Freudian Ethic* (New York: Duell, Sloan and Pearce, 1959); J. A. Gengerelli: "Dogma or Discipline," *Saturday Review of Literature*, XL, 1957, pp. 9-11 and 40. A sensible reply to Gengerelli by a well-educated layman is V. F. Kelly: "Letter to the Editor," *Ibid.*, No. 17, April 27, 1957.

Part III.

EGO PSYCHOLOGY: THE TOTAL
PERSONALITY—1914–1939

Chapter XI. THE TOTAL PERSONALITY: ID, EGO, SUPEREGO

Around the time of the outbreak of World War I Freud began to reformulate some of his basic ideas. Within the next twelve years he had built up a much broader basis for psychoanalytic thought, now generally referred to as "ego psychology," in contrast to the earlier "id psychology." By 1926, with the publication of *The Problem of Anxiety*, the second system of psychoanalytic thought was essentially completed, although the final paper on therapy, "Analysis Terminable and Interminable," was not published until 1937.

Many factors led Freud to revise the system which he had so laboriously built up. Psychoanalysis had begun with the observation that the neurotic has conflicts which involve defenses against unbearable ideas. As has been pointed out, psychoanalysis at first consisted of the exploration of the nature of these unbearable ideas. The general area of the defensive processes—what is now called the ego and what Freud always called, fairly loosely, the ego or the ego instincts—was referred to over and over again but was repeatedly left for future investigation. For a variety of reasons, Freud was not ready to examine the nature of this ego until long after he had clarified the id.

It has been noted that Freud always had in mind a complete system of psychology which would explain the whole of mental functioning. In 1915 he began a book variously titled *Introduction to Metapsychology, Introductory Essays on Metapsychology,* and *A General Review of the Transference Neuroses*. By "metapsychology" he meant a comprehensive description of mental processes along psychoanalytic lines. Unfortunately, only five of the twelve projected essays in this book were ever published; the other seven were destroyed by Freud, for unknown reasons.

As he reflected on what he had built up his ideas began to change. He was always a man who was more concerned with the new than with the meticulous resolution of the old. It is this trait that makes it difficult for the student to follow the ramifications of his thought and that has led to many misinterpretations of what Freud had to say.

While Freud was quite successful in his treatment of the neuroses, the opposite was true with regard to the psychoses; hence, since theory and therapy for him always went hand in hand, the need to understand psychosis was great. Just as sexuality was the key to the neuroses, he saw that ego and ego structure were the keys to psychosis.

Even within the neuroses, the concept of character structure came to be seen as more and more important. The sexual instinct, the id, the unconscious drives that trouble the neurotic are no different from one person to another. Accordingly, the differentiation between the various kinds of neuroses and between the neurotic and the normal person cannot be made on the basis of the existence or the intensity of a sexual drive. There must also be some differences in the way these drives are handled. Actually a careful reading of Freud shows that although he had always paid attention to the nature of defense mechanisms, as they are called today, he had never elaborated them in any systematic form.

Another factor that led to the alteration in the theory was the catastrophe of World War I that shattered the complacent belief in human progress which many European intellectuals had held for some fifty years. The brutality and the violence which the war released surprised everybody, even someone who had preached the irrational nature of man's drives, as long as Freud had.

One technical aspect of the problem of neurosis that appeared in World War I proved a great puzzle and could not be adequately explained by Freudian theory as it then existed. This was the phenomenon of shell shock. In World War II it was rebaptized "combat fatigue"; today it is technically known as "traumatic neurosis." The traumatic neurotic, Freud realized, had dreams that represented the first real deviation from his earlier theory that all dreams are wish-fulfillments. Furthermore, all the other phenomena accompanying traumatic neurosis were intensely puzzling and required a considerable amount of rethinking. Such rethinking Freud did.

Finally and by no means least important was the personal factor involved in the growth of the psychoanalytic movement. By 1910, as already mentioned, there was an international psychoanalytic association with branches in various countries, and the movement seemed well on the way toward continued and harmonious progress. At this point several defections of important personalities occurred that touched Freud deeply. Adler, whom he had appointed as head of the Vienna group, broke with him in 1910 and founded a new school which he was eventually to call Individual Psychology. Even harder for Freud to take was the break with Jung, the Swiss psychiatrist whom he had appointed as president of the International Psychoanalytic Association. Jung started his own school and broke with Freud while he was still the president of the International. Jones comments in his biography that for all his psychoanalytic understanding Freud was a very poor *Menschenkenner;* he had very little insight into the petty grievances and malices that make up so much of many people's lives. Certainly his choice of Adler as president of the Vienna group and as an editor of the journal, and of Jung as president of the International Psychoanalytical Association, demonstrated the high hopes he had placed in these men, their subsequent behavior how completely he had misjudged them.

In Freud's writings after World War I there are numerous references to Adler and Jung, many of them largely irrelevant to the main argument. Freud's need to refute Adler and Jung over and over again is a reflection of his deep shock at the course of events.

Now it cannot be said that either Adler or Jung had too clear a grasp of Freud's views although they worked in the field for a number of years. The basic doctrines of unconscious motivation, psychosexual development and transference-resistance as the basis of therapy were all pretty foreign to them. In some cases they ignored these doctrines entirely so that, for example, Jung's various types of mental functioning are a reversion to a psychology of consciousness, while Adler makes the process of therapy appear so ludicrously simple that a professional psychoanalyst reading him today must get an impression of extreme superficiality.

However, Adler and Jung had two criticisms of the earlier Freudian system which Freud himself came to recognize as valid, although he never explicitly said so. These are that Freud emphasized sex too exclusively; and that he tended to explain symptoms rather than the personality as a whole.

At first Freud reacted to these criticisms by an emphatic rejection and a reassertion of his old position. In *The History of the Psychoanalytic Movement* (1914), he said:

> The view of life which is reflected in the Adlerian system is founded exclusively on the aggressive instinct; there is no room in it for love. We might feel surprise that such a cheerless *Weltanschauung* should have met with any attention at all; but we must not forget that human beings, weighed down by the burden of their sexual needs, are ready to accept anything if only the "overcoming of sexuality" is offered them as a bait.[134]

It is indeed amazing that the same man who called the emphasis on the aggressive impulse a "cheerless view of life" should, only six years later, have postulated the existence of a death instinct.

With regard to the other features of character structure, at first Freud was once again full of disclaimers. He said in *The History of the Psychoanalytic Movement:* "The Adlerian theory was from the very beginning a 'system,' which psychoanalysis was careful to avoid becoming." [135]

Then, however, he quite fairly recognized that Adler had indeed made some contributions to the psychology of the ego, although he made the equally just criticism that Adler overemphasized the ego to the exclusion of the instincts.

TRANSITION FROM ID PSYCHOLOGY TO EGO PSYCHOLOGY

In order to understand the transition from id psychology to ego psychology it is necessary to remember that Freud did not abandon his old position; he merely fitted it into a better framework. Thus the impulses arising at each stage of psychosexual development remain the same. The question, however, is how the ego deals with these impulses in the normal and in the neurotic individual.

Freud's new ideas evolved gradually and were spread out over a series of books and papers. The most formal description of the tripartite structure is in *The Ego and the Id*, published in 1923, although this description has to be supplemented by a variety of other works. It will be easiest and most useful to get an over-all view of the whole of this second system of Freud's, and then to go on to the details.

Freud described the personality as consisting of three areas—the id, the ego, and the superego. The id is the source of all drives, the reservoir of instincts. The word itself was taken from the German analyst, Groddeck, who described the human being as moved by unknown and unknowable forces. The id corresponds to the impulses that form the primary process in the earlier system, except that their contents now include primary aggression.

The ego is that aspect of the psyche that handles reality. The term itself is an outgrowth of the everyday use of the word. In German the word for ego is *Ich*, which is the ordinary word for *I*. In English the word *ego* is used, which is the Latin for *I*. The ego is similar to the secondary process in the old system, although it has been considerably elaborated.

The superego is the composite of the various commands, prohibitions, and ideals that form the personality. It is the heir of the parents, and theoretically arises as a result of the introjection of or the identification with parent figures.

With these three concepts and this new tripartite structure a whole host of phenomena could now be conceptualized and explained that had defied explanation before. Of them the concept of the id is not essentially novel, that of the ego is a refinement of old ideas, while the superego is entirely new.

In theory, Freud saw the ego and the superego as offshoots of the id. In the beginning of life there is only the id. The human being is a mass of primordial urges. He is subject for a time only to the pleasure principle. In order to meet the demands of reality, part of the id splits off and forms the ego. Later on, in the Oedipal period and after, part of the ego again splits off and forms the superego.

THE ID

In the id the most important new idea was that of the aggressive instinct, or, more precisely, the death instinct, which Freud first promulgated in *Beyond the Pleasure Principle*, published in 1920. Here he altered his theory of instincts—a theory with which he was always dissatisfied, and which he frequently referred to as "our mythology"—to make it a dualistic one, postulating the existence of both constructive and destructive drives. The constructive drives he referred to as Eros or the sexual drives in general, while the destructive drives he thought of as a death instinct. The death instinct manifests itself in the form of destructive wishes, first toward oneself (primary masochism) and later toward other people and toward the outside world.

The theory of instincts described in the *Three Essays on Sexuality* had never pleased Freud completely. He revised it in many different ways throughout the course of his life and was continually attempting to make it more adequate wherever he could. Actually he never looked on any of his formulations as in the least degree final.

In the decade preceding the publication of *Beyond the Pleasure Principle*, that is, from 1910 to 1920, Freud's attention had been directed more and more to the problems of guilt and hatred. Over and over again he attempted to derive these very important feelings from his then existing libido theory; and while he always managed to do so, at the same time he always expressed dissatisfaction and hesitancy about the solutions which he found.

Even when he felt most certain of his ground, he would still customarily say that the ego instincts had not been investigated by psychoanalysis and that he would come back to them at some future date. In *Totem and Taboo*, in 1913, he came to the conclusion that the ego instincts were just as important in social life as the sexual instincts, and that, furthermore, the two classes of instincts functioned in dissimilar ways. The ego-social instincts tend to unite men, he said, while the sexual instincts tend to give momentary pleasure and in the long run to disunite men.

Sadism. Even within his libido theory the significance of the sadistic drives dawned on Freud rather late. The anal-sadistic stage and the connection which he drew between the anal-sadistic fixation and the obsessional neurosis were not included in the first description of libidinal development in 1905, but were added later, after the paper "The Disposition to Obsessional Neurosis" in 1913.

When Freud in 1915 came to systematize his whole approach in the work on the transference neuroses (only parts of which have survived), he found himself at considerable difficulty in explaining some of the manifestations of sadism which he had observed. Originally, he had supposed that sadism was a component sexual instinct, so that in effect it subserved the needs of sexuality. Upon more careful reconsideration of the subject in the paper "Instincts and Their Vicissitudes," in 1915, he could not support this point of view any longer. There he stated:

The case of love and hate acquires a special interest from the circumstance that it refuses to be fitted into our scheme of the instincts.[136]

If love and hate cannot be fitted into the scheme of the instincts, whence, then, does hatred arise? As he had repeatedly shown in his studies of the obsessional neurosis, here there is a regression from love to hate, and the ambivalence between love and hate plays a particularly significant role in the symptomatology and character formation. Freud argued that the attitudes of love and hate cannot be made use of for the relations of instincts to their objects, but are reserved for the relations of the total ego to objects. Thus he came to the conclusion that the true origins of the relationship of hate are derived not from the sexual life but from the ego's struggle to preserve and maintain itself. By attaching hatred and sadism to the ego instincts he was, in effect, postulating a more primary sadistic drive which had nothing to do with libidinal wishes as such.

Freud's change of position in 1915 to the point of view that sadism is associated with the ego instincts stands in marked contrast to his earlier position on the question of aggression. The concept of an aggressive impulse had first been proposed by Adler in 1908, at which time it was emphatically rejected by Freud (see p. 170).*

---

* Jones argues that the Adlerian concept of aggression is radically different from the Freudian. This is only partially true, and in any case full credit for priority should be given to Adler.

Freud argued that aggression was something attached to each instinct; that it constituted the motive drive for each instinct and was not a special instinct in itself.

Masochism. At the same time, from a clinical point of view, the significance of masochism began to loom larger and larger. In the paper "Mourning and Melancholia," which was finally published in 1917, although it was written in 1914, Freud for the first time considered seriously the problem of depression and its metapsychology. He recognized that depression was intimately tied up with punishment, and made the point that the punishment in neurotic or psychotic depressions is by an internalized object, in contrast to the punishment by an external object, which the normal person experiences. In the paper, "A Child Is Being Beaten" (1919), he considered at length some clinical observations on beating phantasies in childhood. He argued that the memory of being beaten or of other children being beaten derived ultimately from the incestuous wish to be loved by the father; in the phantasy love was turned into a beating. Thus he was still explaining masochism within the pleasure principle, although with some slight misgivings.

Within the libido theory itself another radical change was brought about by the paper "On Narcissism" in 1914. Among the many points Freud made in that paper was the one to the effect that the reservoir of libido is located in the ego. This made ego-libido a new kind of instinctual concept. This view of the relationship between the libido and the ego again compelled a re-examination of his whole theoretical structure.

Finally, from a metapsychological point of view, he was always trying to get back to the position which he had abandoned in the "Project." There, it will be recalled, he had attempted to lay down a satisfactory physiological basis for his psychological observations; dissatisfied with his results, he abandoned the scheme and never published it. Nevertheless, the idea always beckoned to him, and he tried to come back to it again and again. *Beyond the Pleasure Principle* represents another such attempt.

Beyond the Pleasure Principle. This book has become one of the most provocative and controversial of all of Freud's works.

As the title implies, Freud was eternally testing the pleasure principle and eternally questioning it. Does it explain the facts? When new facts come along, does it explain them as well? At the same time, he was concerned with the economics of psychic energy: if the pleasure principle explains the facts, in what way does it do so?

The book itself is a relatively short one (fifty-eight pages in the Standard Edition), and may be divided into two main parts. After a short introduction in which Freud shows the similarity of his views on the economics or management of pleasure to Fechner's principle of stability or constancy (which more recently has been rephrased in terms of Cannon's principle of homeostasis), he goes on to make a number of remarkable clinical observations.

At first sight all of these observations seem to be instances in which the pleasure principle does not satisfactorily explain the findings. Freud points to the existence of traumatic neurosis, in which the patient comes back to the traumatic scene over and over again, even though he suffers from it. In the dreams of traumatic neurotics there is likewise a return to the traumatic experience. He brings in an observation on children's play, which derived from an observation of his own grandson Ernst, in which he shows how the little child makes a game out of the mother's disappearance, which really must have been an unpleasant experience. In analysis, patients repeat the frightening anxiety-provoking situations of their childhood. Furthermore, there are many types of situations in real life which seem to point to some tendency to repeat, even though the situation repeated is inherently unpleasant. While in theory all of these observations could be explained by some manipulation of the pleasure principle, Freud finds it more satisfactory to point to the *repetition compulsion,* which is common to all of them. This repetition compulsion may sometimes, as in the child's wish to have the same story read to him over and over again, be a simple application of the pleasure principle; more often it may be seen as a shift from something which is passively experienced to something which is actively brought about; this shift helps the individual to master the anxiety involved in passively suffering some trauma.

So far all this is sound clinical observation, and had Freud stopped here, the world would have applauded another brilliant paper by the master. Instead he then went on to speculate about the repetition compulsion, a speculation which led him to the death instinct.

The Death Instinct. The repetition compulsion, he argued, is part of a tendency in nature to reinstate a former state of affairs. Instincts embody such a tendency. Hence, it appears that there are two major classes of instincts—the life instinct, or Eros, and the death instinct. "The aim of all life is death." [137]

Toward the end of the work Freud produced a number of quotations from authorities in biology and a number of biological arguments to bolster his theory.

The death instinct is not, as such, directly observable. Freud argued that it manifests itself clinically only in the ways in which the destructive drive appears, that is, in the vicissitudes of sadism and masochism. Inasmuch as there is now a primary death instinct, this implies that there is also such a thing as *primary masochism.* Previously Freud had always considered masochism to be secondary to the sadistic drives.

The death instinct is certainly a most remarkable idea. At first sight it would appear to be a senseless and contradictory concept. Freud himself was obviously very hesitant about the whole idea. In the book he wrote:

It may be asked whether and how far I am myself convinced of the truth of the hypotheses that have been set out in these pages. My answer would be that I am not convinced myself, and that I do not seek to persuade other people to believe in them. Or, more precisely, that I do not know how far I believe in them.[138]

After his initial hesitation, however, he came to be more and more convinced of the truth of his position.

When Jones expressed some skepticism concerning these conclusions of Freud's, Freud wrote regretting this fact and hoping that he (Jones) would soon come to the same point of view; he himself could no longer see his way without them: they had, in fact, become indispensable to him.[139]

By this time Freud had a wide audience not only among the general public but also among his fellow analysts, many of whom he had himself trained. In spite of the enormous significance attached to anything that came from Freud, the idea of a death instinct met with emphatic repudiation. In a review of the literature up to 1957 Jones found that of the fifty or so papers devoted to the topic since Freud's original publication in 1920, during the first decade only half supported Freud's theory; during the second decade only a third; and during the last, none at all.[140] Even the analysts, such as Melanie Klein, Karl Menninger, and Herman Nunberg, who at least verbally support the idea of the death instinct, use it in a clinical rather than a biological manner.

Attempts have been made to bolster the death instinct by arguments drawn from more recent work in physics and biology. In physics an analogy has been drawn between the death instinct and the law of entropy, the second law of thermodynamics, which leads to the conclusion that the universe is running down. There seems to be a certain parallel between the idea that the universe is running down and will eventually be extinguished and the idea of a death instinct. It has, however, been pointed out that this analogy is a completely inappropriate one, and that arguments derived from physics are totally irrelevant to Freud's theory. Likewise, from the biologic point of view, there is not a particle of evidence to support the idea of a death instinct.

If the concept of a death instinct has been so emphatically repudiated by later psychoanalysts, the question may well be raised—why did Freud resort to it? Clues may be found in his concept of philosophy and in his own scientific development. Again his ambivalence about psychology, which has already been noted, becomes apparent. In his formative years he had been taught that only biology and physiology contained basic truths. Accordingly, psychology, to be on a sound foundation, had to be reduced to them. Even though he created a magnificent psychological structure independent of biological and physiological principles then known, he still yearned for the more secure knowledge of his early days. In *Beyond the Pleasure Principle,* he speaks of finding explanations along "sober Darwinian lines." At another point where he is considering all the obscurities in his explanations he says:

The deficiencies in our description would probably vanish if we were already in a position to replace the psychological terms by physiological or chemical ones. It is true that they, too, are only part of a figurative language, but it is one with which we have long been familiar and which is perhaps a simpler one as well.

On the other hand, it should be made quite clear that the uncertainty of our speculation has been greatly increased by the necessity for borrow-'ing from the science of biology.[141]

Looked at in this light, the theory of the death instinct is an attempt to explain some remarkable psychological observations in terms of physiology and biology. Freud's psychology remains; his biology and physiology have tended to be quietly discarded.

There were also many personal reasons that could explain the assumption of a death instinct. Freud himself considers this possibility. He says:

Perhaps we have adopted the belief [the death instinct] because there is some comfort in it. If we are to die ourselves, and first to lose in death those who are dear to us, it is easier to submit to a remorseless law of nature, to the sublime necessity than to a chance which might perhaps have been escaped.[142]

Throughout Freud's life he always had a sort of morbid interest in death. As far back as anyone can see he seems to have been prepossessed by thoughts about death.[143] Jones relates how Freud, on parting from a friend, would say: "Good-by, you may never see me again." He suffered from repeated attacks of dying. He hated to grow old. He once said that he thought of death every day of his life. After a fainting attack in Munich in 1912 his first remark upon regaining consciousness was: "How sweet it must be to die." Often enough, when he was faced by a strong wish, he tended to explain it by an instinctual drive. In the light of his lifelong concern with death and the strength of his conflicts about it, it may well be supposed that his assumption of a death instinct arose out of his own difficulties.

Aggression. While the death instinct as such has been more or less discarded, its corollary—that of the destructive instinct and the corresponding dual-instinct theory, in which there are two basic instincts, sex and destructiveness—has proved to be one of the most fruitful of Freud's hypotheses. There is such a vast amount of destructiveness in human beings that it cannot be readily explained, as

Freud attempted to do earlier, on the basis of a simple frustration of sexuality. It seems likely that the majority of analysts today would look upon aggression as in some sense a basic drive.

Once Freud had hit upon the idea of aggression, he attached tremendous weight to it. In fact, he said, in *Civilization and Its Discontents* (1930):

> I can no longer understand how we could have overlooked the universality of non-erotic aggression and destruction, and could have omitted to give it its true significance in our interpretation of life . . . I can remember my own defensive attitude when the idea of an instinct of destruction first made its appearance in psychoanalytical literature, and how long it took before I became accessible to it.[144]

However, there is one vital difference between Freud's treatment of the sexual instinct and his later treatment of the aggressive instinct. The vicissitudes of the sexual instinct had been followed, described, and analyzed in the greatest of detail in *Three Essays on Sexuality*. He was able to specify the aim and the object of the sexual instinct, of its representatives at each of the stages of development, and of the partial instincts, all in very clear terms and all in consonance with well-established clinical experience. Other analysts since then have been able to confirm and reconfirm his conclusions.

With the aggressive instinct the case is quite different. Here Freud merely laid down the principle that there is such a thing as the death instinct, which manifests itself in destructive ways, while the larger questions of its development and the related questions of its source, its impetus, its aim and its object, are all left undiscussed. Freud himself recognized that he had left much work undone. In a letter to Marie Bonaparte dated May 27, 1937, he wrote:

> I will try to answer your question [about aggression]. The whole topic has not yet been treated carefully and what I had to say about it in earlier writings was so premature and casual as hardly to deserve consideration.[145]

The revised theory of anxiety. Anxiety is the core problem in neurosis. There are neuroses where anxiety is manifest, on the surface, and there are neuroses where anxiety is completely repressed.

The ordinary definition of the neurotic individual as one who is "nervous" or shows a great deal of anxiety is thus seen to be incorrect. The amount of anxiety which a person displays cannot be immediately determined; it is related to his total ego structure.

Freud's first theory of anxiety, which dates from the 1890's, was that anxiety is dammed-up libido; that is, libido which, unable to find expression in the normal sexual manifestations, then turns into fear or anxiety.

This "toxicological" theory of anxiety held until the publication of *The Problem of Anxiety* in 1926. There a variety of considerations led Freud to the view that anxiety is in the ego, not in the id. Fear is fundamentally, as Darwin had pointed out, a biological response to danger. Anxiety differs from fear only in that in anxiety the danger is not real; it is a threat to the particular individual for subjective reasons. Furthermore, in reflecting on the genesis of anxiety Freud recognized that the instinctual impulse is not immediately transformed into anxiety since the same anxiety can arise from different impulses.

All of these observations and reflections Freud tried to pull together in his second theory of anxiety. Repression does not lead to anxiety, as he had formerly held; now anxiety leads to repression. Anxiety is a signal given by the ego that danger threatens. He then explored the nature of this danger, and came to the conclusion that its essence lay in a fear of separation, or "separation anxiety," as it has since been called. The prototype of this separation anxiety is the birth situation with the actual separation from the mother. In this respect Freud saw some merit in the birth trauma theory of Rank, but he discarded the extreme exaggerations of that theory.

The oral stage. This second theory of anxiety led Freud for the first time back to the oral stage, to the relationship between mother and child before the father enters the picture. It is remarkable that Freud, despite his insistent emphasis on the significance of the infantile factor, recognized the importance of the oral stage only at such a relatively late period in his work. For most of his life he seems to have held on to the idea that nothing could really go wrong between a mother and child and that, accordingly, neurotic difficulties must begin at some later time.

Since Freud's was in some respects a personal system, some explanation for this might be found in the facts of his own life. After he wrote *The Interpretation of Dreams*, he recognized it as a piece of his self-analysis occasioned by his father's death which he referred to as "the most poignant loss in a man's life." [146] Freud's mother, on the other hand, lived to an extreme old age; when she died he was in his seventies. In the course of his self-analysis he had evidently not come to recognize the difficulties that must have existed between himself and his mother; whereas he had clearly seen the Oedipal conflicts early in his career. He even wrote that almost every intimate human emotional relationship which lasts for some time leaves feelings of aversion and hostility, "perhaps with the solitary exception of the relation of a mother to her son." [147]

In any case, once the new theory of anxiety was propounded, and the significance of the oral stage recognized, a new era in psychoanalytic thinking was ushered in. It entered its full swing only after Freud's death, around 1940, when the relationship between mother and child first came to be seriously investigated. From that time on the need of the child for a deep, secure feeling with the mother has been universally recognized, and many recommendations have been made to reorganize infant care in accordance with this need.

THE EGO

The ego is now viewed as that part of the psychic apparatus which deals with reality. The *ego* represents what are called reason and sanity, in contrast to the *id*, which contains the passions. This position was first laid down in *The Ego and the Id* in 1923, and later expanded in a number of ways.

At birth ego and id are undifferentiated. Gradually, as the individual develops, an ego emerges. The first point at which an ego can be said to exist is when bodily sensations are perceived; hence Freud states that the ego is first and foremost a body ego.

The ego is that part of the id which has been modified by the direct influence of the external world acting through the system perception-consciousness (Pcpt-Cs). By its control of perception and consciousness the ego wards off anxiety-provoking situations.

Against the dangers threatening from the external world the eg
is in a good position to defend itself; if necessary, it can take t
flight. This, however, is not possible with regard to internal dange
(instinctual impulses). Freud saw this greater susceptibility t
internal dangers as one source of neurosis.

The ego depends on a neutral displaceable *energy*, which is d
sexualized Eros. This displaceable energy or desexualized libid
could also be described as sublimated energy. Here Freud arriv
at a somewhat different version of the process of sublimation.

For him the ego was a composite of a number of defense mec
anisms, such as sublimation, reaction formation, regression, repre
sion, isolation, undoing, etc. In 1926 he replaced the concept
repression by the concept of defense and saw repression as or
of many defense mechanisms. In 1936, in Anna Freud's book *T*
Ego and the Mechanisms of Defense, she described the vario
defense mechanisms in greater detail and clarified their role in t
functioning of the personality.

Personality structure now centers around the ego. The vario
components of the ego may vary in many different ways, fro
normal to psychotic. In *Analysis Terminable and Interminable*
1937 Freud wrote:

> Now every normal person is only approximately normal: his ego r
> sembles that of the psychotic in one point or another, in a greater or less
> degree, and its distance from one end of the scale and proximity to t
> other may provisionally serve as a measure of what we have indefinite
> spoken of as "modification of the ego." [148]

These modifications or variations of the ego may be either hered
tary or acquired. Every individual has certain characteristic wa
of reacting to the world, and these are a mixture of inborn structur
and environmental influences.

Finally, an ego can be regarded as a strong or a weak ego. T
capacity of the ego to handle reality, both internal and external,
the measure of its strength.

There have been so many developments in ego psychology sin
Freud wrote that no simple summary can be presented here. F
views do indeed form the basis of the later developments but th
have undergone extensive modifications.

THE SUPEREGO

The superego is the wholly novel aspect of ego psychology. Through his concept Freud expands the notion of the Oedipus complex and deals more systematically with intrapersonal identifications and interpersonal relations.

Among both the general public and professionals the image of Freud has long been that of the instinct theorist. To some extent this image was furthered by Freud's own hope that someday a "scientific" biology would explain his psychological findings. In part it stems from the fact that historically in psychoanalytic research instincts were explored before object relations were.

Yet to insist too exclusively on Freud's biological orientation leads to a distortion of the facts, for Freud was always keenly aware of the central role of human relationships. Thus, in 1921, in *Group Psychology and the Analysis of the Ego* he wrote:

The contrast between individual psychology and social or group psychology, which at a first glance may seem to be full of significance, loses a great deal of its sharpness when it is examined more closely. It is true that individual psychology is concerned with the individual man and explores the paths by which he seeks to find satisfaction for his instinctual impulses; but only rarely and under certain exceptional conditions is individual psychology in a position to disregard the relations of this individual to others. In the individual's mental life someone else is invariably involved, as a model, as an object, as a helper, as an opponent; and so from the very first individual psychology, in this extended but entirely justifiable sense of the words, is at the same time social psychology as well. The relations of an individual to his parents and to his brothers and sisters, to the object of his love, and to his physician—in fact, all the relations which have hitherto been the chief subject of psychoanalytic research—may claim to be considered as social phenomena; and in this respect they may be contrasted with certain other processes, described by us as "narcissistic," in which the satisfaction of the instincts is partially or totally withdrawn from the influence of other people.[149]

Beginning with the paper "On Narcissism" in 1914 Freud began to consider more thoroughly the question of object relations. There he postulated the existence of an ego-ideal, which the person uses as a standard by which to measure his actual performance. The object was further developed in the papers "Mourning and Melancholia" in 1917 and "Group Psychology and the Analysis of the Ego" in 1921. Finally, the whole system was crystallized and the ego-ideal was renamed the superego in *The Ego and the Id* in 1923.

Just as the ego is differentiated out of the id, so the superego is differentiated out of the ego. The superego is the heir of the Oedipus complex and arises out of the internalization of the parental images after the Oedipus has been overcome. Freud defines it as follows:

The broad general outcome of the sexual phase governed by the Oedipus complex may, therefore, be taken to be the forming of a precipitate in the ego, consisting of these two identifications [mother and father] in some way combined together. This modification of the ego retains its special position; it stands in contrast to the other constituents of the ego in the form of an ego-ideal or superego.[150]

This definition requires an elaboration of the notion of identification, a topic which Freud considered many times in these years. The earliest identification precedes object cathexis; it is the wish of the child to be like the father (perhaps, Freud says, it is safer to say like the parents: but, as has been noted, he tended to neglect the conflicts with the mother in the early years). In early childhood before and during the Oedipal phase, the child tries to form interpersonal relations or object cathexes. Frequently the child is frustrated in this endeavor. Then the *object cathexes regress to identifications*, for example, frustrated in his wish *to be like* the father, the child falls back on the wish *to be* the father. This formula had originally been discovered in connection with depression, but Freud now came to see the process as one of much greater frequency, and not confined to that illness.

Study of these early identifications led to an important revision of the concept of the Oedipal phase. From now on, Freud says, it is necessary to speak of the *complete Oedipus complex*, involving both sides of the ambivalent conflict toward both parents. He says:

Closer study usually discloses the more complete Oedipus complex which is twofold, positive, and negative, and is due to the bisexuality originally present in children: that is to say, a boy has not merely an ambivalent attitude toward his father and an affectionate object relation toward his mother, but at the same time he also behaves like a girl and displays an affectionate feminine attitude to his father and a correspondng hostility and jealousy toward his mother . . . In my opinion it is advisable in general, and quite especially where neurotics are concerned, to assume the existence of the complete Oedipus complex.[151]

A curious feature of Freud's theory of the superego, one which has been relegated to the background in the course of time, is that the superego retains the character of the father.[152] Today variable weighting could be given to either the father or the mother, depending on the family structure.

To the oft-repeated objection that psychoanalysis fails to consider the spiritual qualities of man Freud could now answer: These spiritual qualities are embodied in the superego. He says:

It is easy to show that the ego-ideal answers in every way to what is expected of the higher nature of man. In so far as it is a substitute for the longing for a father, it contains the germ from which all religions have evolved. The self-judgment which declares that the ego falls short of its ideal produces the sense of worthlessness with which the religious believer attests his longing. As a child grows up, the office of father is carried on by masters and by others in authority; the power of their injunctions and prohibitions remains vested in the ego ideal and continues, in the form of conscience, to exercise the censorship of morals. The tension between the demands of conscience and the actual attainments of the ego is experienced as a sense of guilt. Social feelings rest on the foundation of identifications with others, on the basis of an ego-ideal in common with them.[153]

There is also a collective superego analogous to that of the individual. Social cohesiveness is made possible by the fact that a number of people have similar superego sanctions and prohibitions. This makes the superego of particular importance in the study of society.

The superego is closely allied to the id. *Guilt,* which is superego punishment, results particularly from the projection of hostile impulses onto the parents; in fact the superego is frequently harsher than the parents. This, however, does not alter the general supposition that the superego derives primarily from the parents.

Since Freud's pioneer work the investigation of superego mechanisms has proceeded steadily and many theoreticians have suggested a variety of changes. The most novel findings have come out of the direct study of the first few years of life.

Available English Translations of Freud's Works Cited in Chapter XI.

On the History of the Psychoanalytic Movement. 1914.
Standard Edition, Vol. XIV, pp. 7-64.
Collected Papers, Vol. I, pp. 287-359.
Under title: "The History of the Psychoanalytic Movement." In *The Basic Writings of Sigmund Freud.* New York: Modern Library Giants, Random House, 1938, pp. 933-977.

On Narcissism: An Introduction. 1914.
See bibliographic note to Chapter V.

Instincts and Their Vicissitudes. 1915.
See bibliographic note to Chapter V.

Some Character Types met with in Psychoanalytic Work. 1916.
Standard Edition, Vol. XIV, pp. 311-333.
Collected Papers, Vol. IV, pp. 318-344.

Mourning and Melancholia. 1917.
Standard Edition, Vol. XIV, pp. 243-258.
Collected Papers, Vol. IV, pp. 152-170.
In *A General Selection from the Works of Sigmund Freud.* Edited by J. Rickman. New York: Doubleday Anchor (paperback). pp. 124-140.

Beyond the Pleasure Principle. 1920.
Standard Edition, Vol. XVIII, pp. 7-64.
New York: Boni and Liveright, 1924. New York: Liveright, 1950. London: Hogarth Press and the Institute of Psychoanalysis. 1950. New York: Bantam Books (paperback).
Excerpts in *A General Selection from the Works of Sigmund Freud.* Edited by J. Rickman. New York: Doubleday Anchor (paperback). pp. 141-168.

Group Psychology and the Analysis of the Ego. 1921.
Standard Edition, Vol. XVIII, pp. 69-143.
New York: Liveright, 1940. London and Vienna: International Psychoanalytical Press. 1922.
Excerpts in *A General Selection from the Works of Sigmund Freud.* Edited by J. Rickman. New York: Doubleday Anchor (paperback). pp. 169-209.

The Ego and The Id. 1923.
Standard Edition, Vol. XIX, pp. 12-66.
Above issued as separate volume New York: Norton, 1961. London: Hogarth Press and the Institute of Psychoanalysis. 1927.
Excerpts in *A General Selection from the Works of Sigmund Freud.* New York: Doubleday Anchor (paperback). pp. 210-235.

Inhibitions, Symptoms and Anxiety. 1926.
Standard Edition, Vol. XX, pp. 87-172.
London: Hogarth Press and the Institute of Psychoanalysis. 1936.
Stamford, Conn.: The Psychoanalytic Institute, 1927.
Under title: "The Problem of Anxiety." New York: Psychoanalytic
Quarterly Press and Norton, 1936.

NOTES ON CHAPTER XI

For critical commentary on the *death instinct*, see E. Jones: *The Life
and Work of Sigmund Freud*, Vol. III (New York: Basic Books, 1957),
pp. 272-80. For evaluations by scientists in physics and biology, see C. R.
Kapp: "Comments on Bernfeld and Feitelberg's 'The Principle of Entropy
and the Death Instinct.'" *International Journal of Psychoanalysis*, XII,
1931, p. 22. C. R. Brun: "Ueber Freud's Hypothese vom Todestrieb,"
Psyche, 1953, pp. 81-111.

On the theory of *aggression*, see particularly H. Hartmann, E. Kris and
R. M. Loewenstein: "Notes on the Theory of Aggression," *Psychoanalytic
Study of the Child*, III and IV, 1949, pp. 9-36. D. Beres: "Clinical Notes
on Aggression in Children," *Ibid.*, VII, 1952, pp. 241-63. M. Brenman:
"On Teasing and Being Teased and the Problem of 'moral masochism,'"
Ibid., VII, 1952, pp. 264-83. The important new concept of *neutralization*
is discussed in E. Kris: "Neutralization and Sublimation: Observations on
Young Children," *Ibid.*, X, 1955, pp. 30-46. Interesting physiological material is found in J. C. Lilly: "The Psychophysiological Basis for Two Kinds
of Instincts," *Journal of the American Psychoanalytic Association*, VIII,
1960, pp. 659-70. For an eclectic survey, see J. P. Scott: *Aggression*
(Chicago: University of Chicago Press, 1958).

For a general review of *ego psychology*, see the introduction by David
Rapaport to E. Erikson: *Identity and the Life Cycle* (*Psychological Is-
sues*, 1959). For an over-all survey of some major conceptual changes in
ego psychology since Freud, see R. R. Holt: "Recent Developments in
Psychoanalytic Ego Psychology and their Implications for Diagnostic
Testing." *Journal of Projective Techniques*, XXIV, 1960, pp. 254-63. An
important re-evaluation of many of Freud's basic ideas is in H. Hartmann,
E. Kris and R. M. Loewenstein: "Comments on the Formation of Psychic
Structure," *Psychoanalytic Study of the Child*, II, 1946, pp. 11-38.

For a recent summary on the *superego* see J. Sandler: "On the Concept
of Superego," *Psychoanalytic Study of the Child*, XV, 1960, pp. 128-62.
Also R. Schafer: "The Loving and Beloved Superego in Freud's Structural
Theory," *Ibid.*, pp. 163-88. Clarification of the relationship between early
childhood and the structural components is offered in H. Hartmann and

E. Kris: "The Genetic Approach in Psychoanalysis," *Ibid.*, I, 1945, pp 11-30.

On the *oral stage* the book which ushered in the post-Freudian concern with the mother-child relationship is Margaret Ribble: *The Rights of Infants* (New York: Columbia, 1943). The epoch-making work of R Spitz is reported in a series of papers in the *Psychoanalytic Study of the Child,* especially I, 1945, II, 1946, III and IV, 1949, V, 1950, and VI 1951. From a clinical point of view, most important observations have come from Melanie Klein and her school; see M. Klein: *Contributions to Psychoanalysis* (London: Hogarth, 1948) and M. Klein: *The Psycho analysis of Children* (London: Hogarth, 1932). For a significant applica tion to psychosis, see J. Rosen: *Direct Analysis* (New York: Grune and Stratton, 1953). Various contemporary points of view are expressed in J. Bowlby: "Grief and Mourning in Infancy and Early Childhood," and discussion by A. Freud, M. Schur and R. A. Spitz, *Psychoanalytic Study of the Child,* XV, 1960, pp. 9-94. A report of an interesting experiment and a summary of the literature is in S. Brody: *Patterns of Mothering* (New York: International Universities Press, 1956).

For later views on the problem of *anxiety* see E. R. Zetzel, "The Concept of Anxiety in Relation to the Development of Psychoanalysis," *Journal of the American Psychoanalytic Association,* III, 1955, pp. 369-88 L. Rangell: "On the Psychoanalytic Theory of Anxiety: A Statement of a Unitary Theory," *Ibid.*, pp. 389-414. J. Flescher: "A Dualistic View point on Anxiety," *Ibid.*, 415-46.

Chapter XII. REVISED VIEWS ON NEUROSIS AND THERAPY

From the vantage point of the ego the problems connected with neurosis now had to be reviewed. To begin with, infantile sexuality becomes only one of several factors. Most weight has to be attached to the ego, the relative strength of which determines the outcome of the inner struggle. Thus the task of analysis becomes the strengthening of the ego. The new formula is: Where the id was the ego shall be, instead of the old: Make the unconscious conscious. The old formula, however, is not discarded: it merely plays a subordinate role.

In the process of therapy part of the ego turns out to be sick, part healthy; the therapist makes a pact, as it were, with the healthy part of the ego and both together proceed against the sick.

Freud can now propose a broader yet more simplified classification of mental illnesses, based on the ego concept. A transference neurosis corresponds to a conflict between the ego and the id; a narcissistic neurosis to that between the ego and the superego; and a psychosis to that between the ego and the superego.[154] Nevertheless, quantitative factors still play a decisive role, so that this scheme, like those of earlier days, is primarily of theoretical value.

Freud's penchant for schematic presentations has obscured the fact that his writings in this period led to a much broader and in a sense entirely new concept of neurosis. In the old id psychology, neurosis was a symptomatic affair of the classical type; it was widespread, but still relatively limited in scope.

In ego psychology, however, the horizons are immeasurably broadened. First, Freud sees the ego as a poor creature owing service to three masters and consequently menaced by three dangers—

from the external world, from the id, and from the superego. Clearly each of these dangers can lead to some anxiety and some dysfunction. It is only the conflict between the ego and the id which leads to the classical forms of neurosis; but the other conflicts leave a person just as neurotic in the larger sense.

Furthermore, it becomes clear that certain superego formations can be neurotic even though they produce no apparent symptoms. In effect an analytical ideal can be set up with which whole civilizations can be compared. While Freud had the vision, it has remained for others to work out the details. It is only through the recognition of this analytic ideal that an increasing awareness of the neurotic character of all previous civilizations has developed over the past few decades.

From the technical point of view, when the ego is drawn into the picture, the task of analysis is seen to be much more complicated. Freud considered the question in "Analysis Terminable and Interminable" (1937). He holds that the results of an analysis depend on three main factors: 1. the relative importance of the traumatic element; 2. the relative strength of the instincts; 3. the modifications of the ego in the defensive conflict. It is only in the first instance that a simple outcome in psychoanalysis can be anticipated, one that involves the strengthening of the ego and the replacement of an inadequate childhood decision by a later correct solution. In the other two instances quantitative factors play a major role, and the question of when an analysis is terminated is a thorny one indeed. By and large the goal now is to produce the best possible conditions for the functioning of the ego. Freud says:

> Our object will be not to rub off all the corners of the human character so as to produce "normality" according to schedule, nor yet to demand that the person who has been "thoroughly analyzed" shall never again feel the stirring of passions in himself or become involved in any internal conflicts. The business of analysis is to secure the best possible psychological condition for the functioning of the ego; when this has been done analysis has accomplished its task.[155]

It was in this paper that he recommended that analysts be reanalyzed every five years. Nowadays many training analyses last more than five years to begin with, which deprives Freud's recommendation of its original force. This is but one of many examples of the great changes which have taken place in psychoanalysis in the past quarter-century.

The problem of the *terminated analysis,* which Freud considered at such length in his 1937 paper, had for a long time been of great concern to analysts and still remains a central issue in today's thought. The historical point at which the problem arose can be stated with precision: when Freud switched from catharsis to psychoanalysis. In the course of the switch new questions arose which still await a final resolution.

Termination rests upon one or more of three concepts, all of which have some historical developments:

1) Removal of symptoms

2) Accessibility to a given technique

3) Growth towards a certain goal which is considered psychologically desirable (mental health, genitality, maturity).

1) The *removal of symptoms* remains essentially unchanged as a goal of analysis. The only difference is that knowledge of symptoms expanded considerably, to a point where today any aspect of the character structure may be considered the equivalent of a symptom. This view can be dated from Freud's 1926 book on anxiety.

2) The *accessibility to a given technique:* In principle this has likewise remained unchanged since the beginning of analysis. The basic technique is free association, and it may be said that a patient is analyzable if he can free associate, while he is not analyzable if he cannot free associate. A slight difficulty arises in that there is no entirely clear-cut definition of free association. Nevertheless for all practical purposes the usual statement about the fundamental rule is quite adequate.

The real problem arises not so much with the ability to free associate as with the effect of the technique on the patient. When it is said that schizophrenics, children or mental defectives cannot be analyzed, this means either that the course of free association will provoke some emotional outburst which is undesirable (schizophrenia) or that the individual cannot grasp the idea (child) or that compliance with the rule produces no essential change because the patient cannot grasp what the situation is all about (mental defective).

3) *Growth towards a certain psychologically desirable goal:* It is this element in the concept of analysis and termination which has in the course of time shown the greatest amount of variability. Clearly the variability is dictated by the concept of what is psychologically desirable, which has changed in many different ways.

If Freud's development is traced, seven different discoveries can be specified which led to correspondingly different demands on the analysis and correspondingly different views of what analyzability is and what termination is. These are: a) dreams; b) childhood memories; c) infantile sexuality; d) transference; e) resistance; f) working-through; g) ego structure.

a) *Dreams:*—As soon as Freud discovered the paramount significance of dreams, a new and essentially indeterminate element was introduced into the process of psychoanalysis. For now the patient could be completely free from symptoms, and yet have dreams which pointed to a variety of underlying problems. Naturally the nature of the "healthy dream life" can scarcely be defined with any great precision. In many cases there seems to be no difference, e.g., between the dreams of relative normals and schizophrenics. The search for a criterion in the dream life led to the concept of the termination dream, which has reappeared at various times in the history of psychoanalysis, although Freud himself never went along with it. By and large the notion that one dream or even one series of dreams can determine with absolute certainty the point at which an analysis should be terminated is one which has never appealed to too many analysts.

b) *Childhood memories:*—In the cathartic period Freud held the view that the release of one specific memory could unravel and cure the whole neurotic structure. To a certain extent he held on to this view when he switched to psychoanalysis. He felt that amnesias should be lifted, especially from the vital childhood period of two to four. In the case of the Wolf Man (see above, p. 128) he persisted for five years until the patient recovered some lost memories from this period which seemed to resolve the whole neurosis. (It may however be noted that the Wolf Man had several breakdowns later, in spite of the recovery of these memories.)

As has been seen above (see p. 102) Freud's emphasis on childhood memories went through several stages. Eventually he came to feel that memories and reconstructions were of equal value. In the course of time, analysts have come to believe that while childhood memories are certainly desirable, their mere recovery does not cure the neurosis. As a result this criterion for termination has also had to be abandoned.

c) *Infantile sexuality:*—Next Freud turned his attention to the sexual material of early childhood which the neurotic had repressed, particularly the Oedipus complex. The demand was made that the patient should overcome his Oedipus. In this process Freud did not hesitate to offer elaborate interpretations to the patient after some material had been produced. However, the resolution of the Oedipus complex remains a quantitative rather than a qualitative question, and obviously can lead to many different outcomes.

d) *Transference:*—Freud must have made the observation that in spite of a rich dream life, recovery of childhood memories and full discussion of infantile sexuality many patients did not get better. With these he assumed then that the transference had to be worked out. In the Case of Dora (see above, p. 119) he took himself to task at the end for not going into the transference. Again however, this is a very fluid idea. When can we say that a transference is really worked out? In the course of the history of psychoanalysis there have been many different points of view on this question. Some have held that the patient should become completely neutral to the analyst; others have held that that goal is impossible. Freud himself never tried to answer the question with any precision.

e) *Resistance:*—Resistance is closely allied to transference and the situation here is similar to that in the previous heading. It may be noted here that the positive transference in the male (to a male analyst) and the negative transference in the female (both of these were at one time referred to as an inverse Oedipus complex) were only worked out by analysts after Freud.

f) *Working through:*—The principle of working through meant that the repetition of interpretations over a period of time was absolutely necessary. The patient cannot be expected to get better as a result of one interpretation. This working through could in more conventional psychological terms be called learning. At the same time, once this equation is made, it becomes clear that just when the patient has learned enough about himself is not something that can be specified with any great sharpness.

g) *Ego structure:*—The complications created by the previous discoveries, all of which belong to the period of id psychology, were great enough; those created by the transition to ego psychology were infinitely greater. This is the topic of the 1937 paper.

The particular ways in which the ego must be reconstructed to allow one to say that the analysis has been properly terminated have engaged the attention of analysts ever since Freud's final paper. It can scarcely be said that there is any real agreement in the field, even among members of the same group. Some writers, for example, stress the capacity for self-analysis, others the resolution of the transference. The characteristics of the healthy ego could in general be said to be freedom to work, freedom to love and freedom from symptoms, but when the attempt is made to define these terms more precisely in individual cases wide disagreement results. In spite of all the discussion since 1937, analysts have not really advanced beyond Freud's fluid position that the object of analysis is to strengthen the ego.

Available English Translations of Freud's Works Cited in Chapter XII.

Neurosis and Psychosis. 1924.
　　Standard Edition, Vol. XIX, pp. 149-153.
　　Collected Papers, Vol. II, pp. 25-254.

The Loss of Reality in Neurosis and Psychosis. 1924.
　　Standard Edition, Vol. XIX, pp. 183-187.
　　Collected Papers, Vol. II, pp. 277-282.

Analysis Terminable and Interminable. 1937.
　　Collected Papers, Vol. V, pp. 316-357.

NOTES ON CHAPTER XII

On the *development of psychoanalytic technique* since Freud two crucial papers are K. Eissler: "The Effect of the Structure of the Ego on

Psychoanalytic Technique," *Journal of the American Psychoanalytic Association*, I, 1953, pp. 104-43. T. S. Szasz: "On the Theory of Psychoanalytic Treatment," *International Journal of Psychoanalysis*, XXXVIII, 1957, pp. 166-82.

A *historical survey* may be found in R. Ekstein: "A Historical Survey on the Teaching of Psychoanalytic Technique," *Journal of the American Psychoanalytic Association*, VIII, 1960, pp. 500-516.

For discussions of the *extension of the classical technique*, see L. Stone, "The Widening Scope of Indications for Psychoanalysis," *Ibid.*, II, 1954, pp. 567-94. R. R. Greenson, moderator: "Variations in Classical Psychoanalytic Technique. Papers by A. M. Loewenstein, M. Bouvet, K. R. Eissler, A. Reich, S. Nacht, H. Rosenfeld," *International Journal of Psychoanalysis*, XXXIX, 1958, pp. 200-42.

For a discussion of *group analysis* see E. K. Schwartz and A. Wolf: "Psychoanalysis in Groups: Some Comparisons with Individual Analysis," *Journal of General Psychology*, LXIV, 1961, pp. 153-91. W. L. Hulse (ed.): *Topical Problems of Psychotherapy* (New York: S. Karger, 1960).

On *child analysis* the two classics remain A. Freud: *The Psychoanalytical Treatment of Children* (London: Imago, 1946) and M. Klein: *The Psychoanalysis of Children* (London: Hogarth, 1932).

For so-called *deviant schools* see especially K. Horney: *New Ways in Psychoanalysis* (New York: Norton, 1939); H. S. Sullivan: *Conceptions of Modern Psychiatry* (Washington: W. A. White Psychiatric Foundation, 1947). S. Rado: *The Psychodynamics of Behavior* (New York: Grune and Stratton, 1956). For a comparison of these with the Freudian approach, see R. Fine: "Psychotherapy: A Freudian Point of View," *Annals of Psychotherapy* (American Academy of Psychotherapists, 1959).

For some recent *empirical investigations*, see L. L. Robbins and R. S. Wallerstein: "The Research Strategy and Tactics of the Psychotherapy Research Project of the Menninger Foundation and the Problem of Controls," *Research in Psychotherapy*, (American Psychological Association, 1958). "The Psychotherapy Research Project of the Menninger Foundation," *Bulletin of the Menninger Clinic*, XXIV, No. 4, July, 1960. A. Z. Pfeffer: "A Procedure for Evaluating the Results of Psychoanalysis: A Preliminary Report," *Journal of the American Psychoanalytic Association*, VII, 1959, pp. 418-44.

See also Notes on Chapter VI.

Chapter XIII. THE STRUCTURE OF SOCIETY

After World War I Freud returned to some of the philosophical issues that had intrigued him in his youth but that he had been forced to put aside. He now attempted to extend his system to the broader problems of civilization.

Freud's views on culture contain a number of profound insights that are still the subject of much controversy. Unfortunately, the commonly drawn dichotomy between the "biological" and the "cultural" positions serves merely to confuse the issues. In order to understand what Freud really had to say it is necessary to follow his development historically. (See above, pp. 82-91.)

It has been argued that Freud generalized too much from the particular type middle-class patients whom he saw, and that sexual repression is confined to the middle classes while sexual release is to be found in the lower classes. Oddly enough, this view was expressed by Freud himself before he became a neurologist. In a letter to his fiancée he says:

> The mob give vent to their impulses, and we deprive ourselves . . . this habit of constant suppression of natural instincts gives us the character of refinement. . . . There is a psychology of the common man which is somewhat different from ours.[156]

This early position was maintained by Freud throughout his analytic career. In the paper " 'Civilized' Sexual Morality and Modern Nervousness," 1908, he wrote:

> . . . the injurious influence of civilization reduces itself in the main to the harmful suppression of the sexual life of civilized peoples [or classes] through the "civilized" sexual morality prevalent in them.[157]

His next observation was a more general one but it applied specifically to Western society only. It was that the incidence of nervousness, neuroticism, and sexual difficulties in general is far more widespread than had been thought. Eventually Freud came to the conclusion that in children, at least those brought up according to middle-class standards, neurosis is of universal occurrence. Even here, however, he does not apply his generalization to all societies.

Freud's first attempt to analyze society as a whole was in the book *Totem and Taboo* (1912-13). The major contribution of this work was the thesis that the emotional development of man displays remarkable similarities in all types of different societies or cultures, to use the word most commonly employed today.

The theme of *Totem and Taboo* was put aside for many years, and Freud returned to it only in the late 1920's. His next work along these lines was *The Future of an Illusion* (1927). Here he examined the nature of religion from a psychological point of view and showed that essentially religion is a version of wishful thinking. In the religious system, the adult returns to the dependent, protected, secure atmosphere of his childhood.

Broader questions were touched upon in his final major work on society, *Civilization and Its Discontents* (1930). By this time his first theory of instincts had already been changed, and he was now working with the dual theory. The older formulations, which related primarily to sexuality, therefore, had to be reconsidered in the light of his present position on the instinctual nature of aggression.

Freud now laid less stress on sexuality and held that aggression "constitutes the most powerful obstacle to culture." [158] In civilized society this aggression is internalized by the procedures of education and results in a heightened sense of guilt. The loss of happiness through such increase in guilt is now the price of progress in civilization. Hence, too, guilt is the most important problem in the evolution of culture.

With regard to the break-through and gratification of the aggressive instinct, Freud took essentially the same position that he had taken earlier with regard to the sexual instinct. Aggression will necessarily break through in all societies, regardless of how the society is built up, and inevitably some measures must be taken to

curb man's instinctual wishes. In a way this is a common-sense
point of view rather than a scientific one. Freud holds on to the old
and obvious belief that barbarians simply gratify their impulses
without inhibitions, while civilized men are required to hold themselves in check.

Nevertheless, there is much more to Freud's thinking than the
belief that sooner or later the instinctual needs will break through
The mere fact that they do come out does not prevent man from
taking the proper measures to adjust to the instinctual demands
just as in the individual situation the person can lead a happy life
even though he is not given full permission to satisfy all of his
impulses. For example, Freud says in *Civilization and Its Dis*
contents:

> If the evolution of civilization has such a far-reaching similarity with
> the development of an individual, and if the same methods are employed
> in both, would not the diagnosis be justified that many systems of civiliza
> tion have become "neurotic" under the pressure of the civilizing trends
> To analytic dissection of these neuroses therapeutic recommendation
> might follow which could claim a practical interest. I would not say that
> such an attempt to apply psychoanalysis to civilized society would be
> fanciful or doomed to fruitlessness. But it behooves us to be very careful
> and not to forget that after all we are dealing only with analogies, and
> that it is dangerous, not only with men but also with concepts, to drag
> them out of the region where they originated and have matured. . . . In
> spite of all these difficulties, we may expect that one day someone will
> venture upon this research into the pathology of civilized communities.[15]

At another point in *Civilization and Its Discontents* he wrote:

> We may expect that in the course of time changes will be carried out
> in our civilization so that it becomes more satisfying to our needs and no
> longer open to the reproaches we have made against it. But perhaps we
> shall also accustom ourselves to the idea that there are certain difficulties
> inherent in the very nature of culture which will not yield to any effort
> at reform.[16]

Thus Freud may be considered to be either pessimistic or optimis
tic about the future of civilization, depending upon one's own point
of view. He himself recognized the possibility that the civilization
of his day could be improved in many different ways, although he

did not spell out the ways in which this could be done, but he also insisted that there were inevitably difficulties to be encountered in the paths of any reform, and that these difficulties would necessarily arise because of man's instinctual nature.

The theoretical question, as to whether the manifestations of any given society are the result of biology or culture, of heredity or environment, Freud always answered by saying that clearly they are a combination of the two. He himself stressed the instincts; this was his original contribution. He always recognized, however, that social institutions can alter the phenomena which would otherwise derive directly from the instincts.

In this respect, there is no real difference among the various "schools." Everyone agrees that human behavior is a result of both innate and environmental factors, and that it depends on the circumstances which are to be emphasized. Thus, for example, Malinowski, who for a long time was cited as having "refuted" Freud, says:

The family is the biological grouping to which all kinship is invariably referred and which determines by rules of descent and inheritance the social status of the offspring. As can be seen, this relation never becomes irrelevant to a man and has constantly to be kept alive. Culture, then, creates a new type of bond for which there is no prototype in the animal kingdom. And as we shall see, in this very creative act, where culture steps beyond instinctive endowment and natural precedent, it also creates serious dangers for man. *Two powerful temptations, the temptation of sex and that of rebellion, arise at the very moment of cultural emancipation from nature. Within the group which is responsible for the first steps in human progress there arise the two main perils of humanity: the tendency to incest and the revolt against authority.* [161]

In sum, Freud cannot be said to have had but one single point of view about the problems of culture. He had many insights, he had many opinions, and a number of these changed in the course of time as his own theoretical system changed.

* Italics mine. Dr. Walter Klink, who has kindly called my attention to this passage, rightly comments that were it not for the style this passage could have been written by Freud.

Available English Translations of Freud's Works Cited in Chapter XIII

The Future of an Illusion. 1927.
  Standard Edition, Vol. XXI, pp. 5-56.
  New York: Liveright, 1928. London: Hogarth Press and the Institute
  for Psychoanalysis. 1928. Garden City, New York: Doubleday Anchor
  (paperback).

Civilization and Its Discontents. 1930.
  Standard Edition, Vol. XXI, pp. 64-145.
  London: Hogarth Press and the Institute of Psychoanalysis. 1930. New
  York: Cape and Smith, 1930. Garden City, New York: Doubleday
  1958. New York: Doubleday Anchor (paperback).

NOTES ON CHAPTER XIII

The general problem of the *relationship between psychoanalysis and society* has been much discussed since Freud's work. For some representative views from a variety of points of view: E. Fromm: *The Sane Society* (New York, Rinehart, 1955) argues for a rational reorganization of society. E. Fromm: *Man for Himself* (New York: Rinehart, 1947), proposes a psychoanalytic ethic. H. Marcuse: *Eros and Civilization* (Boston: Beacon, 1955) attempts to portray a society in which positive feelings can receive full recognition. J. L. Halliday: *Psychosocial Medicine* (New York: Norton, 1948) describes the deterioration of personality under depressing economic conditions.

R. Money-Kyrle: *Psychoanalysis and Politics* (New York: Norton, 1951) is the most prominent of the orthodox psychoanalysts who have devoted their attention to this problem. H. Hartmann: *Psychoanalysis and Moral Values* (New York: International Universities Press, 1960), presents a complex analysis of the problem without attempting any clear-cut conclusions.

N. Brown: *Life Against Death: The Psychoanalytical Meaning of History* (Middletown, Conn.: Wesleyan University Press, 1959) has a one-sided thesis of the type which brings psychoanalysis into disrepute. L. S Feuer: *Psychoanalysis and Ethics* (Springfield, Ill.: C. C. Thomas, 1956) has a well-reasoned attempt to integrate the two fields.

A variety of interesting papers may be found in S. Hook, ed.: *Psychoanalysis, Scientific Method and Philosophy.* (New York: New York University, 1959).

See also Notes on Chapters V and IX.

Chapter XIV. THE PROFESSION
OF PSYCHOANALYSIS

With the end of World War I the number of psychoanalysts increased enormously, and for the first time the question of proper training and preparation for the profession of analyst came to the fore. Two questions were involved: the nature of the training institutes to be set up, and the requirements for admission to these institutes.

The first training institute was set up in Berlin in 1922, and their number quickly grew. With few exceptions, all these training institutes were independent bodies, attached neither to universities nor to medical schools.

Although Freud played no significant personal part in the creation of the institutes, naturally his vision inspired much of what went on. In 1927 he wrote:

A scheme of training for analysts has still to be created. It must include elements from the mental sciences, from psychology, the history of civilization and sociology, as well as from anatomy, biology, and the study of evolution. There is so much to be taught in all this that it is justifiable to omit from the curriculum anything which has no direct bearing on the practice of analysis and only serves indirectly (like any other study) as a training for the intellect and for the powers of observation. It is easy to meet this suggestion by objecting that analytic colleges of this kind do not exist and that I am merely setting up an ideal. An ideal, no doubt. But an ideal which can and must be realized. And in our training institutes, in spite of all their youthful insufficiencies, that realization has already begun.[162]

No institute today has carried out Freud's ideal. The core curriculum includes a personal analysis, engaging in supervised analysis, and the essentials of analytic theory. Beyond that, other elements from Freud's scheme are included in varying degrees.

With regard to the prerequisites for admission to the training program, in practice the question boiled down to whether to require a medical degree or not; the nonmedical practitioner is known as a "lay analyst." In this area Freud held very definite and uncompromising views. He was adamantly opposed to restricting psychoanalysis to physicians and strongly in favor of lay analysis.

In theory, Freud held, psychoanalysis is a branch of psychology and he reaffirmed this position over and over again. In his final statement on the subject, he wrote:

I have assumed, that is to say, that psychoanalysis is not a specialized branch of medicine. I cannot see how it is possible to dispute this. Psychoanalysis falls under the head of psychology; not of medical psychology in the old sense, or of the psychology of morbid processes, but simply of psychology. It is certainly not the whole of psychology, but its substructure and perhaps even its entire foundation. The possibility of its application to medical purposes must not lead us astray. Electricity and radiology also have their medical application, but the science to which they belong is none the less physics.[163]

Since psychoanalysis in theory is a branch of psychology, Freud felt that its restriction to medicine would necessarily hamper it in many ways. Many of his own followers were particularly adamant in opposition to Freud on this point; he referred to their position as a resistance or as an attempt at repression. He maintained that the opposition to lay analysis is "the last mask of the resistance against psychoanalysis, and the most dangerous of all."[164]

The subject was of such importance to Freud that he wrote a whole book on *The Question of Lay Analysis*, which was published in 1926. Here he argued that the inclusion in the therapeutic field of suitable people from walks of life other than the medical was to be welcomed, and proclaimed as a principle that it was a matter of indifference whether intending candidates for psychoanalytic training held a medical degree or not. He did not even think that any kind of academic qualification was necessary for membership. Furthermore, he urged those candidates who asked his advice not to spend years of study in obtaining medical qualifications, but to proceed at once to psychoanalytic work.

With regard to scientific knowledge, he again stressed the broader vision that he had of the range to which psychoanalytic knowledge could be put. He said:

For we do not consider it at all desirable for psychoanalysis to be swallowed up by medicine and to find its last resting-place in a textbook of psychiatry under the heading "Methods of Treatment," alongside of procedures such as hypnotic suggestion, autosuggestion, and persuasion, which, born from our ignorance, have to thank the laziness and cowardice of mankind for their short-lived effects. It deserves a better fate and, it may be hoped, will meet with one. As a "depth psychology," a theory of the mental unconscious, it can become indispensable to all the sciences which are concerned with the evolution of human civilization and its major institutions such as art, religion, and the social order. It has already, in my opinion, afforded these sciences considerable help in solving their problems. But these are only small contributions compared with what might be achieved if historians of civilization, psychologists of religion, philologists, and so on, would agree themselves to handle the new instrument of research which is at their service. The use of analysis for the treatment of the neuroses is only one of its applications; the future will perhaps show that it is not the most important one. In any case, it would be wrong to sacrifice all the other applications to this single one, just because it touches on the circle of medical interests.[165]

Analysis, Freud held, could in the future conceivably be called upon to provide some corrective to the intolerable pressures that civilization puts upon mankind. He even expressed the hope that someday it would occur to some American millionaire to apply part of his fortune to providing analytical schooling for the social workers of his country, and so mobilize a corps, "to turn them into a band of helpers for combating the neuroses of civilization." [166]

Available English Translations of Freud's Works Cited in Chapter XIV.

The Question of Lay Analysis. 1926.
    Standard Edition, Vol. XX, pp. 183-258.
    Under title: "The Question of Lay Analysis: An Introduction to Psychoanalysis." New York: Norton, 1950. London: Imago Publishing Co., 1947.
    Under title: "The Problem of Lay Analyses." New York: Brentano, 1927, pp. 25-186.

NOTES TO CHAPTER XIV

The most thorough survey of the *training programs* of the American Psychoanalytic Association is in B. D. Lewin and H. Ross: *Psychoanalytic Education in the U.S.* (New York: Norton, 1960). The best summary of training programs in all forms of psychotherapy is G. Blanck: *Education for Psychotherapy* (New York: Institute for Psychoanalytic Training and Research, 1962).

On the issue of *lay analysis,* see the symposium in the *International Journal of Psychoanalysis,* VIII, 1927, pp. 174-283. For the best recent statement on the subject, see T. S. Szasz: "Psychiatry, Psychotherapy and Psychology," *AMA Archives of General Psychiatry,* I, 1959, pp. 455-63.

The general *need for trained analysts and psychotherapists* is highlighted in *Joint Commission on Mental Illness and Health: Action for Mental Health* (New York: Basic Books, 1961).

Training procedures in analytic institutes are under continual scrutiny. For some recent discussions of training problems, see R. Ekstein, reporter: "The Teaching of Psychoanalytic Technique," *Journal of the American Psychoanalytic Association,* VIII, 1960, pp. 167-74. P. Sloane, reporter: "The Technique of Supervised Analysis," *Ibid.,* V, 1957, pp. 539-47. H. W. Loewald: "Psychoanalytic Curricula—Principles and Structure," *Ibid.,* IV, 1956, pp. 149-61.

Among those who have pressed for far-reaching changes in the training of the analyst Kubie has been most prominent. See L. S. Kubie: "Psychoanalytic Training," Chapter XXII in his *Practical and Theoretical Aspects of Psychoanalysis.* (New York: International Universities Press, 1950). L. S. Kubie: "Medical Responsibility for Training in Clinical Psychology," *Journal of the Association of American Medical Colleges,* VIII, 1948, pp. 1-8. L. S. Kubie: "Problems of Psychoanalytic Training," *Bulletin of the American Psychoanalytic Association,* IV, 1948, pp. 29-36. L. S. Kubie: "The Independent Institute," *Ibid.,* VIII, 8, 1952, pp. 205-8. L. S. Kubie: "A Program of Training in Psychiatry to Break the Bottleneck in Rehabilitation," *American Journal of Orthopsychiatry,* XVI, 1946, pp. 447-54.

A program for psychologists similar to Kubie's for psychoanalysts is proposed in R. Fine: "Pre-Doctoral Training in Psychotherapy," *Proceedings of New York State Psychological Association* (New York, 1960), pp. 16-19.

A useful *interdisciplinary report* is E. A. Rubenstein and M. Parloff (eds.): *Research in Psychotherapy* (American Psychological Association, 1958).

Chapter XV. FREUD'S MAJOR WORKS FROM 1914 TO 1939

As time went on, Freud's writings became to a certain extent less thorough and less systematic. The first major contribution to psychoanalysis, the *Interpretation of Dreams,* has never had to be altered in its essentials. The *Three Essays on Sexuality* remains correct as far as it goes, but has had to be considerably enlarged. *Totem and Taboo* was based on a complete mastery of the best available anthropological literature of the day. The case histories have still never been equalled by any other analyst in a comparable collection.

From 1914 on, however, Freud began to throw out many ideas and make many suggestions which he did not elaborate. Most of them have been examined further by his followers. In many cases he goes beyond his previous views or contradicts them without saying so in so many words. This part of the history of Freud's development is therefore much harder to grasp.

The general description of ego psychology given above derives in each case from a number of Freud's books. Titles are no longer so revealing. *The Ego and the Id,* for example, deals mainly with the superego, while *The Problem of Anxiety* has the most detailed analysis of the defense mechanisms. *Civilization and Its Discontents* unexpectedly attempts a revision of some theoretical formulations regarding hostility. It is almost as though in every new publication Freud changed his mind on essential points. He himself recognized what was happening as a result of this continual stream of new ideas. Kardiner reports that at one meeting of the Vienna Psychoanalytic Society in the early 1920's the members had been quoting

Freud on this or that point for some time. Finally Freud grew impatient and said:

Gentlemen, you do me a great dishonor. Why do you already treat me as if I were dead? Here you are debating among each other what I had said, and I sit at the head of the table, and not one of you thinks of asking me, "What do you think now?" If this is the way you treat me while I am still alive, I can well imagine what will happen when I am really dead.[167]

The later Freud is much less well known than the earlier both to the general public and to the profession. His works are more difficult to understand, they deal with more technical topics, they are not so easy to sum up in simple formulas.

For all these reasons it seems worth while to present in more detail the gist of his later writings. Only the most important, of course, can be dealt with, but these treat all the vital questions which are involved in an understanding of Freud's ego psychology.

ON NARCISSISM: AN INTRODUCTION (1914) *

The paper on narcissism is one of the most important in Freud's works. It represents a turning point in his views, the first systematic shift from id psychology to ego psychology. At the same time, it involves an extension and alteration of the entire libido theory.

The essential, new points in the paper are the following:

1. It describes libido as a quantitatively variable force, the transformations of which explain the manifestations of psychosexuality. This is the *libido theory proper,* which Freud took over from the present paper and included under that heading in all the later editions of the *Three Essays* (see above, p. 77). As noted above, a number of other hypotheses are also subsumed under the libido theory (see pp. 82-91).

2. It contains the first systematic description of the development of *object choice.* This too was later incorporated into the *Three Essays* (see p. 67).

---

* Standard Edition, Vol. XIV, pp. 73-102. For further references see Notes on Chapter Y.

3. It establishes the various meanings of "narcissism," a most useful clinical concept.

4. It makes it possible to speak of the "narcissistic neuroses," in which the patient is unable to establish a relationship with the analyst, in contrast to the transference neuroses, in which he does establish such a relationship. This represents a new classification of mental illness based on the therapeutic reaction.

5. It introduces the concept of the ego-ideal, which was later to become the superego.

At first sight, the paper makes rather difficult reading, and it has led to a good deal of confusion in the literature. When it first appeared, Jones described it as "disturbing." If it is examined more closely, a consistent logical argument appears throughout it. However, it was written at the same time as the polemical paper on "The History of the Psychoanalytical Movement," when Freud was "fuming with rage" because of the secessions of Adler and Jung. That is the reason he now digresses into several side discussions, which today seem essentially irrelevant; he is refuting his former adherents. These side discussions tend to obscure his main points.

The title indicates the main focus of the paper: narcissism or self-love, a topic which had heretofore never been fully considered in the psychoanalytic literature. Freud hopes that the investigation of narcissism will lead to greater clarification of schizophrenia, or of what he preferred to call the paraphrenic disorders.

The schizophrenic is characterized by two things: 1) the turning away of his libido from the external world, and 2) megalomania. This megalomania can be understood as an excessive investment of the ego with libido. Thus, the libido, which ordinarily turns to objects, or other people, in the schizophrenic is turned in upon himself.

This leads Freud to a revision of the libido theory. He now distinguishes ego-libido from object-libido, or love of oneself from love of other people. Ego-libido was previously concealed from his attention because it cannot be observed in its initial form; it can be seen only in terms of the relationship to objects. The original ego-libido is equivalent to a *primary narcissism* in which the person takes himself as a love object. This primary narcissism comes at the stage of pure autoerotism in which there is no object at all. At later stages, the ego-libido goes out to external objects, and then some of this libido may return to the ego; this creates *secondary narcissism*. Essentially, narcissism is now defined as the libidinal complement of the egoistic part of the self-preservative instinct.

If the ego has a libidinal component, then the previous distinction between the sexual instincts and the libidinal instincts, in which the sexual instincts are characterized by libidinal cathexis, while the ego instincts are characterized by rational self-preservative behavior, no longer holds. From now on, Freud saw the essential distinction as that between ego-libido and object-libido.

In this way, the most direct observations on narcissism were incorporated into a libido theory which had had to be revised for that purpose.

Freud then turns his attention to an attempt to understand narcissism as it appears in other ways. He tries to investigate narcissism through three approaches: 1) organic disease; 2) hypochondria; 3) the erotic life of the sexes.

In organic illness, the patient withdraws his libidinal cathexes back upon his own ego, and sends them out again when he recovers. Hypochondria, like organic disease, has the same effect on the distribution of the libido; the major difference is that whereas in an organic illness there is a real disturbance, in hypochondria there is not. Freud stated that he was inclined to class hypochondria as an "actual" neurosis (see p. 14).

In the discussion of the erotic life of the sexes, he, for the first time, considers systematically the choice of object, or the way in which the individual reaches other people. He distinguishes two main early types of object choice: the narcissistic, in which the person chooses somebody who is like himself, and the anaclitic, in which he chooses somebody on whom he can lean. Complete object love of the attachment type is, properly speaking, characteristic of the male. By contrast, in women it is primarily themselves that they love, with an intensity comparable to that of the man's love for them. In terms of narcissism, the man transfers his narcissism to the woman in the love relationship, while the woman maintains her own narcissism unchanged. The man therefore seeks to love, while the woman seeks to be loved. Of course, Freud recognizes this as only a schematic description of events, and one that frequently is violated in actual practice.

In the third section he considers the vicissitudes of narcissism in the development of the normal individual. He finds that one person sets up an ideal in himself by which he measures his actual ego, while another has set up no such ideal. The ideal ego, or the ego-ideal, is now the target of the self-love which was abandoned in childhood.

Once the difference between the ego and the ego-ideal is recognized, it is an obvious step to consider the nature of the person's opinions of himself. Freud observes that there may very well be a special psychical agency that sees to it that narcissistic satisfaction from the ego-ideal is assured, and that, for this purpose, constantly observes the actual ego and measures it by that ideal. Such an agency can easily be recognized as what is ordinarily called "conscience," by means of which a person continually judges whether he is living up to the standards that he has set for himself. Conscience derives first from parental criticism, and subsequently from society.

Freud concludes with some interesting but unsystematic observations on the self-regarding attitude and the ego-ideal. He considers that a truly happy love corresponds to the primal condition in which object-libido and ego-libido cannot be distinguished. One part of self-regard is primary, the residual of infantile narcissism; another part arises out of the fulfillment of the ego-ideal; a third part proceeds from the gratification of object-libido.

A number of the points that he makes here were taken up again in later publications; for instance, the observation that the ego-ideal opens up an important avenue for the understanding of group psychology was elaborated in the book *Group Psychology and the Analysis of the Ego*.

After this first revision of his libido theory, Freud revised it once more. There were some small changes in the paper on "Instincts and Their Vicissitudes" the following year. A major change came about with the introduction of the dual-instinct theory in 1920, in the book *Beyond the Pleasure Principle* (see pages 174-179). He then went on to build up the tripartite theory of the personality—id, ego and superego—in *The Ego and the Id* in 1923. In the course of all this development Freud was more interested in throwing out new ideas than in co-ordinating all the old ones. As a result, the earlier thoughts on narcissism, as embodied in this paper, were never adequately incorporated into his later thinking. This has led to what is generally recognized as a certain amount of confusion among psychologists and psychoanalysts regarding the concept

MOURNING AND MELANCHOLIA (1917) *

Like the earlier paper "On Narcissism," this is one of the building blocks out of which the whole theory of ego psychology emerged It is significant in three respects. First, Freud devoted a paper to the clinical problem of depression or melancholia. Second, in it he undertook an extended discussion of the concept of *identification* which had previously been merely alluded to in passing. And third, through the idea of identification, a change in the content of the unconscious was brought about, which allowed for unconscious persons as well as unconscious ideas or affects, and thus paved the way for the later and more solid idea of the superego.

The paper was part of Freud's book on the transference neuroses of which, as has been mentioned, only five of the twelve chapters were preserved. It was written in 1915, but because of war conditions was not published until 1917.

In the psychoanalytic literature, the writer who had devoted most attention to the problem of depression before this was Abraham.[168] Kraepelinian psychiatry had described manic-depressive psychosis as the benign or circular psychosis, with alternating moods of depression and mania. The psychotic episodes were preceded and followed by so-called free intervals, in which the patient was supposed to be normal. From a psychological point of view it made little sense that a person could be psychotic one day and normal the next. Abraham, in investigating these patients more

* Standard Edition, Vol. XIV, pp. 243-58. For further references see Notes on Chapter XI.

thoroughly, was able to show that the so-called normality was merely an obsessional neurosis that was temporarily under control. Abraham also showed the connection between the depression and the oral phase.

The differences between Freud and Abraham are interesting from the point of view of developmental history. In retrospect, it could be said that Abraham took the libido theory too literally, while Freud felt freer to make changes in it as he thought the occasion required—and this was one of the occasions. Thus, Abraham stressed the libidinal manifestations, while Freud stressed the characterological manifestations which would today be called the interpersonal.

As a matter of fact, Freud sent a copy of the paper to Abraham before publication, and the latter suggested that the oral factor played the part in melancholia that anal erotism does in the obsessional neurosis. To this Freud replied:

Your comments on melancholia I found very valuable. I have unhesitatingly incorporated in my essay what I found useful. The most valuable point was your remark about the oral phase of the libido; the connection you had made between mourning and melancholia is also mentioned. Your request for criticism was easy to fulfill; I was very pleased with everything you wrote. I will only lay stress on two points: that you do not emphasize enough the essential part of my hypothesis, that is, the topographical considerations in it, the regression of the libido, and the abandoning of the unconscious cathexis, and that instead you put sadism and anal erotism in the foreground as the final explanation. Although you are correct in that, you pass by the real explanation. Anal erotism, castration complexes etc., are ubiquitous sources of excitation which must have their share in *every* clinical picture. One time this is made from them, another time that. Naturally, we have the task of ascertaining what is made from them, but the explanation of the disorder can only be found in the mechanism, considered dynamically, topographically, and economically.[169]

Freud looked upon melancholia or depression as a symptom rather than as an illness in its own right. He even allowed for the possibility that an organic factor accounted for some of its manifestations. Nevertheless, he thought that there was enough of a psychological factor to require an explanation.

As the title implies, Freud's argument, which is a masterpiece of logic, proceeds from the parallel between the two states of mourning and of melancholia. Mourning occurs when some person or substitute for a person dear to the individual dies. In melancholia, there is no such apparent death or total loss. Furthermore, in melancholia the patient covers himself with a variety of self-depreciatory attacks, a factor which is absent in normal mourning.

The first parallel readily leads to the assumption that the depressive is reacting to some internalized object or person, in the same way that the mourner is reacting to the real loss of an object. Freud reconstructed the process in this way: There is an attachment to some particular person. Then, owing to some disappointment from this person, the relationship is shattered. Normally, an individual who is denied love by another will simply give up the other person, and try somewhere else. Not so the depressive. The depressed person maintains the attachment, but since he cannot maintain the relationship he incorporates the other person into his ego and continues the relationship there on an internal level. Thus an identification of the ego with the abandoned object is established.

This leads to the second difference between mourning and melancholia: the presence of powerful self-reproaches, torments, and suicidal ideas in melancholia. This can be understood in terms of the vicissitudes of sadism. Freud assumes that the person regresses or falls back to an ambivalent stage, in which sadism, as in the obsessional neuroses, becomes more important than love. This sadism now comes into operation on the substitutive internalized object, abusing it, debasing it, making it suffer, and deriving sadistic gratification from its suffering. By self-punishment, the patient takes revenge on the original object and gets even with the loved one who denied him the love which he craved.

The connection between melancholia and mania, and the alternation of the two states, had been noted by many observers. Freud tries to explain this alternation in terms of the theory which he had built up, but feels that he does not succeed. He notes that in mania the ego seems to be experiencing a sense of triumph, but he is unable to explain the connection between this sense of triumph and the whole depressive state. Later, he came back to this problem and solved it satisfactorily in terms of the superego. In depression the superego punishes the ego, while in mania the ego fuses with the superego and experiences a sense of triumph. Freud likened the processes to the feast and famine practices of primitive peoples: mania is the feast after the preceding famine.

Identification is the earliest type of relationship to an object. It is the first way in which the ego picks out an object, and is expressed in ambivalent fashion. Inasmuch as this choice occurs at the oral or cannibalistic stage of libidinal development, the ego wants to incorporate this object into itself and to devour it. In the normal course of development, the individual outgrows this type of identification, and moves on to different kinds of object-choice and different types of relationships to other people. When object-love is frustrated, the person then regresses to this earlier type of narcissistic identification. This is the process followed in depression and in fact in all the so-called narcissistic disorders. The general formula which is repeated over and over again in Freud's writings for the next few years is: Object cathexes regress to identifications. In other words, the identifications which are seen in the depressive, schizophrenic, or paranoid individual are not the result of a healthy sense of admiration for the parent or other persons, but are the consequence of a frustration in love at the hands of people who are significant for the individual.

The third point relates to the contents of the unconscious. If the object can be incorporated into the ego, and an identification can take place in this way, then the concept of the contents of the unconscious is broadened beyond what it was in the earlier stage. Eventually, this leads to the concept of a superego, which is the internalized representation of the parents.

Inasmuch as Freud had in the paper "On Narcissism," published a short time before, introduced the concept of the ego-ideal, it is not at all clear why he does not apply this concept in the present paper to explain some of the manifestations of depression. Later, he himself provided the formula which is the more common one today, namely that in depression the superego punishes the ego, in much the same way that the parents punish the child in childhood. There is in fact a sado-masochistic conflict between the superego and the ego. In this paper, Freud only pointed to one part of this conflict, that in which the ego rebels and fights against the superego. Apparently, Freud did not feel as yet that he could speak of an ego-ideal in depression. In a letter to Jones on October 27, 1918, he speaks of the conflict between two ego-ideals in the traumatic war neuroses. He notes a certain parallelism with melancholia, where also a new ego has been instituted, but no ideal—merely a new ego on the basis of an object-cathexis that has been abandoned.[170]

Although it has been amended in a number of respects in the course of time, Freud's initial paper on depression remains one of the foundation stones of present-day thinking on the subject.

BEYOND THE PLEASURE PRINCIPLE (1920)*

Beyond the Pleasure Principle is the last and final revision of the theory of instincts. It has already been considered in some details above (see pages 174-179) and no further comments need be added here.

GROUP PSYCHOLOGY AND THE ANALYSIS OF THE EGO (1921) †

Group Psychology and the Analysis of the Ego is Freud's major contribution to social psychology. It is likewise a major step toward the formation of ego psychology. The book is extremely rich in insights and fruitful suggestions, and portrays Freud at his best.

Those who have considered Freud exclusively an instinct theorist will be surprised to learn that he himself never disregarded the relationships of persons to other people. In fact, he always considered psychoanalysis the basis of both individual and social psychology, and could see no really logical difference between the two.

Nevertheless, it is a fact of common observation that the individual when he is in a group appears in many cases to be quite different from the same individual in another group or in an in-

---

* Standard Edition, Vol. XVIII, pp. 7-64. For further references see Note on Chapter XI.

† Standard Edition, Vol. XVIII, pp. 69-143. For further references see Note on Chapter XI.

dividual situation. How this difference comes about, and what it means, is a subject for research.

He proceeds to consider the literature on the subject. He begins with the famous book by Le Bon, *The Psychology of Crowds* (1895). Le Bon points to the similarity of group behavior with the mental lives of primitive people and children. Freud quotes other authorities, some of them in agreement and some of them in disagreement with Le Bon. In general, most authorities looked upon the group as a situation in which the individual could permit himself to regress; he was accordingly in that situation irresponsible, unrepressed, affective rather than intellectual, and, in general, was operating on the level of the child. Only McDougall had pointed out that there were many different kinds of groups, and that the relationship of the individual to the group, and the behavior of the individual in that particular group depended to a considerable extent on the organization of the particular group.

In general Freud is in agreement with such accounts, but he feels that psychoanalysis has something essential to add. This something comes from the libido theory. It is a natural consequence of the libido theory that the essence of the group-mind consists of love relationships, or libidinal ties, or, to use a more neutral expression, emotional ties. In general, previous authorities had made no mention of any such libidinal ties. Freud therefore undertakes to examine what these could be.

As a first approach, he considers two artificial groups: the church and the army. There are many different bases on which groups can be distinguished. Freud chooses to distinguish those with leaders from those without leaders. This emphasis on the role of leader and *leadership*, is one of Freud's major contributions in this work, an idea that before him was generally disregarded and that has frequently been omitted subsequently, despite his work.

He examines the role of the leader in the army and the church. In both, the leader is supposed to love all his subordinates equally, giving them a feeling of equality in his eyes. This, of course, is reminiscent of the situation of the father in the family. The major difference between the army and the church lies in the fact that the army is held together by discipline, while the church is held together by an abstract idea. Naturally, Freud realizes that this is an oversimplification, that abstract ideas play a role in the army also, while discipline, likewise, also has its part in the church. The difference, however, is significant when the leader is lost. In the army, the loss of a leader leads to panic. Leaderless soldiers, for instance, may collapse in the face of dangers which otherwise they would surmount without any difficulty. In the church, on the other hand, the loss of a leader, or the dissolution of a church situation, leads to the release of hostility. Thus, Freud observes that every religious group loves its believers and is intolerant to its enemies, with the result that when the love for the believers is no longer feasible, the hatred for the enemies becomes prominent.

The phenomena of obedience to the leader and of equality in the group require some explanation. All human relationships are governed by ambivalence; how is this ambivalence overcome in a group? It is clear that it cannot be owing to sexual reasons. Perhaps Freud says, it is related to the state of being in love, and perhaps also it is related to the difficult problem of identifications.

In the chapter on identification (Chapter VII) Freud makes a major step forward in theory. Identification, as he has already shown is the earliest expression of an emotional tie with another person Thus, in the boy, identification with the father and sexual desir for the mother for a while coincide without antagonism. Then, the Oedipus complex arises, and these two feelings clash, leading to marked ambivalence. However, the identification, which is a derivative of the oral phase, is ambivalent from the beginning.

Freud recalls the statement he made in *Mourning and Melancholia* that identification appears instead of object-choice, and that object-choice regresses to identification. Pulling all the various statements together, Freud now states that there are three forms of identification: (1) the original form of an emotional tie with an object; (2) in a regressive way identification becomes a substitute for a libidinal object-tie, so to speak, by means of introjection of the object into the ego; and (3) identification may arise with any new perception of a common quality shared with some other person who is not an object of the sexual instinct.

The hypothesis now begins to emerge, that the major libidin

tie between members of a group is in the nature of an identification based upon an important common emotional quality, that is, the third type of identification enumerated above. Freud suggests that this important common quality lies in the nature of the tie with a leader.

He then distinguishes two other forms of identification. In the male homosexual in puberty, the boy identifies himself with his mother, and then relates to other boys in the way that he would like to have had his mother relate to him. This is a form of identification which involves introjection of the lost object into the ego; thus, the homosexual man introjects the mother, and behaves as if he were the mother. The second type of identification which is significant is that in depression, which had already been discussed in the earlier paper. Here Freud singles out especially the fact that depression shows the ego divided into two parts, one of which rages against the second.

In the next section, he takes up being in love and hypnosis. This is one of the many passages in which Freud considered the concept of love in greater detail; as always, he is talking about love as he observes it, and not as it might be ideally.

The simplest case of love is common sensual love. Later, sensual desire is separated from love by the size of the share taken by the aim-inhibited instincts of affection. In this process arises a sexual re-evaluation and idealization of the object—the object is being treated like the person's ego. The object may consume the ego entirely, especially if the love is unhappy. (For example, where a man debases himself or even commits suicide because of an unsatisfactory or unrequited love.) At the same time, in this kind of love, all the functions allotted to the ego-ideal cease to operate with regard to the love-object. The object has been put in the place of the ego-ideal, for example, where the man treats the woman as if she were his ego-ideal.

To distinguish between identification and being in love, it must be ascertained whether the object is put in the place of the ego or of the ego-ideal. In identification, there is an equation of the subject (the other person) and the ego, that is, of the other person and oneself, while in being in love there is an equation of the object and the ego-ideal.

Furthermore, being in love and hypnosis are similar in many respects. The hypnotist has stepped into the place of the subject's ego-ideal. In hypnosis sex is excluded, while in love it is only temporarily held back. The hypnotic relationship can be looked upon as a group of two. This leads to an observation about group formation: inhibited sexual impulses bind people, while gratification tends to sever them. Nevertheless, there are many unanswered questions about hypnosis, such as the manner in which it is produced, its relation to sleep, and still other questions which preclude looking upon hypnosis as an automatic explanation of the problem of the group.

These various considerations allow Freud to lay down the fundamental formula for the group in terms of the libidinal ties between the members of the group, and between the members and the leader. He says that a primary group is a number of individuals who have put one and the same object in the place of their ego-ideal, and have consequently identified themselves with one another in their ego.

In the next two chapters Freud takes up some instinctual and historical considerations. He examines Trotter's idea of an irreducible herd instinct, and rejects it. Trotter, like other writers, pays too little attention to the leader. If the situation is examined genetically, the infant's earliest fear is of the loss of the mother, not of detachment from the herd. Later on, in the family, social feeling derives from envy. This reversal of envy, a negative feeling, into positively toned social feeling occurs under the influence of a common affectionate tie with the parents, and this, in general, occurs in other groups as well.

The nature of the herd instinct is thus reduced to the observation that the family is the basis of human cultural living. As Freud puts it, man is a "horde" animal, not a "herd" animal.

This leads him back to one of his favorite topics, which he has earlier developed in *Totem and Taboo,* that is, the primal horde. Here Freud uses it only in the sense in which Darwin had, as the original type of human family. In this horde, the primal father is the group-ideal which governs the ego in the place of the ego-ideal. A similar type of constellation may be found in many groups.

In the final chapter, entitled "A Differentiating Grade in the Ego," Freud comes to his main theoretical conclusion. He notes that in groups, the individual gives up his own ego-ideal, and substitutes for it the group-ideal of the leader. Of this, of course, the individual is not conscious. Consequently the suggestion arises that there is a process of internalization, what Freud calls a differentiating grade in the ego. The ego now enters into the relation of an object to the ego-ideal, which has been developed out of it, and all the interplay between the external object and the ego as a whole, which has become so familiar from the study of neuroses, may conceivably be repeated within the ego. This first hesitant statement of Freud's later becomes more definite in terms of the internalization of an ego-ideal, which two years later he renamed the superego.

The concept of the ego-ideal is already useful in that it allows Freud to explain the alternation of mania and depression, an explanation, which as has been noted (see above, pages 212-213) had eluded him in the paper on *Mourning and Melancholia*. In *mania*, the ego and the ego-ideal have fused, so that the person in a mood of triumph and self-satisfaction enjoys the abolition of his inhibitions, his concern for others, and his self-torments. On the other hand, the misery of the depressive is the expression of a sharp conflict between the two aspects of the ego, a conflict in which the ego-ideal relentlessly punishes and condemns the ego.

For a long time Freud's contribution to social psychology was virtually ignored.[171] After World War II the situation changed, however, and it became increasingly clear how important Freud could be to the social psychologist. In fact, Krech wrote in 1951:

... it is obvious that much of the current vitality of social psychological theory is due to the influence of psychoanalysis and of those social psychologists trained in, and familiar with, the concepts of psychoanalysis.[172]

However, the acceptance of psychoanalysis by the social psychologist and sociologist has most often been limited to the neoFreudian point of view, which underplays the libidinal-biological elements in human nature.[173] Thus the essential points made by Freud in the present book, on the role of libidinal ties in the formation of groups, the importance of the leader, and the significance of the superego in group behavior have as yet found little application in social psychological theory. Dennis H. Wrong has stated the issues very succinctly:

... there is a difference between the Freudian view on the one hand and both sociological and neo-Freudian conceptions of man on the other. To Freud man is a *social* animal without being entirely a *socialized* animal. His very social nature is the source of conflicts and antagonisms that create resistance to socialization by the norms of any of the societies which have existed in the course of human history.

"Socialization" may mean two quite distinct things; when they are confused an oversocialized view of man is the result. On the one hand socialization means the "transmission of the culture," the particular culture of the society an individual enters at birth; on the other hand the term is used to mean "the process of becoming human," of acquiring uniquely human attributes from interaction with others. All men are socialized in the latter sense, but this does not mean that they have been completely molded by the particular norms and values of their culture. All cultures, as Freud contended, do violence to man's socialized bodily drives but this in no sense means that men could possibly exist without culture or independently of society.[174]

THE EGO AND THE ID. (1923)[*]

It was in this book that the first systematic exposition of Freud's tripartite theory of personality, id, ego, and superego, was contained. Actually, the work concerns itself more with the superego than with the ego; the fullest analysis of the ego in Freud is in the later work, *Inhibitions, Symptoms, and Anxiety* (1926).

As so often, Freud begins with metapsychological considerations. While initially he had assumed that the unconscious and the repressed were synonymous, as time went on he came to see that the unconscious contained more than the repressed. For example, clinical experience shows that the patient resists interpretations ever

[*] Standard Edition, Vol. XIX, pp. 12-66. For further references see Notes on Chapter XI.

though he is totally unconscious of his resistance. Since this resistance stems from the ego, it is clear that part of the ego is unconscious. But if the ego is unconscious, in the old formulation of repression, it would be necessary now to say that one unconscious aspect of the mind is repressing another. This is confusing. Accordingly, Freud felt that he had to substitute for the old antithesis a new one, namely an antithesis between the organized ego and what is repressed and dissociated from it.

In the next chapter Freud picks up the question of how the unconscious becomes conscious. Here he recapitulates his familiar position that this happens through the intermediary of the preconscious. This preconscious, together with the perceptual system (Pcpt), forms the ego.

Now Freud falls back on the terminology of Groddeck, who had said that we are lived by unknown and uncontrollable forces, and who proposed to differentiate id and ego. The ego here is defined as that part of the id which has been modified by the direct influence of the external world, acting through perception and consciousness. This ego has the task of substituting the reality principle for the pleasure principle which reigned supreme in the id. In the ego, perception plays the part which, in the id, devolves upon instinct. The ego thus represents what are called reason and sanity, in contrast to the id, which contains the passions.

In the chapter on the ego and the superego, Freud takes up his old concept of the ego-ideal, and now rechristens it the superego; these two terms are here, and for some time, used synonymously. The superego is less closely connected with consciousness than the rest of the ego.

Freud returns once again to the proposition which he had laid down in the consideration of depression, namely that object-cathexes, or attachments to other people, regress to identifications. He now feels that this is a much more general process than he had considered it before, and sees it as quite common and typical. Thus, when a child's attachments are frustrated, he incorporates the frustrating object into his ego. It follows then that the character of the ego is a precipitate of abandoned object-cathexes and that it contains a record of past object-choices. In the light of this process of internalization the effects of the early identifications in childhood are of necessity profound and lasting.

When these identifications are examined more closely, it appears that the Oedipus complex is more complicated than had originally been thought. Freud, as has been indicated, now recognizes a more complete Oedipus complex, which is twofold—positive and negative, and which is due to the bisexuality originally present in children, so that in this complete Oedipus complex there are both positive and negative feelings toward both parents. This complete Oedipus complex he regards as an especially necessary assumption in the case of neurosis.

The Oedipus complex is resolved or outgrown by the formation of the superego.

Freud considers that the superego retains primarily the character of the father; this is true of both sexes. In this respect his feeling that conflict starts essentially from the Oedipal situation plays an important role. Today it would generally be recognized that some of the superego, in many cases the major portion of it, comes from the mother as well.

The superego is the higher nature of man. The power of authority becomes internalized and invested in the superego. The tension between the superego and the actual attainments of the ego is experienced as a sense of guilt. Social feelings rest upon a superego which is shared by a number of people in a group.

In the next chapter, on the two classes of instinct, Freud comes back to the considerations which he had set forth in *Beyond the Pleasure Principle*. There, he had already said that the death instinct was hard to recognize in its clinical manifestations; the only representative he had been able to point to was sadism. Now he pushes his speculations further. He states that both instincts would be active in every particle of living substance, although in unequal proportions, so that some one substance might be the principal representative of Eros. In the light of the new hypotheses it must necessarily be that the two instincts are fused and blended in a variety of ways, but how this takes place is beyond man's present knowledge. All Freud can point to is some kind of instinctual fusion and de-fusion. Clinically, a de-fusion and the marked emergence of the death instinct (hyperaccentuation of sadism) are among the most noteworthy effects of many severe neuroses, for example, the obsessional neurosis. Ambivalence probably represents a state of incomplete fusion.

Further speculation on the love-hate polarity leads Freud to the assumption, which has been very significant in the subsequent analytic literature, that there exists in the mind a displaceable energy, which is in itself neutral, but which is able to join forces with a neurotic or a destructive impulse, and augment its total cathexis. This neutral displaceable energy, which is probably active both in the ego and in the id, is desexualized Eros, that is, it proceeds from the narcissistic reservoir of libido. From this it can easily be assumed that this displaceable libido is employed in the service of the pleasure principle to obviate accumulations of energy and to facilitate discharge. A certain indifference exists about the manner in which the discharge takes place.

This allows Freud to come to a new view of sublimation. The displaceable energy or desexualized libido can also be described as sublimated energy. Sublimation is now viewed as taking place regularly through the mediation of the ego.

In the final chapter of the book, on the subordinate relationships of the ego, Freud addresses himself principally to the question of the superego. The superego is always in close touch with the id, and can act as its representative in relation to the ego. It reaches deep down into the id, and for that reason is further from consciousness than the ego.

With the concept of the superego certain clinical phenomena can now be better understood. Some patients in analysis exhibit the so-called *negative therapeutic reaction*. This means that even though they grasp every explanation offered to them, tying up their symptoms with the libidinal sources, they continue to get worse in analysis rather than better. With the old id concepts, this phenomenon remained a mystery. With the new, structural concepts, this can be understood as a sense of guilt which is finding atonement in the illness, and is refusing to give up the penalty of suffering. Guilt can now be explained as the punishment by the ego-ideal or superego.

This leads Freud on to a discussion of the whole problem of guilt, to which he had previously not had occasion to pay much attention. In the normal person, guilt is due to tension between the ego and ego-ideal. In two common neuroses the sense of guilt is excessively strong, that is, in obsessional neurosis and in depression. It is also possible for the sense of guilt to be unconscious, as in hysteria.

Guilt may also be related to criminality. Some people, with an exaggeration of the unconscious sense of guilt, then commit crimes in order to be punished. It is as though it is a relief to be able to fasten the unconscious sense of guilt on to something real and immediate. Freud had already considered this problem from another point of view in his paper "Some Character Types Met with in Psychoanalytic Work" (1915).

The harshness of the superego in these and other cases indicates that it is intimately tied up with the sadistic and destructive components. The more a man controls his aggressiveness, the more intense become the aggressive tendencies of his ego-ideal against his ego. It is like a turning round upon the self.

Finally, Freud briefly mentions some other points which he followed up later, especially in *Inhibitions, Symptoms and Anxiety*. The ego, he says, is a poor creature, owing service to three masters, and consequently menaced by three individual dangers—from the external world, from the id, and from the severity of the superego. A different type of anxiety corresponds to each of these three dangers, since anxiety is the expression of a recoil from danger. (This is an early mention of what has since become known as the second theory of anxiety.) The danger from the external world becomes realistic anxiety, that from the id becomes neurosis, and that from the superego, guilt.

INHIBITIONS, SYMPTOMS AND ANXIETY (1926)*

This is Freud's last major theoretical work. It is frequently said that the book marks a new era in the history of psychoanalysis. There are three major innovations in theory in this work, in

---

* Standard Edition, Vol. XX, pp. 87-172. For other references see Notes on Chapter XI.

addition to the usual wealth of insights which virtually every book of Freud's provides. First, it provides a new theory of anxiety; second, it gives the first systematic description of the defense mechanisms, and relates them theoretically to the structure of the ego; third, Freud, for the first time, attaches some real theoretical significance to the oral stage.

1. *The Revised Theory of Anxiety:* Initially, and up to this point in the history of psychoanalysis, Freud had looked upon anxiety as transformed libido. It was held that libido is repressed and then turns into anxiety. In the meantime, Freud's researches on the ego had convinced him that the seat of anxiety is not in the id, as this theory had stated, but in the ego. This concept was made explicit and elaborated in the present work. Anxiety is now seen to be a signal given by the ego to indicate that some danger is impending. Originally, the anxiety was a reaction to helplessness in a traumatic situation, and later, as a signal for help, it is reproduced in the danger situation which is seen as similar to the original trauma.

The prototype for the anxiety reaction is the experience of birth, an idea of Freud's which had been put forth many years before, and had recently been taken up again by Rank. While, as has been noted, Freud disagreed with Rank's extreme use of this idea, he was evidently stimulated by Rank's book on the trauma of birth (1923) to reconsider his own attitude toward the experience of birth and toward the oral stage. It now appeared that the various types of anxiety were all forms of *separation anxiety:* in infancy, the fear is of the loss of the mother, in the Oedipal stage it is the fear of castration (a separation from the genitals), later on it becomes the fear of the superego, which is essentially a fear of the loss of the mother's love. Anxiety situations later in life are reproductions of these earlier ones. The fear of death is a projection of the superego on to the powers of destiny.

Freud now holds that each stage in development has its own particular traumatic situation and its own characteristic form of anxiety.

And anxiety is now seen to lead to repression, instead of the reverse, as Freud had thought for so many years. If anxiety produces repression or other defenses, which it does as well, it then becomes the key to the whole concept of neurosis. Anxiety and the defenses against it become the core of the personality. Since that theory was first expounded this has been the prevalent view among virtually all analysts.

2. *Theory of the Defense Mechanisms:* Careful examination of the various neuroses shows that there are various ways in which the ego handles anxiety. Repression is only one of them. There are also regression, reaction formation, undoing, isolation, and others. Freud therefore proposes again to use the word "defense" as a broader concept than repression, and to consider repression as but one of a number of possible defense mechanisms.

3. *The Oral Stage:* In the light of the fact that anxiety is a fear of separation from the mother, the circumstances surrounding such a separation in the new theory assume a new and special importance for psychoanalysis. Prior to this point, while Freud had mentioned the oral stage from time to time, he had never considered it at any particular length, nor had he attached great theoretical significance to it. For him, the Oedipus complex was always the core of neurosis. But if separation anxiety is now basic, then the relationship between mother and child must have more meaning than he had hitherto attached to it. This natural consequence of Freud's book in many ways marked the transitional stage from the concentration on the Oedipal situation to the profound study of the oral situation which has gone on since.

The book itself makes rather difficult reading. Unlike his usual practice, Freud does not in this work follow one argument consistently throughout; he takes up a number of different points. The central theme however remains that of anxiety, its meaning, its origin, its nature, and its functions.

In the first chapter, Freud takes up the difference between an inhibition and a symptom. An inhibition is seen to be in the ego; a symptom is not.

In the second chapter, Freud begins with the observation that a symptom, as has long been known, is a substitute for instinctual satisfaction; but what happens to the impulse that is repressed? Repression proceeds from the ego; but what part does the ego play? As a result of repression, the intended course of the excitatory process in the id does not occur at all; the ego inhibits or deflects it. Where does the ego get its influence from? Reply: From its connection with the perceptual system. But where does the energy of the ego come from? It is well known that in an external danger there is a recourse to flight. And repression is an equivalent to this attempt at flight.

In the light of all this, Freud can now hold firmly to the idea that the ego is the actual seat of anxiety, and can give up his earlier views that anxiety is in the id.

To return to the impulse: In spite of repression, some substitute for the impulse is found. The ego controls the path to motility and to consciousness, and the substitute remains unconscious. But how can this be reconciled with the view that the ego is so weak?

In the next section, Freud comes back to this question of the weakness of the ego. The ego derives its strength from its connection with the id. The instinctual impulse is repressed, but remains isolated and active. As a rule, repression is followed by a secondary defense struggle against the symptom by the ego. In this struggle, two lines may be taken by the ego:

1. It makes an attempt at restoration or reconciliation—by trying to adapt the symptom to the rest of the personality; for example, hysterical compromises between the Oedipus satisfaction and the need for punishment. This leads to the secondary gains from the illness.

2. Or it continues the repression.

But the symptom, the true substitute for the repressed impulse, continues the role of the repressed impulse. It renews its demands for satisfaction and obliges the ego to defend itself.

In Chapter IV, Freud takes up the question of anxiety in the light of the available clinical material. He compares little Hans and the Wolf Man with regard to their childhood phobias. In both patients, the motive-force of the repression was a fear of castration. But in both, the fear was repressed and came out only in the analysis. Thus, the affect of anxiety came not from libido, but from the repressing agency itself, that is, from the ego.

This led Freud to announce a change in his views, namely that it is anxiety that produces repression, not the reverse, as he had formerly believed.

Why had Freud come to advance his former view? He believed that he had put his finger on a metapsychological transformation of the libido into anxiety. This concept came from the observation that anxiety is produced by certain sexual practices, such as abstinence or *coitus interruptus*. These observations still hold good. How, then, can Freud reconcile the two positions where there seems to be a contradiction?

In Chapter V, Freud tries to resolve this contradiction. At first he considers the neuroses without anxiety, such as conversion hysteria. In this, there is little seen of the ego's struggle against the symptom. But symptom formation is so obscure here that he decides to leave the subject.

He turns next to the obsessional neurosis. The symptoms here are either negative or substitutive. There is a ceaseless struggle against the symptoms, and the roles of the ego and superego are especially important. The fact of *regression* is decisive. At this point Freud comments how necessary it is to distinguish defense from repression. For reaction formation is also a defense.

In the obsessional neurosis the id-superego conflict is especially acute.

In Chapter VI he considers two further ego techniques which deserve attention, that is, the two defense mechanisms, undoing and isolation. Undoing is a magical device which makes the ego believe that something which has happened has really not happened, or the reverse. In isolation, genetically the ego obeys the taboo on touching.

So much for the discussion of the three neuroses. In all three, the motive for defense is the fear of castration, yet this comes to the surface only in the phobias. How is this possible?

In the next chapter, Freud goes back to the infantile phobias of animals in order to find the answer to the question. A digression on the stages of development, in the light of the new instinct theory, points out that there is no need to change the theory. Repression occurs on the genital level; the other defenses occur at lower levels of development.

Anxiety that is felt in the animal phobias is an affective reaction to danger on the part of the ego; and the danger being signaled in this way is the danger of castration. The same applies to the obsessional neurosis—there, too, there is a fear of castration, of the ego by the superego.

Thus, in general, anxiety is a reaction to a situation of danger obviated by the ego's doing something to avoid that situation or to withdraw from it. Symptoms are created so as to avoid a danger situation which is signaled by anxiety.

To this process, traumatic neurosis seems to offer an exception, since it is based on the fear of death, rather than on the fear of castration. Freud shows that this exception is only apparent.

He now points to a rather remarkable correlation: All the dangers seem to be dangers of separation. The first experience of anxiety is birth. Are the others similar?

In the next chapter, Freud recapitulates what is known about anxiety. He reviews the facts: Anxiety is a felt state, it is felt as unpleasure. Anxiety states involve a feeling of unpleasure, acts of discharge, and perceptions of those acts. The anxiety state is a reproduction of some experience that contained the necessary conditions for such an increase of excitation and a discharge along particular paths, and from this experience the unpleasure of anxiety receives its specific character. In man, birth provides a prototypic experience of this kind, and Freud was accordingly inclined to regard anxiety states as reproductions of the trauma of birth.

He next inquired: What is the function of anxiety and on what occasions is it reproduced? Anxiety arose originally as a reaction to a state of danger, and is reproduced whenever a state of that kind occurs. On considering Rank's views in this connection, Freud rejected them. He knows that the child is anxious when alone in the dark, or with a stranger, that is, *when he is missing someone who is loved and longed for*. In this lies the key to anxiety.

The loss of a love-object, that is, the mother, is traumatic because the mother provides gratification. The danger is the accumulation of amounts of stimulation that require being disposed of. When the infant finds that a person is able to remove this overaccumulation for him, the danger shifts from the economic situation to the consequences of the loss of the object. Now it is the absence of the mother that constitutes the danger.

Both as an automatic phenomenon and as a rescuing signal anxiety is seen to be a product of the infant's helplessness.

Further anxiety situations are also separations—castration, and loss of love of the superego. Here, as has been noted, death is a projection of the fears of the superego on to the powers of destiny.

At another point in the book Freud states that he is retracting his earlier views, but he now insists that he is not taking them back, but rather bringing them in line with the present ones. Freud's well-known reluctance to make a sharp break with the past again comes into play here.

Freud finds that each period of the individual's life has its situation of danger and its appropriate form of anxiety.

Next Freud considers the relationship between the formation of symptoms and anxiety. On this question two views exist: 1. Anxiety is a symptom. 2. The symptoms are formed in order to avoid anxiety. In Freud's view, there is a danger situation interposed between the anxiety and the symptom. Thus, symptom formation does put an end to the danger.

Such symptom formation should now more properly be attributed to the defensive process which is similar to the ego's attempt at flight, but which does more—it joins issue with a threatening instinctual process, and somehow suppresses it or deflects it from its aims and renders it innocuous.

But why do people become neurotic? Some determinants of anxiety disappear; others do not. Among the educated classes, all children seem to go through a neurosis; some outgrow it; others do not. Why? This remains a riddle.

In the final chapter Freud says that what is necessary is some factor that will explain why some people are able to subject the affect of anxiety to normal control, while others come to grief in this process. Two attempts at explanation had been offered by Adler and Rank, neither of which is adequate.

Freud comes back to his favorite position that in the individual it is the quantitative relationships that are important and decisive.

On a broader scale, there are three conditions that lay the

groundwork for the formation of neurosis—the biological fact of man's long state of helplessness, the phylogenetic fact of the existence of a latency period, and the psychological fact that it is easier to put up defenses against the dangers threatening from the external world than against the dangers from within.

THE QUESTION OF LAY ANALYSIS (1926) *

The question of lay analysis was for Freud perhaps the most important organizational problem that concerned him after World War I. He attributed both practical and theoretical importance to the need to train nonmedical persons in the theory and practice of analysis.

Things were brought to a head by an accusation of quackery against Dr. Theodor Reik in Vienna in 1926. Freud immediately stepped forward on Reik's behalf and intervened with the authorities. The case was dropped. It provided Freud, however, with an opportunity to write this book.

In the book he undertakes to marshal all the arguments for and against lay analysis. The book takes the form of a dialogue with an impartial person, whom Freud later identified as one of the public officials whom he had spoken to on behalf of Dr. Reik. In spite of the thirty-five years that have elapsed since its publication, the book is still essentially valid and contains the basic arguments in favor of permitting nonmedical people to practice analysis.

The crux of Freud's position may be summed up in two propositions: First, the growth of the knowledge of psychoanalysis had shown increasingly that psychoanalysis is a branch of psychology, and not of medicine. This had been explicitly stated by Freud when the International Psychoanalytical Association was founded in 1910. Second, the practice of analysis can be acquired only by a special kind of training which, then and now, is still independent of both medicine and psychology. Freud wrote:

I lay stress on the demand that no one should practice analysis who has not acquired the right to do so by a particular training. Whether such a person is a doctor or not seems to me immaterial." [175]

* Standard Edition, Vol. XX, pp. 183-258. For other references see Notes on Chapter XIV.

In order to clarify the question of quackery in psychoanalysis he first sketched out to the impartial person an outline of the theory of psychoanalysis, one of the many such that he penned in his life time. This demonstrated that while medical questions do and may enter in particular cases, medicine and psychoanalysis are essentially separate disciplines.

A quack, says Freud, is one who undertakes treatment without possessing the knowledge and capacity for it. Taking his stand on this definition, he asserts that doctors form a preponderating contingent of quacks in analysis. They very frequently practice analytic treatment without having learned it and without understanding it

He argues that medicine not only fails to instruct the future physician in psychology or in the techniques of analysis, but gives him a false and negative attitude toward the subject.

In the light of the prevailing scientific and political conditions he advocated a policy of laissez faire toward the whole subject

He readily granted that physicians are necessary at some points in the practice of analysis, particularly in determining the question of differential diagnosis. This, however, is by no means to be construed as an argument against lay analysis.

Freud considers three separate interests—those of the patients, of the doctors, and of science.

With regard to the patient, Freud is interested only in having the person who treats him well qualified in the area, and here he holds previous training in medicine to be irrelevant.

From the point of view of the physician, medical training is already long enough, and to demand that he add psychoanalytic training to this would be both scientifically and economically undesirable.

From the point of view of science Freud argued particularly for the value of analysis to other disciplines. The knowledge of analysis can be acquired only by a personal analysis. He expressed the opinion that the use of analysis for the treatment of neuroses is only one of its applications; the future, he thought, would show that it is perhaps not the most important one. (In a sense, this has in fact turned out to be the case.)

But even with regard to the problem of therapy, Freud thought

:he lay analyst was needed to combat widespread neuroses and
undo the harm imposed by civilization. In this connection he wrote:

> Our civilization imposes an almost intolerable pressure on us, and it
> :alls for a corrective. Is it too fantastic to expect that psychoanalysis, in
> spite of its difficulties, may be destined for the task of preparing mankind
> 'or such correctives? [176]

CIVILIZATION AND ITS DISCONTENTS (1930) *

The book contains Freud's mature reflections on the subject of
:ivilization and the contributions which psychoanalysis can make
o its understanding.

The immediate predecessor of the book is a little monograph
entitled "The Future of an Illusion" (1927), in which Freud takes
up the meaning of religion. Here his view is that religion is an
expression of man's craving for authoritative figures to help him over-
:ome the feeling of helplessness and the anxiety which it engenders.

The book under discussion is written in a popular vein and reads
very easily. After some introductory comments about religion, in
vhich Freud reasserts his position that religion is an illusion, he
liscusses suffering. Suffering comes either from bodily pain, external
langers, or relations with one's fellow men. After some remarks
about the first two he comes to the third, the question of relations
vith one's fellow men. This is the heart of the book.

Civilization is built up on instinctual privations, a view which
'reud had long maintained. It must seek a satisfying solution
between individual claims and those of the civilized community.
n contrast with his previous views, however, Freud now takes
he position that the instinctual privation which is of the greatest
significance and which is hardest to handle relates to aggression.
While cultures may mitigate the severity of the renunciation, to a
:ertain extent some suffering is inevitable.

Civilization holds aggressiveness in check by means of the process
of internalization or introjection. This leads to the formation of a
superego in the individual as well as in the group.

* Standard Edition, Vol. XXI, pp. 64-145. For other references see Notes on
Chapter XIII.

Freud makes a new theoretical point in that he states that guilt relates not to any privation but specifically to the renunciation of aggression. It is this aggression, then, that enters into the superego and makes it much more severe than would otherwise be the case. Thus, characteristically, a person who is unable to find expression for his aggression has a very harsh superego, while one who releases his aggression freely may have a relatively mild one.

Freud's whole exposition in this work is of a tentative character, as though he were thinking out loud and had not himself come to any final conclusions. While culture involves suffering, he holds that this varies from one society to another. The neurosis of culture is embodied in a collective superego which may perhaps someday be brought under therapeutic control.

If the book is compared with *Totem and Taboo*, it must be considered much inferior to the previous work. There Freud had combed the entire anthropological literature, extracted its relevant features and offered an explanation of the phenomena based on psychoanalytic understanding. Here he merely expressed some philosophical opinions. Actually, *Civilization and Its Discontents* is important only because of the changes displayed in Freud's position and not because of any profound insights in its own right.

ANALYSIS TERMINABLE AND INTERMINABLE (1937) *

This paper sums up Freud's final views on neurosis and therapy. Twenty-three years had passed since Freud's last major statement on the problem of analysis, in his 1914 paper "Remembering, Repeating, and Working-Through." In the intervening period there had been many developments in the theory of psychoanalysis, and it was certainly important to see how Freud attempted to apply this theory to the actual analytical situation.

The question which the essay tries to answer is: Under what circumstances can it be said that an analysis is properly terminated? The major changes which had taken place since 1914 related particularly to the ego and it was to this aspect of the problem that Freud devoted a major portion of the paper.

* Collected Papers, Vol. V, pp. 316-57.

From the point of view of the id it is easy enough to say when an analysis is finished: The symptoms disappear.

From the point of view of the ego, however, it is far more complicated. Even if the symptoms disappear, there may be many ego traits or character traits which both the patient and the analyst will be trying to change, and here the criteria of change are much less concrete. Eventually, Freud could only say in broad outline that the goal of analysis is to secure the best possible psychological conditions for the functioning of the ego.

The paper follows a very logical argument, which will be summarized below.

Analysis is a long and tedious process; can it be shortened? Several attempts to do so have been made but have not been found to resolve the whole problem.

Is there such a thing as a natural end to an analysis, or is it really possible to conduct it to such an end? In order to answer this question it is necessary to decide what is meant by "the end of analysis." By it can be meant either a practical end in which enough psychopathology has been cleared away to make one satisfied with the results, or a theoretical state in which no further change would take place if the analysis were to continue.

Three main factors on which the results of an analysis depend are: 1. the relative importance of the traumatic factor; 2. the relative strength of the instincts; and 3. the modifications of the ego in the defensive conflict.

Only when the *traumatic factor* predominates can we look for a simple and clear-cut achievement in psychoanalysis, involving the strengthening of the ego and the replacement of an inadequate childhood decision by a correct solution. When the other two factors, the strength of the instincts and unfavorable modifications of the ego, are present, the analysis is far more difficult. Here the question to be asked is: What are the obstacles to cure?

It already becomes clear that if the more exacting demands made upon therapeutic analysis are to be fulfilled its duration, whether as a means or an end, is not to be shortened.

Is it possible for analysis permanently and definitely to resolve a conflict between instinct and ego or to settle a pathogenic instinctual demand upon the ego? The *strength of the instinct* determines the answers to this question. In theory, the real achievement of analytic therapy is the subsequent correction of the original process of repression, with the result that the quantitative factor no longer has the upper hand. In fact, the results are variable. Analysis does indeed sometimes succeed, although not invariably, in undoing the effect of a quantitative increase in the strength of the instinct. Thus, in theory analysis is always right in its claim to cure neurosis by assuring control over instinct while, in practice, its claim is not always justified.

If the instincts are excessively strong, the ego fails in its task Hence the therapeutic purpose will be achieved only when a greater measure of analytic help can be given to the patient's ego.

Two further questions must be handled together: Can future conflicts be guarded against? And is it practical and advisable to stir up latent conflicts? These goals must be rejected. If any instinctual drive is not active now and does not manifest itself in any way, it cannot be influenced by analysis.

Analysis works by *a modification* of the ego, by making a compact with the patient's ego; for such a pact the ego must be normal. But like normality in general, the normal ego is an ideal fiction.

Modifications of the ego are either congenital or acquired. Freud takes up the acquired ones first. The ego uses the defense mechanisms which had been described the year before in the book by his daughter, Anna Freud: *The Ego and the Mechanisms of Defense.* These mechanisms, however, may in themselves become dangerous. They reappear in the analysis as resistances, as a result of which recovery itself becomes a new danger.

The therapeutic effect of analysis depends on the making conscious of what is represented within the id. But there turns out to be a resistance to the discovery of resistance, and the defense mechanisms become resistances, not only to the bringing into consciousness of id contents, but also to the whole process of analysis and so, to the cure.

The outcome of analysis in this sense depends principally on the strength and depth of the roots of the resistances constituting the ego modifications. Once more the significance of the quantitative factor

ust be appreciated and once more it must be borne in mind that
nalysis has only certain limited quantities of energy at its disposal.

There are primary congenital variations in the ego. Still other
esistances of another type exist which can no longer be localized
nd which seem to be created by certain fundamental aspects of
he mental apparatus. These are: (1) adhesiveness of libido; (2)
nobility of libido; (3) loss of plasticity. There are others as well.

In connection with resistances, the strongest impression is the
eeling that there is a force at work which is defending itself by all
ossible means against recovery and is clinging tenaciously to illness
nd suffering. The instinct to destruction certainly plays a role here.

The personal characteristics of the analyst also play a role (this
s usually referred to as the countertransference). Analysts do not
holly come up to the standard of psychic normality which they set
or their patients; these defects impede the analyst in his work.

The analyst acquires his qualifications in his own analysis. For
ractical purposes this can only be short and incomplete. Unfor-
unately, many analysts use analysis as a defense and remain un-
hanged. Because of this, every analyst ought periodically himself
o reenter analysis again at intervals of, say, five years. "So not only
he patient's analysis but that of the analyst himself has ceased to
e a terminable and has become an interminable task." [177]

This does not mean by any means that analysis is an endless
rocess. As in Freud's own self-analysis, specific conflicts can be
esolved, but deeper self-understanding can go on all through life.

Two themes create extraordinary trouble—penis envy in women
nd passivity in men. Ferenczi had said that these two must be
vercome for an analysis to be complete, but Freud felt that this
vas asking a great deal. It is in these points that he felt that bedrock
ad been reached; he considered these to be biological facts.

It is sometimes said that this final essay of Freud on therapy is
 pessimistic one. He points to the many difficulties which lie in the
vay of complete analysis, stresses its interminable nature in some
espects, and points to hazards in other respects which may make
nalysis laborious or impossible. At the same time he offers a system-
tic examination of the process of analysis. It is only through this
ystematic approach and its relationship to theory that a decision

can be reached whether analysis is adequately terminated or n
Freud would have described himself as neither an optimist nor
pessimist, but a realist. While he was fully aware of the mar
obstacles to success in analysis, he was equally well aware of tl
great therapeutic achievements of analysis. As he once put i
analysis is not a panacea, yet it is far superior to any of the availab
alternatives.

Part IV.

RETROSPECT AND PROSPECT

In his *Autobiography* in 1925 Freud wrote:

Looking back, then, over the patchwork of my life's labors, I can say
that I have made many beginnings and thrown out many suggestions.
Something will come of them in the future, though I cannot myself tell
whether it will be much or little. I can, however, express a hope that I
have opened up a pathway for an important advance in our knowledge.[178]

It is time to reflect on how "much or little" has come of Freud.

To begin with, it is necessary to be clear about just what Freud
said. It has been shown above that his thought underwent many
changes in the course of his life; perhaps it is easiest to begin with
a resume of his development.

Freud began as a neurologist in the 1880's. At that time virtually
nothing was known of the neuroses, his particular province. For the
first decade, roughly, he functioned as a physician investigating the
neuroses, in much the same way that other physicians investigate
other illnesses. He was an inordinately ambitious young man and
hoped to achieve fame and fortune by resolving the riddle of
hysteria.

In these early years he made a number of discoveries which fore-
shadowed his later views but still fell far short of them. He saw
neurosis as a defense against inner conflict which was aroused by
some traumatic experience in childhood. Such conflict leads to
dammed-up tension, which could be either discharged or abreacted.
Yet the whole conflict was unconscious, and Freud perfected a
cathartic method which could make the unconscious conscious.
"Unconscious," however, was still used in a superficial sense and did
not have the deeper meaning it was later to acquire. Freud claimed

241

a considerable measure of success with therapeutic methods base
on these insights, and in 1895 published a book in conjunction wit
Breuer, *Studies on Hysteria*, which described these successes.

Then, in 1895, began his self-analysis. It lasted some five yea
and revolutionized his entire way of thinking as well as his whol
inner life. The many ways in which his self-analysis left its impri
on the entire history of psychoanalysis have been stressed above.

To begin with, Freud's self-analysis proceeded by way of dream
and he gradually opened up the secret of the dream by laborious
piecing together the many associations to the dream elements an
showing how meaning could be found in them. This resulted in th
publication of *The Interpretation of Dreams* in 1900, with its fu
theory of the unconscious.

When dream analysis failed to resolve his inner conflicts, he wer
further into his childhood memories and uncovered his Oedipu
complex and the whole world of infantile sexuality. Eventually thi
led to the libido theory and the *Three Essays on Sexuality* in 190£
which should also be looked upon as a piece of Freud's self-analysi

In attempting to apply the results of his self-analysis to hi
patients, Freud came up against numerous obstacles, which he calle
resistances. These resistances could be traced to the transferenc
phenomenon, the carry-over to the person of the analyst of th
infantile responses to the parents.

With the idea of transference Freud could also understand som
of his own otherwise unexplained attachments in life, such as tha
with Fliess and the long-sustained hope that Fliess would finall
provide the necessary physiological and biological truths for him

These three concepts—the unconscious, the libido theory, and trans
ference–resistance—form the core of the first psychoanalytic system
that of id psychology, which was crystallized and elaborated in th
period from 1900 to 1914. This part of psychoanalysis was so care
fully worked out that it has become an integral part of all contem
porary psychological and psychoanalytic theory; it has only beer
fitted into a larger framework.

Freud soon saw that his system of psychoanalytic psycholog
could be applied in numerous ways. In medicine he was able tc
resolve the problem of the classical neuroses: he classified the

enomena, even provided most of the terminology in use today, emonstrated the connections between the neuroses and infantile xuality, and showed how they could be cured by psychoanalysis.

the social sciences he turned his attention particularly to anthrology and art and demonstrated how the adoption of a psychoalytic point of view allows the scholar to explain data which otherise remain inaccessible to man's understanding, or can be treated ly in a superficial way.

When, around the outbreak of World War I, Freud tried to stematize his views he ran up against unexpected difficulties. The stem was only approximately correct; many refinements were eded. Accordingly he went on to devise the second system of sychoanalytic psychology, that of ego psychology. Ego psychology es not refute id psychology; it just places it in a broader perective.

In the main, ego psychology was worked out in the years from 14 to 1926. These were years of war, hardship and—later—for eud himself, serious physical illness. Accordingly it need not me as a surprise that the insights of ego psychology were not orked out with the same meticulous care which he had lavished n id psychology. In the new system he mainly established the undations on which others since have built.

Ego psychology posits a tripartite structure of the mind—id, ego nd superego. The id is the reservoir of instincts; the ego the sychic agency that handles reality; the superego the conscience, r the introjection of the parents.

In the id the most novel element is the shift from sexuality as the ajor instinct to the assumption of two major instincts, Eros and he death instinct, which clinically manifests itself as aggression. he earlier theory of anxiety was revised: Instead of seeing anxiety s the transformation of libido, Freud saw it as a signal given by he ego to announce a danger. Investigation showed that the danger ituations all embodied separation, and separation anxiety was enceforth seen as the basic type of anxiety. This led Freud for the rst time to a more extended consideration of the oral stage, and he relationship between the mother and child.

The ego is a composite of many defense mechanisms which

manage the impulses, deal with reality, and handle the superego
The superego is the heir to the parents, their introjection or inter
nalization. Thus Freud was led for the first time to a consideratio
of early identifications.

Like the first system, that of id psychology, ego psychology wa
applied in many ways, particularly to medicine and the social sc
ences. Neurosis could now be seen as one of many pathologica
reactions, and the meaning of the term could be expanded unt
it became virtually synonymous with personality structure. In h
analysis of society Freud now saw aggression as at least as basi
as sexuality, sometimes even more so.

By this time Freud had numerous followers who amended h
views in many ways and took up where he had left off. Hencefort
Freud is not the only psychoanalyst, and numerous argumen
spring up about "Freudian" vs. "non-Freudian" positions.

Two personal peculiarities of Freud have served to obscure th
main trends of his development. First, although he recognized fror
an early date that he was a psychologist, a certain ambivalenc
about psychology always remained with him. Somehow he hope
that biology or physiology would provide more certain answers, an
although the echo of this hope became fainter and fainter as tim
went on, it never disappeared entirely. Second, Freud was relucta
to give up an old position entirely. Although careful study shows o
how many different points he did change his mind, it is rare t
find a frank admission to that effect in his writings. This has create
the wholly erroneous notion that everything that he wrote retair
equal validity, whereas the fact is that much of what he said h
himself later dismissed or contradicted.

Psychoanalysis is a new science in the history of mankind. Th
creative achievement of Freud is on a par with other bold concep
tions, such as Darwin's and Einstein's, which have revolutionize
man's thinking. At the same time it is not necessary to make a go
out of a man. It must be recognized that Freud left many gaps i
the structure of psychoanalysis, that some of his views do not hol
up in the light of later scientific research, and that a host of abl
workers has learned from Freud and added much to what Freu
left his fellow men.

While it is not possible here to go into the subsequent history of psychoanalysis in any detail, it is worth while to summarize briefly the major changes which have occurred since Freud.

1. The *oral stage* has been studied far more intensively, especially since about 1940. Here the emphasis has shifted from libidinal gratification as such to a minute examination of the relationship between mother and child.

2. Other *libidinal stages* have been explored much more fully, and a vast mass of additional data has been accumulated regarding human development. A good deal of this has come out of research in nonanalytic settings, but inspired by the basic research framework of psychoanalysis.

3. *Object relations* or *interpersonal relations* have been subjected to much more careful scrutiny. The contributions here have come more often from sources which consider themselves "non-Freudian" (see discussion below).

4. The concept of *neurosis* has been deepened and extended in all directions. The classical neuroses now form but a small part of the clinical material with which the contemporary psychoanalyst deals. It has been shown that it is possible to treat psychoanalytically even the most deteriorated psychotics. Character disturbances of all kinds, once considered unamenable to psychoanalysis, are now routinely treated, of course with various modifications of technique. The treatment of psychotics, child analysis, group analysis, and many other variations unknown in Freud's day, are now commonly seen. Naturally, the relationship of these to classical analysis remains a much-disputed point. However, it can already be said that when Freud commented that he had all the world as his patient, he did not realize how literally this was to come to pass.

5. The early observations on hysteria were extended to all illness and the totally new field of *psychosomatic medicine* has come into being, grown, and developed. While new findings appear almost every day, the concept of psychosomatics has already recast both the theory and the practice of medicine.

6. Many efforts have been made to make psychoanalysis a *general psychology*. This was already Freud's vision, but it has been made more explicit by Hartmann, Rapaport and others. Hartmann's

concept of the autonomous ego has been particularly useful in this respect.

7. A whole new field has grown up, *clinical psychology,* which rests primarily upon the Freudian view of perception as an emotion-laden process rather than the classical view of perception as a reflection of the external world.

8. The role of *culture* in the formation of personality has been the topic of innumerable studies. Anthropologists have made a particularly important contribution to this area.

9. The *applications* of psychoanalysis to other disciplines have expanded enormously. It is safe to say that by now there is no social science which has not been enriched to some extent by the insights of psychoanalytic psychology.

10. The deeper significance of psychoanalysis as a *philosophical approach to life* has come to be appreciated. If psychoanalysis has discovered that all mankind is neurotic in a certain sense, it can also suggest ways for mankind to get out of the impasse.

11. Finally there has been an enormous expansion of *psychoanalysis as a profession.* One of the major obstacles to the expansion of the field remains the shortage of qualified workers.

After this brief survey three questions remain to be considered: the relationship of psychoanalysis to psychiatry, of psychoanalysis to psychology, and of Freudian psychoanalysis to other "schools."

NOTES ON CHAPTER XVI

For general summaries of *psychoanalytic theory subsequent to Freud,* see M. Gill: "The Present State of Psychoanalytic Theory," *Journal of Abnormal and Social Psychology,* LVIII, 1959, pp. 1-8. L. Bellak (ed.): "Conceptual and Methodological Problems in Psychoanalysis," *Annals of the New York Academy of Sciences,* LXXVI, 1959, pp. 971-1134. L. Bellak: "Psychoanalytic Theory of Personality. Notes Toward a Systematic Textbook of Psychoanalysis," In *J. L. McCary* (ed.): *Psychology of Personality* (New York: Logos Press, 1956). H. Hartmann, E. Kris and R. M. Loewenstein: "Comments on the Formation of Psychic Structure," *Psychoanalytic Study of the Child,* II, 1946, pp. 11-38. D. Rapaport: "The Structure of Psychoanalytic Theory," *Psychological Issues* (New York: International Universities Press, 1960).

On the theory of *libidinal stages,* see also H. Hartmann: "Psychoanalysis and Developmental Psychology," *Psychoanalytic Study of the Child*, V, 1950, pp. 7-17. E. Kris: "Notes on the Development and on Some Current Problems of Psychoanalytic Child Psychology," *Ibid.*, pp. 24-46. L. A. Spiegel: "A Review of Contributions to a Psychoanalytic Theory of Adolescence," *Ibid.*, VI, 1951, pp. 375-94.

On *object relations* or *interpersonal relations* see H. S. Sullivan: *Conceptions of Modern Psychiatry* (Washington: W. A. White Psychiatric Institute, 1947). Also E. Jacobson: "Sullivan's Interpersonal Theory of Psychiatry," *Journal of the American Psychoanalytic Association*, III, 1955, pp. 149-56.

On *neurosis*, see especially O. Fenichel: *The Psychoanalytic Theory of Neurosis* (New York: Norton, 1945).

On *psychosomatic medicine*, see F. Weiss and O. English: *Psychosomatic Medicine* (Philadelphia: Saunders, 1943). F. Dunbar: *Emotions and Bodily Changes* (New York: Columbia University Press, 1955). H. Selye: *The Stress of Life* (New York: McGraw-Hill, 1956). F. Deutsch (ed.): *The Psychosomatic Concept in Psychoanalysis* (New York: International Universities Press, 1953).

On *psychoanalysis and psychology*, see Notes on Chapter XVII.

On the *applications* of psychoanalysis to the *social sciences* see the appropriate sections in J. Frosch, (ed.): *Annual Survey of Psychoanalysis*.

On the more *philosophical questions* involved in psychoanalysis, see M. Brierley: *Trends in Psychoanalysis* (London: Hogarth, 1951), Chap. VI. R. E. Money-Kyrle: "Psychoanalysis and Ethics." *International Journal of Psychoanalysis*, XXXIII, 1952, pp. 225-34. J. D. Sutherland (ed.): *Psychoanalysis and Contemporary Thought* (London: Hogarth, 1958). F. Alexander: "Impressions from the Fourth International Congress of Psychotherapy," *Psychiatry*, XXII, 1959, pp. 89-95.

On the *professional* aspects of psychoanalysis, see Notes on Chapter XIV.

Chapter XVII. PSYCHOANALYSIS, PSYCHIATRY AND PSYCHOLOGY

PSYCHIATRY

Technically Freud was a psychiatrist, as have been the majority of psychoanalysts. The relationship between psychoanalysis and psychiatry has for this and other reasons always been a central concern to the profession. It almost seems as if every psychoanalyst sooner or later finds himself compelled to say something on the subject; the literature contains innumerable contributions.

Probably the prevalent view today is that psychiatry provides the description of mental illness, while psychoanalysis gives us the dynamic understanding. Thus Kraepelin and Freud are somehow combined and reconciled. It is doubtful whether on closer examination such a view is tenable.

Clarity can only be reached by reviewing the historical development. Physicians began to take an active interest in the mentally ill around the time of the French Revolution. Their interest was aroused by the humanitarian wish to rescue the patient from the clutches of the demonologists, who were primarily the clergy. This interest however could be justified only by an organic hypothesis: The mentally ill must have some medical illness, most probably something wrong with their brain. Thus was born the concept of "mental illness" by analogy with physical illness, a concept which scarcely existed before 1800. Medical research would tackle this illness as it tackled all others; it would classify the phenomena, find the causes, and effect a cure. Primarily the physician was concerned with the psychotic; some slight attention was paid to the very severe neurotic, but the normal was left entirely out of the picture, as would be expected from a situation dominated by this kind of orientation.

The hope that research would uncover the brain or other lesions which cause the mental aberrations has been realized in but a few instances; general paresis and epilepsy are the best known. In the vast majority of disorders, however, persistent research has failed to reveal any consistent organic findings.[179]

Kraepelin summed up both the orientation and the results of a century of research in his classification of the psychoses. The division into dementia praecox and manic-depressive psychosis somehow seemed to confirm the illusion that one could make "diagnoses" of these "mental illnesses" in much the same way that one can diagnose physical illness. The logical errors inherent in this point of view have repeatedly been stressed, most clearly and most recently by Szasz.[180]

In the field of the neuroses the situation was entirely different. Before Freud neuroses were generally ignored and always poorly understood. It was Freud who provided most of the basic descriptive material for the neuroses similar to what Kraepelin had done for the psychoses. But, of course, Freud went much further—he provided in addition a dynamic understanding and an effective therapy.

Inevitably study of psychosis and neurosis raises questions of what is normal. Here psychiatry, medically oriented, could only say that the normal person is one who is without illness; psychoanalysis on the other hand could offer a variety of psychological insights.

Thus if the initial hypothesis on the basis of which the physician took over the care of the mentally ill, is re-evaluated, the conclusion must be that it has not been confirmed. From our present-day point of view normal, neurotic, and psychotic represent differences of degree. As Ernest Jones put it in 1929 in an address delivered on the occasion of the opening of Columbia University Psychiatric Institute (New York):

All mental morbidity is . . . a state of schizophrenia, although Professor Bleuler has proposed to reserve this term for the most striking of its forms. What we meet with clinically as mental disorder represents the endless variety of the ways in which the threatened ego struggles for its self-preservation. In the nature of things, therefore, our conception of it can be cast only in terms of active dynamic strivings.[181]

If historically psychiatry represents an assumption of organic etiology which has not been confirmed, psychoanalysis stands for a psychological point of view. The meaning of the term "psychoanalysis" has become confused for a variety of reasons; it is being used in this book in the sense of a theoretical system of psychology, that is, psychoanalytic psychology.

It is this psychological point of view which currently dominates most of psychiatry and clinical psychology. The concept of neurosis has expanded to become almost coterminous with personality; the differences between normal, neurotic, and psychotic are matters for research, not arbitrary fiat. Whole societies can be severely disturbed; many have been and many are.

Insensibly then an entirely different attitude has crept into the field—medicine has been replaced by psychology. At the same time most of the practitioners of this new psychology have been physicians, technically psychiatrists. Unwilling to break with tradition completely, they speak of themselves as psychoanalytic psychiatrists or often dynamic psychiatrists.

Arguments have arisen about whether "psychoanalysis" is applicable to those patients whose ego is too "fragile." The confusion here arises from looking at "psychoanalysis" in too narrow a sense. Virtually all psychotherapy today derives from the fundamental dynamic insights of Freud, and can therefore justifiably be called psychoanalytic psychotherapy. By now modifications of technique have been developed which allow for the application of psychoanalytic therapy to almost any type of patient.

The medical problems met with in psychoanalytic treatment are no different from those encountered in other life situations. In any case, following Freud's thinking, it has been customary to keep psychotherapy as pure as possible, so that the patient with a medical problem would be referred to another physician for treatment of that problem.

Some comments are in order about the somatic treatments which have appeared since the 1930's—shock treatments, brain surgery, and more recently the tranquilizing drugs. In practice these techniques may often be useful. In theory however the prime need of the patient is for psychological understanding. The deplorable shortage of competently trained practitioners plays a considerable role here.

In sum, then, the heart of psychiatry today is psychoanalytic understanding and treatment. Medical problems may arise here, as in any other human enterprise and of course have to be treated by appropriate specialists in medicine and neurology. This however does not affect the fundamental position. Were it not for the force of tradition, and the effect on a varying public opinion, the psychiatrist might just as well call himself a psychologist or a psychoanalyst.

PSYCHOLOGY

The relationship between psychoanalysis and psychology is as complicated, baffling, and confused as that between psychoanalysis and psychiatry. Psychoanalysis, following Freud, looks upon itself as a system of psychology yet it has as a rule been condemned or at best ignored by the official departments of psychology in the universities. Often enough, psychoanalysis is roundly rejected as "unscientific." At the same time even a casual glance at any contemporary textbook of psychology shows how heavily the author has borrowed from psychoanalysis, especially in those areas which touch upon personality functioning. Again it is only a review of the historical picture which can shed light upon what is happening.

Psychology, in Freud's early days, was still intimately tied up with philosophy, which meant that it leaned heavily on speculation. In order to free itself from philosophy and to achieve status as a science, it sought to emulate physics and chemistry and began to place a heavy emphasis on the experimental method. This led to the behaviorist movement, which from about 1910 on has been the dominant theoretical position in American psychology. Behaviorism stressed the objective, the observable, the measurable.

At the same time this emphasis on objectivity seriously curtailed the scope of psychology. As G. Stanley Hall pointed out in 1920,[182] it was precisely those areas of human functioning that were neglected by academic psychology that were intensively investigated by Freud—the unconscious, the abnormal, sex, and affectivity generally. When these areas were approached by strictly objective methods the results were either meaningless or trivial.

Furthermore, behavioristic psychology set itself squarely against two of the traditional concepts in psychology—the mental and the instinctual. It argued that they were not amenable to scientific clarification, and should therefore be discarded. For a long time they were discarded; however, the only result was that the experimental and academic psychologists were kept at a great distance from human concerns.

With the advent of clinical psychology at the time of World War II, psychologists returned to a direct study of people, and considerable changes were brought about. Those who went through Freud's experiences in doing psychotherapy made the same or similar observations about the unconscious, psychosexual development, transference, resistance, and ego structure.

Psychologists who underwent a personal analysis also repeated Freud's experience—they too found that it served to open a whole new world to them.[183] Self-analysis was again shown to be one of the crucial keys to understanding.

The behaviorists pinned their greatest hopes on learning theory. Eventually, they felt, the laws of learning applicable to all organisms would be uncovered and the problems of psychology would be resolved. As with the medical hypothesis in psychiatry, the learning theory hypothesis of the behaviorist has not been confirmed. There are just as many puzzles and disagreements among learning theorists as among psychoanalysts. Some have even expressed the opinion that

> ... All this work on learning is a maze of "crucial experiments," none of which is ever quite confirmed and any one of which almost certainly has been contradicted.[184]

Mowrer has perhaps made the contemporary learning theorist's criticism of behaviorism most explicit. He says:

> If, for example, we sometimes speak of "consciousness" (a tabued word for the Behaviorists), this is not just a friendly gesture to the past or

concession to common sense; it represents instead the growing conviction that the objective study of behavior has now reached the point where some such concept is essential if systematic progress in theory construction is to go forward. . . .

There is, however, a sense in which learning theory is severely limited. At best, it gives us a picture of the basic, biologically determined principles, or *laws*, of learning. It has little or nothing to say about what living organisms, and human beings in particular, *ought* to learn or what they in fact *do* learn. . . .[185]

Another factor that has gradually become clear is that in their criticism of psychoanalysis psychologists frequently resorted to sheer speculation. E. g., Woodworth, in his widely-used textbook, at one point considers Freud's theory of dreams.[186] He objects to Freud's theory on the grounds that it fails to take account of the easy-running recall mechanism; it overdoes the unconscious; and it overdoes the libido. What he fails to state is that Freud's conclusions were derived from extensive empirical research, while Woodworth himself had never bothered to collect dreams and try to understand them.

At the same time it has become clear since about 1940 that many areas of cognitive functioning are strongly influenced by affective factors. The "new look" in perception theory is only one facet of this growing awareness. Thus psychoanalysis becomes relevant even in the most traditional and best-explored areas of psychology.

In psychological writings, the meaning of psychoanalysis, as of psychiatry, is often confused. At times it is taken as a restricted form of therapy (classical analysis); at other times some one doctrine is singled out for special attack. Psychoanalysis can only be understood in its broad context as a psychoanalytic psychology.

At times the accusation is heard that psychoanalysis does not lend itself to "scientific validation" and does not offer "testable hypotheses." By now this accusation, unfortunately too often repeated, has been many times refuted. There are certainly a great many hypotheses deriving from psychoanalysis which have been tested in many ways.

Actually, a good deal of psychoanalysis has already been incorporated into general psychology, in spite of what might be called official antagonism. This incorporation has been obscured or concealed by a curious attitude often adopted toward Freud by many textbook writers—whatever part of psychoanalysis is accepted is described as general psychology; what is rejected is labeled "psychoanalysis" or "Freudian." A number of years ago Kris, Herma and Shor [187] demonstrated how this worked in the case of the dream: More and more of psychoanalytic dream theory was accepted as time went on, but at every point whatever was accepted was termed psychological knowledge, while what was rejected remained Freud's theory. The same holds for other areas of psychoanalysis. The result has been that the student is usually left with the erroneous notion that psychoanalysis is somehow a fanatical or lunatic fringe theory which has little to do with "scientific" psychology.

Some outstanding psychologists have, however, always appreciated the fructifying role of psychoanalysis in psychological theory. Boring, in the 1950 edition of his classic *History of Experimental Psychology*, put it this way:

> It was Freud who put the dynamic conception of psychology where psychologists could see it and take it. They took it, slowly and with hesitation, accepting some principles while rejecting many of the trimmings. It is not likely that the history of psychology can be written in the next three centuries without mention of Freud's name and still claim to be a general history of psychology.[188]

In the present-day environment there is a growing rapprochement between psychoanalysis and general psychology from both directions. Psychoanalysis is becoming increasingly interested in research which is nontherapeutic in nature, while general psychology is learning more and more about the dynamic factors in human behavior which psychoanalytic psychology has been pointing out for many decades. There can be little doubt that as time goes on this rapprochement will grow even closer.

NOTES ON CHAPTER XVII

Perhaps the best exposition of the *relationship between psychoanalysis and psychiatry* is the address delivered by Ernest Jones at the opening of the Psychiatric Institute of Columbia University (New York) in 1929. Reprinted in E. Jones: "Psychoanalysis and Psychiatry," *Papers on Psychoanalysis, 5th edition* (London: Bailliere, Tindall and Cox, 1948), Chapter XIX. Some other representative papers are: A. Staercke: "Psychoanalysis and Psychiatry," *International Journal of Psychoanalysis*, II, 1921, pp. 361-415. J. Rickman: "The Development of Psychological Medicine (1950)," Chapter XVIII in *Selected Contributions to Psychoanalysis* (New York: Basic Books, 1957). S. Rado: "Psychoanalysis and Psychiatry," *International Journal of Psychoanalysis*, XVII, 1936, pp. 202-5. C. P. Oberndorf: "Psychoanalysis and Psychiatry," *American Journal of Psychiatry*, V, 1926, pp. 605-14. R. Knight: "The Relationship of Psychoanalysis to Psychiatry," *Ibid.*, CI, 1945, pp. 777-82. E. Jones: "Psychiatry Before and After Freud." In *Four Centenary Addresses* (New York: Basic Books, 1956), pp. 67-91. M. Gitelson: "Psychoanalysis and Dynamic Psychiatry." *Archives of Neurology and Psychiatry*, LXVI, 1951, pp. 280-88. A. Brill: *Freud's Contribution to Psychiatry* (New York: Norton, 1944). L. Binswanger: "What are the Tasks Arising for Psychiatry from the Progress of the New Psychology?" *Zeitschrift fuer die Gesamte Neurologie und Psychiatrie*, XCI, 1924, pp. 402-36. T. S. Szasz: "Psychiatry, Psychotherapy and Psychology." *AMA Archives of General Psychiatry*, I, 1959, pp. 455-63.

For the growing *impact of psychoanalysis on the presentation of psychiatric material*, see successive editions of any standard textbook, such as Strecker and Ebaugh or Noyes.

The best recent summary of all points of view on *schizophrenia* is L. Bellak (ed.): *Schizophrenia* (New York: Logos Press, 1958).

As can be seen in the Notes to Chapter X, Freud had few adherents among the psychologists prior to World War I. The outstanding exception was G. S. Hall: *Preface to S. Freud: A General Introduction to Psychoanalysis* (New York: Garden City Publishing Company, 1920).

The first work which signalled a marked change in attitude was *Psychoanalysis as Seen by Analyzed Psychologists* (American Psychological Association, 1953), a reprint of articles published in 1940. The *application of psychoanalysis to the social sciences* is discussed in C. S. Hall and G. Lindzey: "Psychoanalytic Theory and Its Application in the Social Sciences," Chapter IV, in G. Lindzey (ed.): *Handbook of Social Psychology* (Reading (Mass.): Addison-Wesley, 1954). See also D. Krech: "Psychological Theory and Social Psychology." In H. Helson (ed.): *Theoretical Foundations of Psychology* (Princeton (N.J.): Van Nostrand, 1951) and D. H. Wrong: "The Oversocialized Conception of Man in Modern Sociology," *American Sociological Review*, 26, 1961, pp. 183-93.

Notable chiefly for its faulty conception of *methodology* is R. R. Sears: "Survey of Objective Studies of Psychoanalytic Concepts," *Social Science Research Council Bulletin*, 1943, No. 51. More sophisticated discussions of the topic may be found in E. Pumpian-Mindlin (ed.): *Psychoanalysis as Science* (New York: Basic Books, 1952).

Much attention has been devoted to a synthesis of *psychoanalysis and learning theory*. See especially E. R. Hilgard: *Theories of Learning* (New

York: Appleton-Century-Crofts, 1956), 2nd edition, Chap. IX, and O. H. Mowrer: *Learning Theory and Behavior* (New York: John Wiley, 1960).

The most comprehensive presentation of *psychoanalysis as a complete psychology* is D. Rapaport: "The Structure of Psychoanalytic Theory," *Psychological Issues* (New York: International Universities Press, 1960). A different approach is adopted in R. Fine: *Principles of Psychoanalytic Psychology* (Unpublished lectures given at the University of Amsterdam, Netherlands, 1961). See also G. Murphy: "Psychoanalysis as a Unified Theory of Human Behavior," *Psychiatry*, XXIII, 1960, pp. 341-6.

Some significant *research studies* are R. Gardner, P. S. Holzman, G. S. Klein, H. Linton and D. P. Spence: "Cognitive Control," *Psychological Issues* (International Universities Press, 1959), G. S. Blum: "A Clinical Psychologist Views Psychoanalytic Theory. A Study of the Psychoanalytic Theory of Psychosexual Development," *Genetic Psychology Monographs*, XXXIX, 1949, pp. 7-99. D. R. Miller: "Studies of Denial in Fantasy," Chap. II in H. P. David and J. C. Brengelman (eds.): *Perspectives in Personality Research* (New York: Springer, 1960).

For discussions of *research in psychoanalytic psychology* see L. Bellak: "Research in Psychoanalysis," *Psychoanalytic Quarterly*, XXX, 1961, pp. 519-48, and J. Sandler: "The Hampstead Index as an Instrument of Psychoanalytic Research," to be published in *International Journal of Psychoanalysis*.

Some idea of the *change in attitude* towards psychoanalysis in psychological texts may be obtained by comparing more recent books with older ones. See e.g. R. S. Woodworth: *Psychology* (New York: Henry Holt, 1937), typical of that day. L. F. Shaffer and E. J. Shoben: *The Psychology of Adjustment* (Boston: Houghton, Mifflin, 1956) lean far more heavily on psychoanalytic ideas, as do a large number of contemporary books on personality, though usually without explicitly stating so. Interesting data on the presentation of Freud in psychology texts is contained in E. Kris, H. Herma and J. Shor: "Freud's Theory of the Dream in American Textbooks," *Journal of Social and Abnormal Psychology*, XXXVIII, 1943, pp. 319-34.

A comparison of Piaget and Freud is attempted in P. H. Wolff: *The Developmental Psychologies of Jean Piaget and Psychoanalysis* (Psychological Issues, International Universities Press, 1960).

Chapter XVIII. THE "SCHOOLS"
OF PSYCHOANALYSIS

Both among the general public and professional circles psycho-analysis is seen as divided into many warring factions or schools.* One writer's description of psychoanalysis incorporates this supposed division into its title.[189]

The two early deviants, Adler and Jung, gave rise to the statement, repeated for many years, that there were three main schools of psychoanalysis—Freud, Adler and Jung. As time has gone on, the influence of these latter two has tended to recede. As already noted, neither of them fully grasped the first psychoanalytic system, with its concepts of the unconscious, psychosexual development, and transference-resistance.

This criticism is not applicable to the later deviants, who began to appear in the 1930's—Sullivan, Horney, Fromm, Kardiner, Rado, etc. This so-called culturalist school has generally accepted the findings of the early Freud but has differed with him on others. Few people today, for example, would question the role of the unconscious, or the existence of psychosexual stages of development, or the vital significance of the transference in therapy. Thus the question becomes: What is being accepted and what is being rejected?

It is possible in psychoanalysis, as in so many other fields, to say the same thing in many different ways. When Sullivan, for instance, speaks of satisfaction and security he is actually talking about the id and the ego; when he speaks of awareness he is talking of consciousness; his "dynamisms" differ in no essential from the Freudian

---

* Several years ago the writer met a prominent clergyman at a social gathering. As soon as he heard that I was a psychoanalyst, he asked: "What denomination?"

defense mechanisms. A recent book by two prominent members of the Sullivan group amounted to little more than a rediscovery of the unconscious.[190]

When it is possible to reformulate psychoanalysis in so many different ways, talk about "schools" becomes highly misleading. It would seem to be much more fruitful to talk about problems. In the interest of further progress it is better to say boldly: There are no schools, there are only issues.

Thus a considerable amount of ink has been spilled on the meaningless debate of the "biological" vs. the "cultural" orientation. Obviously both play a role for all workers in the field, and the real problem is one of clarifying how much weight should be assigned to each for any particular problem.

Or again the argument is sometimes raised that Freudian analysts are too "passive" in therapy and that other schools are more "active." To be "Freudian" is therefore to be "passive"; while to be "non-Freudian" is to be "active." This kind of cliché formulation does great violence to the varied and intricate interpersonal processes that are involved in the analytic situation. To achieve clarity one must bear in mind the nature of the total analytic relationship, the transference, and the needs of any particular patient. All this requires the careful presentation of data, earnest attempts at understanding, not the slinging of formulas.

In the present-day status of analytic theory there are large numbers of unresolved issues. Such fundamental questions as the classification of personality, the relationship of clinical neurosis to childhood experience, even the nature of free association require investigation. For many years the journals have been full of articles which attempt to clarify basic ideas. Only empirical research concentrating on these issues will be able to resolve the many problems arising.

In conclusion, some attempt can be made to answer Freud's query as to whether much or little has come out of his work. Psychoanalysis has expanded into hitherto unknown territory, it has evolved entirely novel techniques, and marched on to innumerable new discoveries. Yet the core of psychoanalytic understanding still remains the imperishable insights that mankind owes to Freud.

NOTES ON CHAPTER XVIII

The most comprehensive *survey* from the *schools point of view* is R. L. Munroe: *Schools of Psychoanalytic Thought* (New York: Dryden, 1955). This work contains bibliographies relevant to the major figures who take positions different from Freud.

See also J. A. C. Brown: *Freud and the Post-Freudians,* paperback (Penguin, 1961). K. Horney: *New Ways in Psychoanalysis* (New York: Norton, 1939). P. Mullahy: *Oedipus: Myth and Complex* (New York: Grove, 1955). C. Thompson: *Psychoanalysis: Its Evolution and Development* (New York: Hermitage, 1950).

A useful discussion of some basic issues may be found in R. Ekstein: "Ideological Warfare in the Psychological Sciences," *Psychoanalytic Review,* XXXVI, 1949, pp. 144-51. R. Ekstein: "Tower of Babel in Psychology and Psychiatry. Towards a Theory of Determinants in Psychology." *American Image,* II, 1950, pp. 77-141.

See also Notes on Chapter V and other appropriate chapters for discussions of different points of view on specific issues.

FOOTNOTES

1. Quoted in Jones, *The Life and Works of Sigmund Freud,* I, pp. 40-41.

2. P. F. Cranefield. "Josef Breuer's Evaluation of His Contribution to Psychoanalysis," *Int. J. of Psychoanalysis,* XXXIX, 1958, pp. 319-22.

3. *Standard Edition,* XX, p. 16. (Abbr. S.E. See p. 272, Note 89.)

4. *The Origins of Psychoanalysis,* pp. 119-20.

5. *Ibid.,* p. 162.

6. *Ibid.,* p. 269.

7. *Ibid.,* p. 129.

8. *Ibid.,* p. 134.

9. *Ibid.,* p. 169.

10. *Ibid.,* p. 264.

11. *Ibid.,* pp. 244-45.

12. Luise von Karpinska. *"Ueber die Psychologischen Grundlagen des Freudismus,"* *Int. Z. f. Psychoanalyse,* II, 1914.

13. "On Psychotherapy." *S.E.,* VII, p. 260.

14. O. Fenichel. *The Psychoanalytic Theory of Neurosis,* p. 563.

15. "Studies on Hysteria." *S.E.,* II, p. 154 and pp. 268 ff.

16. *Ibid.,* pp. 160-61.

17. Jones, *op. cit.,* I, p. 320.

18. D. Anzieu. *L'Auto-Analyse.* Presses Universitaires de France, Paris, 1959.

19. Jones, I, p. 327.

20. *S.E.,* XI, p. 145.

21. *The Origins of Psychoanalysis,* pp. 234-235.

22. Collected Papers, V, p. 314.

23. *S.E.,* XIV, p. 20.

24. *S.E.,* IV, p. xxvi.

25. *New Introductory Lectures on Psychoanalysis,* pp. 154-55.

26. *S.E.,* XIX, p. 142.

27. *Ibid.,* VII, p. 151.

28. *Ibid.,* XIX, p. 141.

29. Cf. paper by H. H. Hart. "A Scarcely Recognized Factor in the Oedipus Complex," Bull. of the Philadelphia Assn. for Psychoanalysis, VI, 1956, pp. 54-7.

30. "History of the Psychoanalytic Movement 1914." S.E., XIV, p. 44.

31. S.E., XIV, p. 190.

32. Quoted in L. Bellak. "Free Association: Conceptual and Clinical Aspects," Int. J. of Psychoanalysis, XL, 1961, Parts I and II.

33. For an excellent discussion of the rendering of Freud's German into English see L. W. Brandt: "Some Notes on English Freudian Terminology," J. of Am. Psychoanalytic Association, 1961, pp. 331-39.

34. Jones, op. cit., I, p. 360.

35. S.E., IV, p. xxxii.

36. Ibid., IV, p. xxiii.

37. Ibid., V, p. 396.

38. Ibid., p. 397.

39. Ibid., p. 182.

40. C. Fisher: "A Study of the Preliminary Stages of the Construction of Dreams and Images," J. Amer. Psychoanalytic Association, V, 1957, pp. 5-60. Also, other papers by Fisher and associates in the same journal.

41. W. Kleitman and Dement, W. "The Relation of Eye Movements during Sleep to Dream Activity: An Objective Method for the Study of Dreaming," J. Exp. Psychology, LIII, 1957, pp. 339-46.

42. D. R. Goodenough, Shapiro, A., Holden, M., and Steinschriber, L. "A Comparison of Dreamers and Nondreamers," J. Abnormal and Social Psychology, LIX, 1959, pp. 295-302.

43. W. Dement: "The Effect of Dream Deprivation," Science, CXXXI, 1960, pp. 1705-7.

44. S.E., VI, p. 272.

45. Ibid., p. 5-6.

46. Ibid., p. 7.

47. H. Ebbinghaus. Memory. Teachers College, Columbia University, 1913.

48. S.E., VI, p. 239.

49. For the best recent exposition of this position see N. R. Hanson, Patterns of Discovery (Cambridge: University Press, 1958).

50. S.E., XX, p. 36.

51. "The Infantile Genital Organizaton: An Interpolation Into the Theory of Sexuality," S.E., XIX, pp. 141-45.

52. S.E., Vol. XII, p. 316.

53. An Outline of Psychoanalysis, p. 30.

54. The section in the Three Essays on the libido theory was added in 1915 after the publication of the paper. Cf. Strachey, S.E., VII, p. 126.

55. S.E., IX, p. 175.

56. S. Ferenczi. *Sex in Psychoanalysis*, p. 303.

57. K. Abraham. *Selected Papers on Psychoanalysis*, pp. 394-95.

58. *S.E.*, VII, p. 229.

59. *Ibid.*, XII, p. 168.

60. *Ibid.*, XVIII, p. 101.

61. *Letters of Sigmund Freud*, selected and edited by Ernst Freud, p. 308.

62. Martin Freud. *Sigmund Freud: Man and Father*.

63. Jones, *op. cit.*, II, pp. 292-94.

64. *S.E.*, XI, p. 187.

65. *Ibid.*, XI, p. 190.

66. *Ibid.*, IV, p. 130.

67. Jones, *op. cit.*, II, p. 285.

68. E. Jones, *Papers on Psychoanalysis*, 5th ed., Chaps. XXV-XXVII.

69. *S.E.*, VII, p. 133.

70. E. Jones, *Free Associations*, pp. 145-46.

71. *S.E.*, VII, p. 172.

72. *Ibid.*, VII, p. 205.

73. A. Kardiner, A. Karush and L. Ovesey. "A Methodological Study of Freudian Theory," *J. of Nervous and Mental Disease*, CXXIX, 1959, Nos. 1-4.

74. G. Zilboorg. *A History of Medical Psychology*, p. 143.

75. S. Freud. "Report on My Studies in Paris and Berlin (1886)." *Int. J. Psychoanalysis*, XXXVII, 1956, pp. 2-7.

76. *S.E.*, II, p. xxxi.

77. *Ibid.*, VII, p. 278.

78. L. Binswanger. *Sigmund Freud: Reminiscences of a Friendship*, p. 27.

79. *S.E.*, XVIII, p. 60.

80. *Ibid.*, VII, p. 131.

81. *Ibid.*, VII, p. 217.

82. Binswanger, *op. cit.*, p. 81.

83. M. Fortes. "Malinowski and Freud," *Psychoanalysis and the Psychoanalytic Review*, XLV, 1958-59, pp. 120-145.

84. B. Malinowski. *Sex and Repression*, p. 136.

85. *Op. cit.*, p. 38.

86. Fortes, *op. cit.*, p. 125.

87. Jones, *op. cit.*, III, p. 139.

88. *S.E.*, Vol. XX, p. 37.

89. A. Kardiner. *The Individual and His Society*, p. 3.

90. *S.E.*, XIV, p. 16.

91. *Ibid.*, VII, p. 252.

92. *Ibid.*, VII, p. 253.

93. *Ibid.,* VII, p. 177.

94. See T. S. Szasz: "On the Theory of Psychoanalytic Treatment," *Int. J. Psychoanalysis,* XXXVIII, 1957, pp. 166-82.

95. *S.E.,* XII, p. 141.

96. *Ibid.* VII, p. 116.

97. *Ibid.,* XII, p. 104.

98. *Ibid.,* p. 111.

99. E. Glover. *The Technique of Psychoanalysis.* Appendix.

100. *S.E.,* XX, p. 42.

101. *Ibid.,* XII, pp. 155-56.

102. *A General Introduction to Psychoanalysis,* pp. 323-24.

103. Jones, *op. cit.,* II, p. 241.

104. See page 14.

105. *S.E.,* XII, p. 237.

106. *Ibid.,* pp. 236-37.

107. F. Deutsch. "A Footnote to Freud's 'Fragment of an Analysis of a Case of Hysteria,'" *Psychoanalytic Quarterly,* XXVI, 1957, pp. 159-67.

108. *S.E.,* X, pp. 148-49.

109. *Ibid.,* pp. 276-78.

110. Jones, *op. cit.,* II, p. 268.

111. The quotations from the case history are taken from Freud's account.

112. See the works of Melanie Klein and John Rosen, among others.

113. The Wolf Man: "How I Came Into Analysis With Freud." *J. Amer. Psychoanalytic Assn.,* VI, 1958, pp. 348-52.

114. *S.E.,* XVII, p. 99.

115. *Ibid.,* p. 36.

116. *Ibid.,* p. 85.

117. *Ibid.,* XIV, p. 52.

118. *Letters of Sigmund Freud,* op. cit., p. 396.

119. *S.E.,* XIII, p. 100.

120. *Ibid.,* XII, p. 82.

121. Jones, *op. cit.,* II, p. 353.

122. *S.E.,* XIII, p. 26.

123. *Ibid.* pp. 156-57.

124. *Ibid.,* XIII, p. 35.

125. A. L. Kroeber. "Totem and Taboo, An Ethnologic Psychoanalysis," *Amer. Anthropologist,* XXII, 1920, pp. 48-55.

126. "Totem and Taboo in Retrospect," *Amer. J. of Sociology,* XLV, 1939, pp. 446-51.

127. C. Kluckhohn. "Universal Categories of Culture," In A. L. Kroeber (ed.) *Anthropology Today,* pp. 507-23.

128. Jones, *op. cit.,* III, p. 332.

129. *A General Introduction to Psychoanalysis,* pp. 327-28.

130. *S.E.,* VIII, p. 16.

131. *Ibid.,* XI, p. 136.

132. *Ibid.,* pp. 60-62.

133. Jones, *op. cit.,* II, p. 57.

134. *S.E.,* XIV, p. 58.

135. *Ibid.* p. 52.

136. *Ibid.,* p. 133.

137. *Ibid.,* XVIII, p. 38.

138. *Ibid.,* p. 59.

139. Jones, *op. cit.,* III, p. 276.

140. *Ibid.,* p. 266.

141. *S.E.,* XVIII, p. 60.

142. *Ibid.,* p. 45.

143. Jones, *op. cit.,* III, pp. 278-80.

144. *Civilization and Its Discontents,* p. 99.

145. Jones, *op. cit.,* III, p. 464.

146. *S.E.,* IV, p. xxvi.

147. *Ibid.,* XVIII, p. 101.

148. *Collected Papers,* V, p. 337.

149. *S.E.,* XVIII, p. 69.

150. *The Ego and the Id,* p. 44.

151. *Ibid.,* pp. 42-43.

152. *Ibid.,* p. 80.

153. *Ibid.,* p. 49.

154. *Collected Papers,* II, p. 254.

155. *Ibid.,* V, p. 354.

156. Jones, *op. cit.,* I, pp. 190-91.

157. *S.E.,* IX, p. 185.

158. *Civilization and Its Discontents,* p. 102.

159. *Ibid.,* pp. 141-42.

160. *Ibid.,* pp. 92-93.

161. B. Malinowski. *Sex and Repression in Savage Society,* pp. 223-24.

162. *S.E.,* XX, p. 252.

163. *Ibid.*

164. Jones, *op. cit.,* III, p. 298.

165. *S.E.,* XX, p. 248.

166. *Ibid.* p. 250.

167. B. Nelson, (ed.). *Freud and the 20th Century,* p. 50.

168. K. Abraham: *Selected Papers on Psychoanalysis,* Chap. VI and XII.

169. Jones, *op. cit.,* II, p. 329.

170. *Ibid.,* p. 252.

171. F. B. Karpf. *American Social Psychology*, 1932.

172. D. Krech. "Psychological Theory and Social Psychology." In H. Helson (ed.): *Theoretical Foundations of Psychology*.

173. See C. S. Hall and Lindzey, G. Psychoanalytic Theory and its Application in the Social Sciences. Chap. IV in G. Lindzey, (ed.). *Handbook of Social Psychology*.

174. D. H. Wrong. "The Oversocialized Conception of Man in Modern Sociology," *Amer. Sociological Review*, XXVI, No. 2, April, 1961.

175. *S.E.*, XX, p. 233.

176. *Ibid.*, pp. 249-50.

177. *Collected Papers*, V, p. 353.

178. *S.E.*, XX, p. 70.

179. Cf. L. Bellak, (ed.). *Schizophrenia*.

180. T. S. Szasz: "Psychiatry, Psychology and Psychotherapy," *AMA Archives of General Psychiatry*, I, 1959, pp. 455-63.

181. E. Jones. *Papers on Psychoanalysis (5th ed.)*, p. 375.

182. G. S. Hall. Preface to S. *Freud: A General Introduction to Psychoanalysis*.

183. *Psychoanalysis as seen by Psychoanalyzed Psychologists*. Amer. Psychological Assn., 1953.

184. Quoted in O. H. Mowrer. *Learning Theory and Behavior*, p. ix.

185. *Ibid.*, p. 7.

186. R. S. Woodworth. *Psychology*, pp. 505-07.

187. E. Kris, H. Herma and Shor, J. "Freud's Theory of the Dream in American Textbooks," *J. of Abn. Soc. Psychology*, XXXVIII, 1943, pp. 319-34.

188. E. G. Boring. *A History of Experimental Psychology*, (2nd ed.), p. 707.

189. R. Munroe. *Schools of Psychoanalytic Thought*.

190. Cf. R. Fine. "Review of 'E. Tauber and M. Green: Prelogical Experience.'" *Contemporary Psychology*, V, No. 3, March, 1960.

BIBLIOGRAPHY

1. Abraham, K. *Selected Papers on Psychoanalysis*. New York: Basic Books, 1953.
2. Adler, A. *Individual Psychology*. New York: The Humanities Press, 1951.
3. Adler, K. A., and Deutsch, D. (eds.). *Essays in Individual Psychology*. New York: Grove Press, 1959.
4. Alexander, F. "Impressions from the Fourth International Congress of Psychotherapy," *Psychiatry*, XXII, 1959, pp. 89-95.
5. ———. *Our Age of Unreason, A Study of the Irrational Forces in Social Life*. Philadelphia and New York: Lippincott, 1942.
6. ———. *The Western Mind in Transition: An Eyewitness Story*. New York: Random House, 1960.
7. *Annual Survey of Psychoanalysis*. Frosch, J. (ed.). New York: International Universities Press, 1950—.
8. Anzieu, D. *L'Auto-Analyse*. Paris: Presses Universitaires de France, 1959.
9. Axelrad, S. "On Some Uses of Psychoanalysis," *Journal of the Amer. Psychoanalytic Assn.*, VIII, 1960, pp. 175-218.
10. Baumeyer, F. "The Schreber Case." *International Journal of Psychoanalysis*, XXXVII, 1956, pp. 61-74.
11. Beane, F., McLaughlin, F., Marburg, R. "The Metapsychology of Narcissism," *Psychoanalytic Study of the Child*. XIV, 1914, pp. 9-28. New York: International Universities Press.
12. Bellak, L. "Free Association: Conceptual and Clinical Aspects," *International Journal of Psychoanalysis*, XLII, 1961, Parts I and II.
13. ———. "Research in Psychoanalysis." *Psychoanalytic Quarterly*, XXX, 1961, pp. 519-48.
14. ——— (ed.). "Conceptual and Methodological Problems in Psychoanalysis," *Annals of N. Y. Academy of Sciences*, LXXVI, pp. 971-1134. New York: 1959.
15. ———. (ed.). *Schizophrenia*. New York: Logos Press, 1958.
16. ———. "Psychoanalytic Theory of Personality. Notes Toward a

Systematic Textbook of Psychoanalysis." In McCary, J. L. (ed.). *Psychology of Personality*. New York: Logos Press, 1956.

17. Benedek, T. "Parenthood as a Developmental Phase: A Contribution to Libido Theory," *Journal of Amer. Psychoanalytic Association*, VII, 1959, pp. 389-417.

18. Beres, D. "Clinical Notes on Aggression in Children," *The Psychoanalytic Study of the Child*, VII, 1952, pp. 241-63. New York: International Universities Press.

19. Binswanger, L. *Sigmund Freud: Reminiscences of a Friendship*. New York: Grune and Stratton, 1957.

20. ———. "What Are the Tasks Arising for Psychiatry from the Progress of the New Psychology?" *Zeitschrift fuer die gesamte Neurologie und Psychiatrie*, XCI, 1924, pp. 402-36.

21. Blau, A. "In Support of Freud's Syndrome of Anxiety (Actual) Neurosis," *International Journal of Psychoanalysis*, XXXIII, 1952, pp. 363-72.

22. Blanck, G. *Education for Psychotherapy*. New York: Institute for Psychoanalytic Training and Research, 1962.

23. Blum, G. S. "A Clinical Psychologist Views Psychoanalytic Theory. A Study of the Psychoanalytic Theory of Psychosexual Development." *Genetic Psychology Monographs*, XXXIX, 1949, pp. 7-99.

24. ———. *Psychoanalytic Theories of Personality*. New York: McGraw-Hill, 1953.

25. Boring, E. G. *A History of Experimental Psychology*. (2nd ed.). New York: Appleton-Century-Crofts, 1950.

26. Bowlby, J. "Grief and Mourning in Infancy and Early Childhood." *Psychoanalytic Study of the Child*, XV, 1960, pp. 1-94. New York: International Universities Press.

27. Brandt, L. W. "Some Notes on English Freudian Terminology," *Journal of the Amer. Psychoanalytic Association*, IX, 1961, pp. 331-39.

28. Breland, K. and Breland, M. "The Misbehavior of Organisms," *American Psychologist*, XVI, 1961, pp. 681-84.

29. Brenman, M. "On Teasing and Being Teased; and the Problem of 'Moral Masochism.'" *Psychoanalytic Study of the Child*, VIII, 1952, pp. 264-85. New York: International Universities Press.

30. Brenner, C. "An Addendum to Freud's Theory of Anxiety," *International Journal of Psychoanalysis*, XXXIV, 1953, pp. 18-24.

31. Brierley, M. *Trends in Psychoanalysis*. The International Psychoanalytical Library No. 39. London: The Hogarth Press and the Institute of Psychoanalysis, 1951.

32. Brill, A. *Freud's Contribution to Psychiatry.* New York: Norton, 1944.

33. Brody, S. *Patterns of Mothering.* New York: International Universities Press, 1956.

34. Bronowski, J. and Mazlish, B. *The Western Intellectual Tradition from Leonardo to Hegel.* New York: Harper and Brothers, 1960.

35. Brown, J. A. C. *Freud and the Post-Freudians.* Baltimore: Penguin Books, 1961.

36. Brown, N. O. *Life Against Death: the Psychoanalytical Meaning of History.* Middletown, Conn., Wesleyan University Press, 1959.

37. Brun, C. R. "Ueber Freud's Hypothese vom Todestrieb." *Psyche,* 1953, pp. 81-111.

38. Bunker, H. A. "From Beard to Freud." In *Medical Review of Reviews.* 412th Issue, March, 1930.

39. Child, I. L. and Whiting, J. M. *Child Training and Personality.* New Haven: Yale University Press, 1953.

40. Colby, K. "An Experiment on the Effects of an Observer's Presence on the Imago System During Psychoanalytic Free Association," *Behavioral Science,* V, No. 3, July, 1960.

41. ———. *Energy and Structure in Psychoanalysis.* New York: The Ronald Press Company, 1955.

42. Cranefield, P. F. "Josef Breuer's Evaluation of His Contribution to Psychoanalysis," *International Journal of Psychoanalysis,* XXXIX, 1958, pp. 319-22.

43. H. D. *Tribute to Freud.* New York: Pantheon, 1956.

44. David, H. P. and Brengelman, J. C. (eds.). *Perspectives in Personality Research.* New York: Springer, 1960.

45. Dember, W. N. *Psychology of Perception.* New York: Holt and Company, 1956.

46. Dement, W. "The Effect of Dream Deprivation," *Science,* CXXXI, 1960, pp. 1705-7.

47. ——— and Kleitman, W. "The Relation of Eye Movements during Sleep to Dream Activity: An Objective Method for the Study of Dreaming," *Journal of Experimental Psychology,* LIII, 1957, pp. 339-46.

48. de Monchaux, D. "Pooling of Case Material: A Methodological Project." *Clinical Studies in Psychoanalysis,* Research Project of the Hampstead Child Therapy Clinic, by A. Freud. Proc. Royal Society of Medicine, LI, 1958.

49. Deutsch, F. "A Footnote to 'Freud's Fragment of an Analysis of a Case of Hysteria.'" *Psychoanalytic Quarterly,* XXVI, 1957, pp. 159-67.

50. Dorcus, R. M. and Shaffer, G. W. *Textbook of Abnormal Psychology*. Baltimore: Williams and Wilkins Company 1934; 2nd ed., 1939; 3rd ed., 1945.

51. Dunbar, H. F. *Emotions and Bodily Changes: A Survey of Literature on Psychosomatic Interrelationships*. New York: Columbia University Press, 1935; 2nd ed., 1938; 3rd ed., 1946; 4th ed., 1954.

52. Ebbinghaus, H. *Memory*. New York: Teachers College, Columbia University, 1913.

53. Eissler, K. "The Effect of the Structure of the Ego on Psychoanalytic Technique," *Journal of the American Psychoanalytic Association*, I, 1953, pp. 104-43.

54. Ekstein, R. "A Historical Survey on the Teaching of Psychoanalytic Technique," *Journal of the American Psychoanalytic Association*, VIII, 1960, pp. 500-16.

55. ———. "Ideological Warfare in the Psychological Sciences," *Psychoanalytic Review*, XXXVI, 1949, pp. 144-51.

56. ———, reporter. "The Teaching of Psychoanalytic Technique," *Journal of the American Psychoanalytic Association*, VIII, 1960 pp. 167-74.

57. ———. "Tower of Babel in Psychology and Psychiatry. Toward a Theory of Determinants in Psychology," *American Imago* II, 1950, pp. 77-141.

58. Ellenberger, H. "The Unconscious Before Freud," *Bulletin of the Menninger Clinic*, XXI, 1957.

59. English, O. and Weiss, E. *Psychosomatic Medicine*, Philadelphia W. B. Saunders and Company, 1943.

60. Erikson, E. "Identity and the Life Cycle," *Psychological Issues* I, 1959, No. 1. New York: International Universities Press, 1959

61. ———. "The Dream Specimen of Psychoanalysis," *Journal of the American Psychoanalytic Association*, II, 1954, pp. 5-56.

62. ———. *Childhood and Society*. New York: W. W. Norton, 1950

63. Escalona, S. and Heider, G. M. *Prediction and Outcome*. New York: Basic Books, 1959.

64. Farrow, E. P. *A Practical Method of Self-Analysis* (Foreword Freud, Sigmund). New York: Norton, 1943. Under title *Psycho analyze Yourself; A Practical Method of Self-Analysis Enabling a Person to Remove Unreasoning Fears and Depression from His Mind*. New York: International Universities Press, 1945 2nd ed., 1948.

65. Federn, P. *Ego Psychology and the Psychoses*. New York: Basic Books, 1952.

66. Feldman, S. *Mannerisms of Speech and Gestures in Everyday Life.* New York: International Universities Press, 1959.

67. Fenichel, O. *Problems of Psychoanalytic Technique.* New York: Psychoanalytic Quarterly, Inc., 1941.

68. ———. *The Psychoanalytic Theory of Neurosis.* New York: Norton, 1945.

69. Ferenczi, S. and Rank, O. *The Development of Psychoanalysis.* New York and Washington: Nervous and Mental Diseases Publishing Company, 1925.

70. Ferenczi, S. *Sex in Psychoanalysis.* Boston: Badger, 1916.

71. Feuer, L. S. *Psychoanalysis and Ethics.* Springfield, Ill.: C. C. Thomas, 1956.

72. Fine, R. "Pre-Doctoral Training in Psychotherapy," *Proceedings of N. Y. State Psychological Association.* (New York, 1960) pp. 16-19.

73. ———. *Principles of Psychoanalytic Psychology.* Lectures given at the University of Amsterdam, Netherlands, 1961. (In press.)

74. ———. "Review of 'E. S. Tauber and M. R. Green: Prelogical Experience,'" *Contemporary Psychology,* V, No. 3, 1960.

75. ———. "Review of E. Fromm: 'Sigmund Freud's Mission,'" *Psychoanalysis and the Psychoanalytic Review,* XLVI, 1959-1960, pp. 119-25.

76. ———. "Psychotherapy: A Freudian Point of View," *Annals of Psychotherapy.* American Academy of Psychotherapists, Monograph No. 1, I, No. 1, July, 1959.

77. ———. "The Logic of Psychology," *Psychoanalysis and the Psychoanalytic Review,* XLV, 1958-59, pp. 15-44.

78. ———. "Psychoanalysis and Learning Theory," *Psychoanalysis,* V, No. 4, Winter, 1957.

79. Fisher, C. "A Study of the Preliminary Stages of the Construction of Dreams and Images," *Journal of the American Psychoanalytic Association,* V, 1957, pp. 5-60.

80. Flescher, J. "A Dualistic Viewpoint on Anxiety," *Journal of the American Psychoanalytic Association,* III, 1955, pp. 415-46.

81. Fletcher, R. *Instinct in Man.* New York: International Universities Press, 1957.

82. Fliess, R. *The Revival of Interest in the Dream.* New York: International Universities Press, 1953.

83. Fortes, M. "Malinowski and Freud," *Psychoanalysis and the Psychoanalytic Review,* XLV, 1958-59, pp. 120-45.

84. Fraiberg, L. *Psychoanalysis and American Literary Criticism.* Detroit: Wayne State University Press, 1960.

85. Freud, Anna. *The Ego and the Mechanisms of Defense*. New York: International Universities Press, 1946.

86. ———. *The Psychoanalytical Treatment of Children*. London: Imago Publishing Co., 1946.

87. Freud, Martin. *Sigmund Freud: Man and Father*. New York: Vanguard Press, 1958.

88. Freud, Sigmund. "Report on My Studies in Paris and Berlin (1886)," *International Journal of Psychoanalysis*, XXXVII, 1956, pp. 2-7.

89. ———. *The Standard Edition of the Complete Psychological Works of Sigmund Freud*. Translated from the German under the general editorship of James Strachey, in collaboration with Anna Freud, assisted by Alix Strachey and Alan Tyson. London: The Hogarth Press and the Institute of Psychoanalysis, 1955— This is the standard edition, referred to in the text as *S.E.*, which is still in the process of publication. It is intended to replace all previous translations.
    For a complete bibliography of Freud's works, see below, pp. 285-293.

90. Fromm, E. *Man for Himself; An Inquiry into the Psychology of Ethics*. New York: Rinehart, 1947.

91. ———. *Sigmund Freud's Mission*. New York: Harper and Brothers, 1959.

92. ———. *The Sane Society*. New York: Rinehart and Co., 1955.

93. Galdston, I. (ed.). *Freud and Contemporary Culture*. New York: International Universities Press, 1957.

94. Gengerelli, J. A. "Dogma or Discipline?" *Saturday Review*, XL, No. 12, March 23, 1957, pp. 9-11 and 40.

95. Gero, G. and Rubinfine, D. L. "On Obsessive Thoughts," *Journal of the American Psychoanalytic Association*, III, 1955, pp. 222-43.

96. Gill, M. "The Present State of Psychoanalytic Theory," *Journal of Abnormal and Social Psychology*, LVIII, 1959, pp. 1-8.

97. Gitelson, M. "Psychoanalysis and Dynamic Psychiatry," *Archives of Neurology and Psychiatry*, LXVI, 1951, pp. 280-88.

98. Glover, E. *The Technique of Psychoanalysis*. New York: International Universities Press, 1955.

99. Goodenough, D. R., Shapiro, A., Holden, M., Steinschriber, L. "A Comparison of Dreamers and Nondreamers," *Journal of Abnormal and Social Psychology*, LIX, 1959, pp. 295-302.

100. Greenacre, P. (ed.), *The Affective Disorders*. New York: International Universities Press, 1953.

101. Greenson, R. R., moderator. "Variations in Classical Psycho-Analytic Technique: An Introduction," *International Journal of Psychoanalysis,* 39, 1958, pp. 200-1.

102. Grinker, R. R. "Reminiscences of a Personal Contact with Freud," *American Journal of Orthopsychiatry,* X, 1940, pp. 850-55.

103. Guillain, G. *J. M. Charcot, 1825-1893, His Life—His Work.* Edited and translated by Bailey, P. New York: Paul B. Hoeber, Inc., 1959.

104. Gutheil, E. *A Handbook of Dream Analysis.* New York: Liveright, 1951.

105. Hall, G. S. *Preface to S. Freud: A General Introduction to Psychoanalysis.* New York: Garden City Publishing Co., 1920.

106. Halliday, J. L. *Psychosocial Medicine: A Study of the Sick Society.* New York: W. W. Norton, 1948.

107. *Handbook of Social Psychology,* Lindzey, G. (ed.). Cambridge: Addison-Wesley Publishing Company, 1954.

108. Hanson, N. R. *Patterns of Discovery.* Cambridge: University Press, 1958.

109. Hart, H. H. "A Scarcely Recognized Factor in the Oedipus Complex," *Bulletin of the Philadelphia Association for Psychoanalysis,* VI, 1956, pp. 54-7.

110. Hartmann, H. *Ego Psychology and the Problem of Adaptation.* New York: International Universities Press, 1958.

111. ———. "Psychoanalysis and Developmental Psychology." *Psychoanalytic Study of the Child,* V., 1950, pp. 7-17. New York: International Universities Press.

112. ———. *Psychoanalysis and Moral Values.* (New York Psychoanalytic Institute. Freud Anniversary Lecture Series, 1959.) New York: International Universities Press, 1960.

113. ———. Kris, E., Loewenstein, R. M. "Comments on the Formation of Psychic Structure," *Psychoanalytic Study of the Child,* II, 1946, pp. 11-38. New York: International Universities Press.

114. ———. "The Genetic Approach in Psychoanalysis." *Psychoanalytic Study of the Child,* I, 1945, pp. 11-30.

115. ——— and Loewenstein, R. M. "Notes on the Theory of Aggression." *Psychoanalytic Study of the Child,* III/IV, 1949, pp. 9-36. New York: International Universities Press.

116. ———. "Comments on the Psychoanalytic Theory of the Ego." *Psychoanalytic Study of the Child,* V, 1950, pp. 74-96. New York: International Universities Press.

117. Hilgard, E. *Theories of Learning,* 2nd ed. New York: Appleton-Century-Crofts, 1956.

118. Hitschmann, E. "Freud's Conception of Love," *International Journal of Psychoanalysis*, XXXIII, 1952, pp. 421-28.

119. Hoffman, F. J. *Freudianism and the Literary Mind.* Baton Rouge: Louisiana State University Press, 1945.

120. Hollingsworth, H. H. *Abnormal Psychology: Its Concepts.* New York: Ronald Press, 1930.

121. Holt, R. R. "Recent Developments in Psychoanalytic Ego Psychology and Their Implications for Diagnostic Testing." *Journal of Projective Techniques*, XXIV, 1960, pp. 254-63.

122. Hook, S. (ed.). *Psychoanalysis, Scientific Method and Philosophy.* New York: New York University Press, 1959.

123. Horney, Karen. *New Ways in Psychoanalysis.* New York: Norton, 1939.

124. ———. *Self-Analysis.* New York: Norton, 1942.

125. Hulse, W. (ed.). *Topical Problems of Psychotherapy*, II, New York: S. Karger, 1960.

126. *Index of Psychoanalytic Writings.* Ed. by Grinstein, A. New York: International Universities Press, 1957.

127. Jacobi, J. *The Psychology of Jung; an Introduction.* New Haven: Yale University Press, 1943.

128. Jacobson, E. "Sullivan's Interpersonal Theory of Psychiatry." *Journal of the American Psychoanalytic Association*, III, 1955, pp. 149-56.

129. ———. "The Self and the Object World." *Psycho-Analytic Study of the Child*, IX, 1954, pp. 75-127. New York: International Universities Press.

130. Jastrow, J. *Freud: His Dream and Sex Theories.* World, McClelland, 1940. Under title *The House that Freud Built.* New York: Greenberg, 1932.

131. Joint Commission on Mental Illness and Health. *Action for Mental Health.* New York: Basic Books, 1961.

132. Jones, E. *Free Associations: Memoirs of a Psychoanalyst.* New York: Basic Books, 1959.

133. ———. *The Life and Work of Sigmund Freud.* Three volumes. New York: Basic Books, 1953-1957. Referred to in the text as Jones, I, II, and III.

134. ———. *Sigmund Freud: Four Centenary Addresses.* New York: Basic Books, 1956.

135. ———. *Papers on Psychoanalysis.* 5th edition. London: Bailliere Tindall and Cox, 1948.

136. Jung, C. G. *Psychological Types; or, The Psychology of Individuation.* New York: Harcourt, Brace, 1923.

137. Kapp, C. R. "Comments on Bernfeld and Feitelberg's 'The Principle of Entropy and the Death Instinct,'" *International Journal of Psychoanalysis*, XII, 1931, pp. 82-6.

138. Kardiner, A. "Freud—The Man I Knew, the Scientist and His Influence." In *Freud and the Twentieth Century*, Nelson, B. (ed.). New York: Meridian Books, 1957.

139. ———. *The Individual and His Society*. New York: Columbia University Press, 1939.

140. ———, Karush, A., Ovesey, L. "A Methodological Study of Freudian Theory," *Journal of Nervous and Mental Disease*, CXXIX, 1959, Nos. 1-4.

141. ———. *The Psychological Frontiers of Society*. New York: Columbia University Press, 1945, 1946, 1947.

142. Karpf, F. B. *American Social Psychology*. New York: McGraw-Hill, 1932.

143. Karpinska, Luise von. "Ueber die Psychologischen Grundlagen des Freudismus," *Internationale Zeitschrift fuer Psychoanalyse*, II, 1914, pp. 305-26.

144. Katan, M. "Schreber's Hereafter: Its Building-Up and Its Downfall," *Psychoanalytic Study of the Child*, XIV, 1959, pp. 314-82. New York: International Universities Press.

145. Kaufman, I. "Some Ethological Studies of Social Relationships and Conflict Situations," *Journal of the American Psychoanalytic Association*, VIII, 1960, pp. 671-85.

146. Kaywin, L. "An Epigenetic Approach to the Psychoanalytic Theory of Instincts and Affects," *Ibid.*, pp. 613-58.

147. Kelly, V. F. "What Is Important?" (In "Letters to the Editor"), *Saturday Review*, XL, No. 17 (April, 27, 1957).

148. Klein, G. S., Gardner, R., Holzman, P. S., Linton, H. and Spence, D. P. *Cognitive Control*. (Psychological Issues, I, No. 4.) New York: International Universities Press, 1959.

149. Klein, G. S. "Consciousness in Psychoanalytic Theory," *Journal of the American Psychoanalytic Association*, VII, 1959, pp. 5-34.

150. Klein, M. *Contributions to Psychoanalysis*. London: Hogarth Press, 1948.

151. ———, Heimann, P., Money-Kyrle, R. E. *New Directions in Psychoanalysis*. New York: Basic Books, 1955.

152. ———. *The Psychoanalysis of Children*. New York: W. W. Norton, 1932.

153. Kluckhohn, C. "Universal Categories of Culture." In *Anthropology Today*, Kroeber, A. L. (ed.). Chicago: University of Chicago Press, 1953.

154. Knight, R. "The Relationship of Psychoanalysis to Psychiatry," *American Journal of Psychiatry*, CI, 1945, pp. 777-82.

155. Kramer, M. "On the Continuation of the Analytic Process after Psycho-Analysis (A Self-Observation)," *International Journal of Psychoanalysis*, XL, 1959, pp. 17-25.

156. Krech, D. "Psychological Theory and Social Psychology." *Theoretical Foundations of Psychology*, Helson, H. (ed.). New York: Van Nostrand, 1951.

157. Kris, E. "Neutralization and Sublimation: Observations on Young Children," *Psychoanalytic Study of the Child*, X, 1955, pp. 30-46. New York: International Universities Press.

158. ———. "Notes on the Development and on Some Current Problems of Psychoanalytic Child Psychology." *Psychoanalytic Study of the Child*, V, 1950, pp. 24-46. New York: International Universities Press.

159. ———. *Psychoanalytic Explorations in Art*. New York: International Universities Press, 1952.

160. ———. Series of papers in *The Psychoanalytic Study of the Child*. New York: International Universities Press, 1945-1960.

161. ———, Herma, H. and Shor, J. "Freud's Theory of the Dream in American Textbooks," *Journal of Abnormal and Social Psychology*, XXXVIII, 1943, pp. 319-34.

162. Kroeber, A. L. (ed.). *Anthropology Today: An Encyclopedic Inventory*. Chicago: University of Chicago Press, 1953.

163. ———. "Totem and Taboo, An Ethnologic Psychoanalysis." *American Anthropologist*, XXII, 1920, pp. 48-55.

164. ———. "Totem and Taboo in Retrospect." *The American Journal of Sociology*, XLV, 1939, pp. 446-51.

165. Kubie, L. S. "The Independent Institute; Should Institutes for Training in Psychoanalysis Be Independently Organized or a Subdivisions of Departments of Psychiatry in Medical Schools?" *Bulletin of the American Psychoanalytic Association*, VIII, 1952, pp. 205-208.

166. ———. "Medical Responsibility for Training in Clinical Psychology," *Journal of the Association of American Medical Colleges*, IV, 1943, pp. 582-98.

167. ———. *Practical and Theoretical Aspects of Psychoanalysis*. New York: International Universities Press, 1950.

168. ———, reporter, "Problems of Psychoanalytic Training," *Bulletin of the American Psychoanalytic Association*, IV, 1948, pp. 29-3

169. ———. "A Program of Training in Psychiatry to Break the Bottleneck in Rehabilitation." *American Journal of Orthopsychiatry: A Journal of Human Behavior*, XVI, 1946, pp. 447-54.

170. Landis, C. "Psychoanalytic Phenomena," in *Psychoanalysis as Seen by Psychoanalyzed Psychologists*. Washington: American Psychological Association, 1953.

171. La Piere, R. *The Freudian Ethic*. New York: Duell, Sloan and Pearce, 1959.

172. Lewin, B. D. *The Psychoanalysis of Elation*. New York: W. W. Norton, 1950.

173. ———, Ross, H. *Psychoanalytic Education in the U. S.* New York: W. W. Norton, 1960.

174. ———. "Sleep, the Mouth and the Dream Screen," *Psychoanalytic Quarterly*, XV, 1946, pp. 419-34. In *The Yearbook of Psychoanalysis*. Lorand, Sandor (ed.). III, pp. 61-73. New York: International Universities Press, 1947.

175. Lilly, J. C. "The Psychophysiological Basis for Two Kinds of Instincts: Implications for Psychoanalytic Theory," *Journal of the Psychoanalytic Association*, VIII, 1960, pp. 659-70.

176. Loewald, H. W., reporter. "Psychoanalytic Curricula—Principles and Structure," *Ibid.*, IV, 1956, pp. 149-61.

177. Loewenstein, R. R. (ed.). *Drives, Affects, Behavior*. New York: International Universities Press, 1953.

178. Lorand, S. *Technique of Psychoanalytic Therapy*. New York: International Universities Press, 1946.

179. MacAlpine, I. and Hunter, R. A. (ed.). *Daniel Paul Schreber: Memoirs of My Nervous Illness*. London: W. Dawson, 1955.

180. Madison, P. *Freud's Concept of Repression and Defense*. Minneapolis: University of Minnesota Press, 1961.

181. Malinowski, B. *Sex and Repression in Savage Society*. New York: The Humanities Press, 1927.

182. Marcuse, H. *Eros and Civilization: A Philosophical Inquiry into Freud*. Boston: Beacon Press, 1955.

183. Marmor, J. "Orality in the Hysterical Personality," *Journal of the American Psychoanalytic Association*, I, 1953, pp. 656-71.

184. Matte-Blanco, I. "Expression in Symbolic Logic of the Characteristics of the System Ucs vs. the Logic of the System of Ucs," *International Journal of Psychoanalysis*, XL, 1959, pp. 1-5.

185. Menninger, K. *Theory of Psychoanalytic Technique* (Menninger Clinic Monograph Series, No. 12). New York: Basic Books, 1958.

186. Money-Kyrle, R. E. "Psychoanalysis and Ethics." In Klein, M., Heimann, P. (ed.). *New Directions in Psychoanalysis*. New York: Basic Books, 1955.

187. ———. *Psychoanalysis and Politics. A Contribution to the Psychology of Politics and Morals*. New York: W. W. Norton, 1951.

188. Mowrer, O. H. *Learning Theory and Behavior*. New York: John Wiley and Sons, 1960.

189. Mullahy, P. *Oedipus: Myth and Complex*. New York: Grove Press, 1955.

190. Munroe, R. *Schools of Psychoanalytic Thought*. New York: Dryden, 1955.

191. Murphy, G. "Psychoanalysis as a Unified Theory of Human Behavior," *Psychiatry*, XXIII, 1906, pp. 341-46.

192. ———— and Solley, C. S. *Development of the Perceptual World*. New York: Basic Books, 1960.

193. ————. *Historical Introduction to Modern Psychology*. New York: Harcourt, Brace, 1949.

194. Myerson, A. "The Attitude of Neurologists, Psychiatrists and Psychologists toward Psychoanalysis," *American Journal of Psychiatry*, XCVI, 1939, pp. 623-41.

195. Nelson, B. (ed.). *Freud and the Twentieth Century*. New York: Meridian Books, 1957.

196. Niederland, William. "The 'Miracled-up' World of Schreber's Childhood." *Psychoanalytic Study of the Child*, XIV, 1959, pp. 383-413. New York: International Universities Press.

197. ————. "Schreber's Father," *Journal of the American Psychoanalytic Association*, VIII, 1960, pp. 492-99.

198. ————. "Three Notes on the Schreber Case," *Psychoanalytic Quarterly*, XX, 1951, pp. 579-91.

199. Noyes, A. P. *Modern Clinical Psychiatry*. Philadelphia: W. B. Saunders Company, 1934. 2nd ed., rewritten and enlarged, 1939; 3rd ed., 1953. 4th ed., 1956. 5th ed., with Kolb, L. C., 1958.

200. Oberndorf, C. P. *A History of Psychoanalysis in America*. New York: Grune and Stratton, 1953.

201. ————. "Psychoanalysis and Psychiatry," *American Journal of Psychiatry*, V, 1926, pp. 605-14.

202. Orr, D. W. "Transference and Counter-Transference: A Historical Survey," *Journal of the American Psychoanalytic Association*, II, 1954, pp. 621-70.

203. Ostow, M. "Psychoanalysis and Ethology," Ibid., VIII, 1960, 526-34.

204. Penrose, L. S. "Freud's Theory of Instinct and Other Psychobiological Theories," *International Journal of Psychoanalysis*, XII, 1931, p. 22.

205. Pfeffer, A. Z. "A Procedure for Evaluating the Results of Psychoanalysis: A Preliminary Report." *Journal of the American Psychoanalytic Association*, VII, 1959, pp. 418-44.

206. Posinsky, S. H. "Instincts, Culture and Science." *Psychoanalytic Quarterly*, XXVII, 1958, pp. 1-37.

207. *Psychoanalysis as Seen by Analyzed Psychologists*. Washington: American Psychological Association, 1953. Reprinted from articles in the *Journal of Abnormal and Social Psychology*, XXXV, 1940.

208. *Psychoanalysis and Contemporary Thought*. Sutherland, J. D. (ed.). New York: Grove Press, 1959.

209. *Psychoanalysis, Scientific Method and Philosophy*. S. Hook (ed.). New York: New York University Press, 1959.

210. *The Psychosomatic Concept in Psychoanalysis*. Deutsch, F. (ed.). New York: International Universities Press, 1953.

211. "The Psychotherapy Research Project of the Menninger Foundation," *Bulletin of the Menninger Clinic*, XXIV (July, 1960), 4.

212. Pumpian-Mindlin, E. (ed.). *Psychoanalysis as Science*. New York: Basic Books, 1952.

213. Puner, H. W. *Freud: His Life and His Mind (A Biography)*. New York: Howell, Soskin, 1947.

214. Rado, S. "Psychoanalysis and Psychiatry," *International Journal of Psychoanalysis*, XVII, 1936, pp. 202-5.

215. ———. *Psychoanalysis of Behavior*. New York: Grune and Stratton, 1956.

216. Randall, J. H. *The Making of the Modern Mind: A Survey of the Intellectual Background of the Present Age*. Boston: Houghton-Mifflin Company, 1926; rev. ed., 1940.

217. Rangell, L. "The Nature of Conversion," *Journal of the American Psychoanalytic Association*, VII, 1959, pp. 632-62.

218. ———. "On the Psychoanalytic Theory of Anxiety: A Statement of a Unitary Theory," Ibid., III, 1955, pp. 389-414.

219. Rank, O. *Art and the Artist*. New York: Tudor Publishing Co., 1932.

220. Rapaport, D. "On the Psycho-Analytic Theory of Affects," *International Journal of Psychoanalysis*, XXXIV, 1953, pp. 177-98.

221. ———. "The Structure of Psychoanalytic Theory." *Psychological Issues*, II, No. 2, Monograph No. 6. New York: International Universities Press, 1960.

222. ———. Introduction to: Erik Erikson, "Identity and the Life Cycle." *Psychological Issues*, I, New York: International Universities Press, 1959.

223. ———. *Emotions and Memory*. Baltimore: The William and Wilkins Company, 1942.

224. Reich, W. *Character Analysis*. New York: Orgone Institute Press, 1945.

225. Reichard, S. "A Re-Examination of 'Studies in Hysteria,'" *Psychoanalytic Quarterly*, XXV, 1956, pp. 155-57.

226. Reider, N. reporter: "Re-evaluation of the Libido Theory," *Journal of the American Psychoanalytic Association*, IV, 1956, pp. 162-69.

227. Reik, T. *From Thirty Years with Freud*. New York: Farrar and Rinehart, 1940.

228. Ribble, M. *The Rights of Infants; Early Psychological Needs and their Satisfaction*. New York: Columbia University Press, 1943.

229. Rickman, J. *Selected Contributions to Psychoanalysis*. New York: Basic Books, 1957.

230. Rieff, P. *Freud: The Mind of the Moralist*. New York: Viking Press, 1959.

231. Robbins, L. L., reporter. "The Borderline Case," *Journal of the American Psychoanalytic Association*, IV, 1956, pp. 550-62.

232. ―――― and Wallerstein, R. S. "Research Strategy and Tactics of the Psychotherapy Research Project of the Menninger Foundation and the Problem of Controls." *Research in Psychotherapy* (Proceedings of a Conference, Washington, D. C., April 9-12, 1958.) Washington: American Psychological Association, 1959.

233. Roheim, G. *Psychoanalysis and Anthropology*. New York: International Universities Press, 1950.

234. Rosen, J. *Direct Analysis*. New York: Grune and Stratton, 1953.

235. Ross, N. "An Examination of Nosology According to Psychoanalytic Concepts." *Journal of the American Psychoanalytic Association*, VIII, 1960, pp. 535-51.

236. Rubinfine, D. "A Survey of Freud's Writings on Earliest Psychic Functioning." *Journal of the American Psychoanalytic Association*, IX, 1961, pp. 610-25.

237. ――――, reporter. "The Problem of Identity," *Ibid.*, VI, 1958, pp. 132-42.

238. Rubenstein, E. A. and Parloff, M. (eds.) *Research in Psychotherapy*. Washington: American Psychological Association, 1958.

239. Russell, B. A *History of Western Philosophy and Its Connection with Political and Social Circumstances from Earliest Times to the Present Day*. New York: Simon and Schuster, 1945.

240. Sachs, H. *The Creative Unconscious*. Cambridge: Sci-Art Publishers, 1942.

241. Sandler, J. "The Hampstead Index as an Instrument of Psychoanalytic Research." To be published in *International Journal of Psychoanalysis*.

242. ———. "On the Concept of Superego." *Psychoanalytic Study of the Child*, XV, 1960, pp. 128-62. New York: International Universities Press.

243. Schafer, R. "The Loving and Beloved Superego in Freud's Structural Theory," *Ibid.*, pp. 163-88.

244. Schwartz, E. K. and Wolf, A. "Psychoanalysis in Groups: Some Comparisons with Individual Analysis," *The Journal of General Psychology*, LXIV, 1961, pp. 153-91.

245. Scott, J. P. *Aggression.* Chicago: University of Chicago Press, 1958.

246. Sears, R. "Survey of Objective Studies of Psychoanalytic Concepts," *Social Science Research Council Bulletin*, 1943, No. 51.

247. Seldes, G. *Can These Things Be!* New York: Brewer, Warren and Putnam, 1931.

248. Selye, H. *The Stress of Life.* New York: McGraw-Hill, 1956.

249. Shaffer, L. F. and Shoben, E. J. *The Psychology of Adjustment.* Boston: Houghton-Mifflin, 1956.

250. Sloane, P., reporter. "The Technique of Supervised Analysis," *Journal of the American Psychoanalytic Association*, V, 1957, pp. 539-47.

251. Slochower, H. "Psychoanalysis and Literature." In *Progress in Clinical Psychology*, IV, Abt, L. Brower, D. (eds.). New York: Grune and Stratton, 1960.

252. Spiegel, L. A. "A Review of Contributions to a Psychoanalytic Theory of Adolescence," *Psychoanalytic Study of the Child*, VI, 1951, pp. 375-94. New York: International Universities Press.

253. Spitz, R. A. with Wolf, K. M. "Autoerotism. Some Empirical Findings and Hypotheses on Three of Its Manifestations in the First Year of Life." *Ibid.*, III-IV, 1949, pp. 85-120. New York: International Universities Press.

254. ——— "Hospitalism. An Inquiry into the Genesis of Psychiatric Conditions in Early Childhood." *Ibid.*, I, 1945, pp. 53-74. New York: International Universities Press.

255. ——— "Hospitalism: A Follow-Up Report." *Ibid.*, II, 1946, pp. 113-17. New York: International Universities Press.

256. ——— "The Psychogenic Diseases in Infancy: An Attempt at Their Etiologic Classification." *Ibid.*, VI, 1951, pp. 255-75. New York: International Universities Press.

257. ———. "Relevance of Direct Infant Observation." *Psychoanalytic Study of the Child*, V, 1950, pp. 66-73. New York: International Universities Press.

258. Staercke, A. "Psychoanalysis and Psychiatry," *International Journal of Psychoanalysis*, II, 1921, pp. 361-415.

259. Stone, L. "The Widening Scope of Indications for Psychoanalysis." *Journal of the American Psychoanalytic Association*, II, 195 pp. 567-94.

260. Stoodley, B. H. *The Concepts of Sigmund Freud*. Glencoe, Ill. The Free Press, 1959.

261. Strecker, E. A. and Ebaugh, F. G. *Practical Clinical Psychiatry* Philadelphia: Blakiston Company, 1925; 2nd ed., 1928; 3rd ed 1931; 4th ed., 1935. With section on "Psychopathological Problems of Childhood," by Kanner, L., 5th ed., 1940. 6th ed., 194 With Ewalt, J. R., 7th ed., 1951.

262. Sullivan, H. S. "Conceptions of Modern Psychiatry." The Fir: William Alanson White Memorial Lectures. *Psychiatry*, III, 194 pp. 1-117.

263. "Symposium on Lay Analysis," *International Journal of Psycho analysis*, VIII, 1927, pp. 174-283.

264. Szasz, T. S. "Psychiatry, Psychotherapy and Psychology." *AM. Archives of General Psychiatry*, I, 1959, pp. 455-63.

265. ———. "The Myth of Mental Illness," *The American Psycho ogist*, XV, 1960, pp. 113-18.

266. ———. "On the Theory of Analyzability: Technical and Theoret ical Observations," *Psychoanalytic Quarterly*, XXIX, 1960, p 478-506.

267. ———. "On the Theory of Psychoanalytic Treatment," *Inte national Journal of Psychoanalysis*, XXXVIII, 1957, pp. 166-8:

268. Thompson, C. *Psychoanalysis: Its Evolution and Developmen* New York: Hermitage House, 1950.

269. Valenstein, A., reporter. "The Psychoanalytic Concept of Chara ter," *Journal of the American Psychoanalytic Association*, V 1958, pp. 567-75.

270. Weigert, E. V. "Counter-Transference and Self Analysis of tl Psycho-Analyst." *International Journal of Psychoanalysis*, XXX 1954, pp. 242-46.

271. Whiting, J. M. and Child, I. L. *Child Training and Personalit A Cross-Cultural Study*. New Haven: Yale University Press, 195:

272. Whyte, L. L. *The Unconscious Before Freud*. New York: Bas Books, 1960.

273. Wittels, F. *Freud and His Time*. New York: Liveright, 1931.

274. Wolf Man, The. "How I Came into Analysis with Freud *Journal of the American Psychoanalytic Association*, VI, 195 pp. 348-52.

275. Wolff, P. H. *The Developmental Psychologies of Jean Piaget an Psychoanalysis*. (Psychological Issues, II, No. 1.) New Yor International Universities Press, 1960.

276. Woodworth, R. S. *Psychology.* New York: Henry Holt and Company, 1937.

277. Wortis, J. *Fragments of an Analysis with Freud.* New York: Simon and Schuster, 1954.

278. Wrong, D. H. "The Oversocialized Conception of Man in Modern Sociology," *American Sociological Review,* XXVI, 1961, pp. 183-93.

279. Zetzel, E. R. "The Concept of Anxiety in Relation to the Development of Psychoanalysis," *Journal of the American Psychoanalytic Association,* III, 1955, pp. 369-88.

280. Zilboorg, G. *A History of Medical Psychology.* New York: W. W. Norton and Company, 1941.

CHRONOLOGICAL LIST OF FREUD'S WRITINGS ON PSYCHOANALYSIS

General Note

The best single source for Freud's writings is the Standard Edition (see Bibliography above, reference 89). Twenty-four volumes are planned.

The most authoritative bibliography of Freud's work is in *The Index of Psychoanalytic Writings*, edited by Alexander Grinstein (see Bibliography above, reference 126). The following list is adapted from that *Index*. Most prefaces, obituaries, letters of minor consequence, and duplications have been omitted. The present list also contains several works that have appeared since the publication of the *Index*.

In some cases two dates are given. The first refers to the date when the work in question was actually published; the second to the date when it was written.

Freud's works are referred to by title and the year in which they were published. In order to distinguish works published in the same year from one another, Grinstein has added a letter beginning "a" to the year in which the work appeared. Thus, e.g., in 1913 there are 1913a, 1913b, 1913c, and so on to 1913l. This usage has become customary in the psychoanalytic literature and is adhered to throughout the present volume.

Apart from the Standard Edition, two useful collections of books and papers are:

The Basic Writings of Sigmund Freud. Modern Library Giant. New York: Random House.

Collected Papers. 5 volumes. London: Hogarth Press and the Institute of Psychoanalysis. New York: Basic Books.

Virtually all the books and papers in these two collections have by now been retranslated and published in the Standard Edition. In some cases different titles have been given to the retranslations.

1873–1939

1960a—*Letters of Sigmund Freud*, selected and edited by Ernst Freud. New York: Basic Books, 1960

1887–1902

1950a—*The Origins of Psychoanalysis*. Letters to Wilhelm Fliess. Drafts and Notes: 1887–1902

1888

1888b—"Hysteria." Contribution to Villaret, A. *Handwoerterbuch der gesamten Medizin*

1888b—"Hystero-epilepsy." Contribution to Villaret, A. *Handwoerterbuch der gesamten Medizin*

1892

1893a (1892)—*On the Psychical Mechanism of Hysterical Phenomena. Preliminary Communication*. In collaboration with Josef Breuer

1940 (1892)—*On the Theory of the Hysterical Attack*

1892–1893

1892–93b—*A Case of Successful Treatment by Hypnotism With some Remarks on the Origin of Hysterical Symptoms Through "Counterwill"*

1893

1893c—*Some Points in a Comparative Study of Organic and Hysterical Paralysis*

1893f—*Charcot*

1893h—*Lecture on the Psychical Mechanism of Hysterical Phenomena*

1894

1894a—*The Defense Neuro-Psychoses*

1895b (1894)—*On the Grounds for Detaching from Neurasthenia a Particular Syndrome: The Anxiety Neurosis*

1895c (1894)—*Obsessions and Phobias*

1895

895d—*Studies on Hysteria*
895f—*A Reply to Criticisms of My Paper on Anxiety Neurosis*
895g—*On Hysteria*

1896

896a—*Heredity and the Etiology of the Neuroses*
896b—*Further Remarks on the Defense Neuro-Psychoses*
896c—*The Etiology of Hysteria*

1898

898a—*Sexuality in the Etiology of the Neuroses*
898b—*The Psychical Mechanism of Forgetting*

1899

899a—*Screen Memories*
901c (1899)—*Autobiographical Note*
941c (1899)—*A Premonitory Dream Fulfilled*

1900

900a (1899)—*The Interpretation of Dreams*

1901

901a—*On the Dream*
901b—*The Psychopathology of Everyday Life*

1904

904a—*Freud's Psychoanalytic Procedure*
904d—*A Note on Human Magnetism*
905a (1904)—*On Psychotherapy*
906e (1904)—*Letters to Wilhelm Fliess*

1905

905b—*Psychical Treatment*
905c—*Jokes and Their Relation to the Unconscious*
905d—*Three Essays on Sexuality*
905e (1901)—*Fragment of an Analysis of a Case of Hysteria*
906a (1905)—*My Views on the Part Played by Sexuality in the Etiology of the Neuroses*

1905–1906

1905–1906—*Psychopathic Characters on the Stage*

1906–1931

1955b—*Letters to Arthur Schnitzler*

1906

1906c—*Psychoanalysis and the Establishment of Facts in Legal Proceedings*

1907

1907a—*Delusions and Dreams in Jensen's* Gradiva
1907b—*Obsessive Acts and Religious Practices*
1907c—*The Sexual Enlightenment of Children*
1907d—*An Unknown Autobiographical Letter by Freud. On the Reading of Good Books*

1908

1908a—*Hysterical Phantasies and Their Relation to Bisexuality*
1908b—*Character and Anal Erotism*
1908c—*On the Sexual Theories of Children*
1908d—*"Civilized" Sexual Morality and Modern Nervousness*
1908e—*Creative Writers and Daydreaming*

1909

1910a (1909)—*Five Lectures on Psychoanalysis*
1909a—*Some General Remarks on Hysterical Attacks*
1909b—*Analysis of a Phobia in a Five-Year Old Boy*
1909c—*The Family Romance of Neurotics*
1909d—*Notes upon a Case of Obsessional Neurosis*

1910

1910c—*Leonardo da Vinci and a Memory of his Childhood*
1910d—*The Future Prospects of Psychoanalytic Therapy*
1910e—*The Antithetical Sense of Primal Words*
1910g—*Contributions to a Discussion on Suicide*
1910h—*A Special Type of Object Choice in Men*
1910i—*The Psychoanalytic View of Psychogenic Visual Disturbances*
1910j—*Two Instances of Pathogenic Phantasies Revealed by the Patients Themselves*
1910k—*"Wild" Psychoanalysis*
1910l—*A Typical Example of a Disguised Oedipus Dream*

1911

1911a—*Additions to the Interpretation of Dreams*

1911b—*Formulations Regarding the Two Principles in Mental Functioning*

1911c—*Psycho-Analytic Notes Upon Autobiographical Account of a Case of Paranoia (Dementia Paranoides)*

1911d—*The Significance of a Sequence of Vowels*

1911e—*The Handling of Dream Interpretaton in Psychoanalysis*

1911f—*Great Is Diana of the Ephesians*

1911i—*A Contribution to the Forgetting of Proper Names*

1913m (1911)—*On Psychoanalysis*

1958a (1911)—*Dreams in Folklore* (in collaboration with D. E. Oppenheim). New York: International Universities Press, 1958

1911–1938

Letters to Theodor Reik

1912

1912b—*The Dynamics of Transference*

1912c—*Types of Onset of Neurosis*

1912d—*The Most Prevalent Form of Degradation in Erotic Life*

1912e—*Recommendations to Physicians Practising Psychoanalysis*

1912f—*Contributions to a Discussion of Masturbation*

1912g—*A Note on the Unconscious in Psychoanalysis*

1912h—*Paragraph in* Offener Sprechsaal *on Observations of Coitus*

1912i—*Request for Examples of Childhood Dreams*

1912–1913

1912–13—*Totem and Taboo*

1913

1913a—*A Dream Which Bore Testimony*

1913c—*Further Recommendations on the Technique of Psychoanalysis. On Beginning the Treatment*

1913d—*The Occurrence in Dreams of Material from Fairy Tales*

1913f—*The Theme of the Three Caskets*

1913g—*Infantile Mental Life. Two Lies Told by Children*

1913h—*Observations and Examples from Analytic Practise*

1913i—*The Disposition to Obsessional Neurosis*

1913j—*The Claims of Psychoanalysis to Scientific Interest*

1913k—*Foreword to Bourke, John Gregory,* Scatologic Rites of All Nations

1913l—*Childhood Dreams of Special Importance*

1914

1914a—*Fausse Reconnaissance (déjà raconté) in Psychoanalytic Treatment*

1914b—*The Moses of Michelangelo*

1914c—*On Narcissism: An Introduction*

1914d—*The History of the Psychoanalytic Movement*

1914e—*A "Great Achievement" in a Dream*

1914f—*Some Reflections on Schoolboy Psychology*

1914g—*Further Recommendations on the Technique of Psychoanalysis. Remembering, Repeating and Working-Through*

1918b (1914)—*From the History of an Infantile Neurosis*

1915

1915a—*Further Recommendations on the Technique of Psychoanalysis. Observations on Transference-Love*

1915b—*Reflections on War and Death*

1915c—*Instincts and Their Vicissitudes*

1915d—*Repression*

1915e—*The Unconscious*

1915f—*A Case of Paranoia Running Counter to the Psychoanalytical Theory of the Disease*

1916

1916a—*On Transience*

1916b—*A Mythological Parallel to a Visual Obsession*

1916c—*A Connection between a Symbol and a Symptom*

1916d—*Some Character Types Met with in Psychoanalytic Work*

1916–1917

1916–17—*A General Introduction to Psychoanalysis*

1917

1917a—*A Difficulty in the Path of Psychoanalysis*

1917b—*A Childhood Recollection from* Dichtung und Wahrheit

1917c—*On Transformation of Instinct as Exemplified in Anal Erotism*

1917d—*A Metapsychological Supplement to the Theory of Dreams*

1917e—*Mourning and Melancholia*

1918a (1917)—*The Taboo of Virginity*

1918

1919a (1918)—*Lines of Advance in Psychoanalytic Therapy*

1919

1919e—"A Child Is Being Beaten." *A Contribution to the Study of the Origin of Sexual Perversions*

1919h—*The "Uncanny"*

1919k—*E. T. A. Hoffmann on the Function of Consciousness*

1919j—*On the Teaching of Psychoanalysis at Universities*

1920

1920a—*The Psychogenesis of a Case of Homosexuality in a Woman*

1920b—*A Note on the Prehistory of the Technique of Analysis*

1920d—*Associations of a Four-Year-Old Child*

1920f—*Supplements to the Theory of Dreams*

1920g—*Beyond the Pleasure Principle*

1955c (1920)—*Memorandum on the Electrical Treatment of War Neuroses*

1921

1921c—*Group Psychology and the Analysis of the Ego*

1941d (1921)—*Psychoanalysis and Telepathy*

1922

1922a—*Dreams and Telepathy*

1922b—*Certain Neurotic Mechanisms in Jealousy, Paranoia and Homosexuality*

1922f—*Some Remarks on the Unconscious*

1933b (1922)—*Why War?*

1940c (1922)—*Medusa's Head*

1923

1923a—*Two Encyclopaedia Articles*

1923b—*The Ego and the Id*

1923c—*Remarks on the Theory and Practice of Dream Interpretation*

1923d—*A Neurosis of Demoniacal Possession in the Seventeenth Century*

1923e—*The Infantile Genital Organization of the Libido*

1923f—*Josef Popper-Lynkeus and the Theory of Dreams*

1924

1924b—*Neurosis and Psychosis*

1924c—*The Economic Problem in Masochism*

1924d—*The Passing of the Oedipus Complex*

1924e—*The Loss of Reality in Neurosis and Psychosis*

1924f—*A Short Account of Psychoanalysis*
1924h—*Communication of the Editor*
1925d (1924)—*An Autobiographical Study*

1925

1925a—*A Note upon the "Mystic Writing Pad"*
1925c—*To the Opening of the Hebrew University*
1925d—*The Resistances to Psychoanalysis*
1925g—*Josef Breuer: Obituary*
1925h—*Negation*
1925i—*Some Additional Notes upon Dream Interpretation as a Whole*
1925j—*Some Psychological Consequences of the Anatomical Distinction Between the Sexes*

1926

1926c—Foreword to E. Pickworth Farrow's **A Practical Method of Self-Analysis**
1926d—*Inhibitions, Symptoms and Anxiety*
1926e—*The Question of Lay Analysis*
1926f—*Psychoanalysis: Freudian School*
1941e (1926)—Address to Members of the B'nai B'rith

1927

1927a—*Postscript to a Discussion on Lay Analysis*
1927b—*Postscript to my Paper on the Moses of Michelangelo*
1927c—*The Future of an Illusion*
1927d—*Humor*
1927e—*Fetishism*

1928

1928a—*A Religious Experience*
1928b—*Dostoyevsky and Parricide*

1930

1930a—*Civilization and Its Discontents*
1930e—*Address Delivered in the Goethe House at Frankfurt*

1931

1931a—*Libidinal Types*
1931b—*Female Sexuality*
1931d—*The Specialist Opinion in the Halsmann Case*

1932

1932a—*The Acquisition and Control of Fire*
1932c—*My Contact with Josef Popper-Lynkeus*
1933a (1932)—*New Introductory Lectures on Psychoanalysis*

1932–1935

Letters to Joseph Wortis

1934

Letter to Havelock Ellis

1935

1935b—*The Subtleties of a Parapraxis*
1951a (1935)—*A Letter on Homosexuality*

1936

1936a—*A Disturbance of Memory on the Acropolis*

1937

1937c—*Analysis Terminable and Interminable*
1937d—*Constructions in Analysis*

1937–1939

1939a (1937–1939)—*Moses and Monotheism*

1938

1938a—*A Note on Anti-Semitism*
1940a (1938)—*An Outline of Psychoanalysis*
1940b (1938)—*Some Elementary Lessons in Psychoanalysis*
1940e (1938)—*The Splitting of the Ego in the Defensive Process*
1941f (1938)—*Findings, Ideas and Problems*

SELECTED LIST OF COMMENTARIES ON FREUD

In spite of the enormous reaction which he evoked, there are surprisingly few books devoted exclusively to Freud. No doubt some day some analytically-trained historian will come along who will disentangle the numerous emotional crosscurrents of the repercussions of Freud and psychoanalysis over the years. The following list contains the more important works available, written from different points of view.

For full details on each book see the reference number in the bibliography, indicated in parentheses.

1. Ernest Jones. *The Life and Work of Sigmund Freud.* 3 volumes. 1953-1957. This is the definitive biography of Freud, written by one of his most illustrious disciples. Jones played an active part in the psychoanalytic movement; and his book is an original source book as well as a biography. (133) A one-volume abridgment by Trilling and Marcus was issued in 1961.

2. J. A. C. Brown. *Freud and the Post-Freudians.* 1961. Summation of various positions and attitudes. (35)

3. Erich Fromm. *Sigmund Freud's Mission.* 1959. A dubious polemic. (91)

4. I. Galdston (ed.). *Freud and Contemporary Culture.* 1957. Centenary addresses by a number of authorities. (93)

5. E. R. Hilgard, *Theories of Learning,* 2nd ed., 1956. Chapter IX. Excellent discussions of Freud and learning theory. (117)

6. Karen Horney: *New Ways in Psychoanalysis.* 1939. This and Clara Thompson's book (*see* No. 12 below) contain the standard culturalist criticisms of Freud. (123)

7. P. Mullahy: *Oedipus: Myth and Complex.* 1948. A summation of various attitudes by a Sullivanian. (189)

8. R. Munroe: *Schools of Psychoanalytic Thought.* 1955. An eclectic text. (190)

9. G. Murphy: *Historical Introduction to Modern Psychology*. 1949. Chapters XXII and XXIII. Relates Freud and psychoanalysis to historical development in other areas of psychology. (193)

10. P. Rieff: *Freud: The Mind of the Moralist*. 1959. A scholarly study without a well-defined thesis. (230)

11. B. Stoodley: *The Concepts of Sigmund Freud*. 1959. A sociological re-examinaton of Freud which takes issue with the traditional biological interpretation. (260)

12. Clara Thompson: *Psychoanalysis: Its Evolution and Development*. 1950. Culturalist critique. (268) *See* comment on No. 6 above.

13. F. Wittels: *Freud and His Time*. 1931. A discursive account by one of Freud's early students. (273)

14. G. Zilboorg: *A History of Medical Psychology*. 1941. Chapter XI. Relates Freud to the history of psychiatry. (280)

INDEX